360° of Reading:

A Literature Guide for the College Bound

© 2007 W.E. Poplaski
All Rights Reserved.

No part of this publication may be reproduced, stored in a retrieval system, or transmitted, in any form or by any means, electronic, mechanical, photocopying, recording, or otherwise, without the written permission of the author.

First published by Dog Ear Publishing
4010 W. 86th Street, Ste H
Indianapolis, IN 46268
www.dogearpublishing.net

ISBN: 978-159858-379-3
Library of Congress Control Number: 2007935986

This book is printed on acid-free paper.

Printed in the United States of America

Brief Table of Contents

PREFACE..	I
BOOK REFERENCES....................................	1
FICTION..	1
Novels / Short Stories.................................	1
Drama..	139
Narrative Poetry...	166
Poetry, Collected Works.............................	176
NONFICTION..	189
History / Biography / Social Science............	189
Science / Math..	284
Philosophy / Religion / Spirituality................	323
LONG BOOKS...	338
APPENDIX...	**361**
INDICES..	**363**
Author Index..	363
Authors by Country Index...........................	369
African Authors...	369
Asian Authors...	369
Australian & Pacific Island Authors..............	370
European Authors..	370
Middle Eastern Authors..............................	371
North American Authors.............................	372
South American & Caribbean Authors............	375
African-American Authors Index.................	376
Women Authors Index................................	376
Date of First Publication Index....................	378
Keyword Index...	389
'*'-Level Books (less challenging)................	401
'**'-Level Books (challenging)....................	404

Table of Contents

PREFACE…………………………………..	1
BOOK REFERENCES……...……………….	1
FICTION……………………………………..	1
Novels / Short Stories……..……………….	1
18 Best Stories by Edgar Allan Poe *…..…....	1
1984……………………………………...	2
The Adventures of Huckleberry Finn *……….	3
The Alchemist: A Fable About Following Your Dream ……..……………………………...	4
Alfred and Guinevere *………………………...	5
All Quiet on the Western Front *……..……….	6
Animal Farm *……………...…………………...	7
April Morning *……………………….....…….	8
Arabian Nights and Days ………..…………….	9
As I Lay Dying **…..……………...................	10
At Swim-Two-Birds ** ……………………....	11
Atticus…..…………………………..……	12
The Autobiography of an Ex-Colored Man.......	13
The Awakening…..……………………..……..	14
Balzac and the Little Chinese Seamstress…..….	15
The Baron in the Trees ………… ……………..	16
Becoming Madame Mao………………………	17
Bel Canto…………………………………....	18
The Bell Jar **…………………………..…...	19
A Bend in the River………………………....	20
Brave New World……………………….….	21
Bridge of San Luis Rey……………………..….	22
The Bridges at Toko-Ri *……………………...	23
Brighter Sun *……..……...……………………	24

Candide **	25
A Canticle for Leibowitz **	26
The Catcher in the Rye	27
Cat's Cradle	28
Changes: A Love Story	29
Chocolat	30
A Christmas Carol *	31
Chronicle of a Death Foretold	32
The Color Purple	33
Cry, the Beloved Country	34
The Crying of Lot 49 **	35
The Curious Incident of the Dog in the Night-Time	36
Darkness at Noon **	37
The Day of the Locust	38
Death Comes for the Archbishop	39
A Death in the Family	40
Dinner at the Homesick Restaurant	41
Dracula	42
Elbow Room	43
A Farewell to Arms	44
Ficciones	45
The Fixer	46
Flatland: A Romance of Many Dimensions **	47
Flowers for Algernon	48
The Following Story **	49
Fools and Other Stories	50
Frankenstein	51
From a Crooked Rib	52
Girl with a Pearl Earring *	53
Go Tell It on the Mountain *	54
Going After Cacciato	55
The Good Earth *	56
A Good Man is Hard to Find *	57
Goodbye, Columbus	58
The Great Gatsby	59

Heart of Darkness…………………………....	60
Hound of the Baskervilles *………………….	61
Housekeeping…………….…………………….	62
How the Garcia Girls Lost Their Accents *…..	63
Howards End………....……………………….	64
The Human Comedy *……………………..…	65
The Illustrated Man *…………………………	66
Interpreter of Maladies……………………….	67
The Joy Luck Club…………………..……….	68
Joys of Motherhood…………………………...	69
The Jungle…………………………………….	70
The Kingdom of This World………………….	71
Kokoro **………………….…..……………...	72
Life of Pi………………………………….…...	73
Like Water for Chocolate……………………...	74
Lord of the Flies…………………….…………	75
Lost Horizon *………………………….……..	76
Lost in the City *……………………….……...	77
Medicine River………………………………..	78
The Mistress of Spices……………………...…	79
Native Speaker…………………….…………...	80
Night…………………………………….……..	81
Now in November…………………………….	82
The Odyssey *………………………………...	83
Of Mice and Men *……………………………	84
Old Man and the Sea *…………………….…..	85
One Flew Over the Cuckoo's Nest…………….	86
The Optimist's Daughter…………………...….	87
The Orchid House……………………………..	88
The Outsiders *……………………………….	89
The Palm-Wine Drinkard and My Life in the Bush of Ghosts………………………………..	90
The Painted Bird **………………………...….	91
Pedro Paramo……………………………….....	92
Persepolis: The Story of a Childhood *………	93
A Personal Matter……………………………...	94

The Plague	95
The Power and the Glory	96
The Prisoner of Zenda *	97
The Professor's House	98
Purple Hibiscus	99
Rabbit, Run	100
The Red Badge of Courage *	101
The Red Tent	102
Rip Van Winkle and Other Stories *	103
Roofwalker	104
The Screwtape Letters	105
The Sea	106
The Secret Life of Bees	107
Seize the Day	108
A Separate Peace	109
Shame **	110
The Sheltering Sky	111
Shizuko's Daughter *	112
Siddhartha **	113
Silas Marner	114
Snow Flower and the Secret Fan *	115
So Long, See You Tomorrow	116
Something Wicked This Way Comes *	117
The Spy Who Came in from the Cold	118
Sula	119
The Swallows of Kabul	120
Their Eyes Were Watching God	121
Things Fall Apart	122
To Kill a Mockingbird *	123
To the Lighthouse **	124
Too Loud a Solitude **	125
The Trial	126
Uncle Tom's Cabin	127
Waiting for the Vote of the Wild Animals	128
Waiting for the Barbarians	129
Walk in the Light & Twenty-Three Tales	130

The War of the Worlds *	131
Weep Not, Child	132
Where We Once Belonged	133
Wide Sargasso Sea	134
Winesburg, Ohio *	135
A Yellow Raft in Blue Water	136
You Know Me Al	137
Zorba the Greek	138
Drama	139
3 by Shakespeare: A Midsummer Night's Dream, Romeo and Juliet and Richard III	139
The Cherry Orchard	140
The Complete Greek Tragedies: Aeschylus II	141
The Complete Greek Tragedies: Euripides V	142
The Complete Greek Tragedies: Sophocles I	143
The Crucible *	144
The Death of a Salesman *	145
A Doll's House	146
Faust Part One	147
Glengarry Glen Ross	148
The Importance of Being Earnest	149
Life Is a Dream	150
The Lion and the Jewel *	151
Long Day's Journey into Night *	152
Lost in Yonkers *	153
A Man for All Seasons	154
Miss Julie	155
Murder in the Cathedral	156
'night, Mother **	157
No Exit and Three Other Plays **	158
Our Town *	159
The Piano Lesson *	160
A Raisin in the Sun *	161
Saint Joan	162
A Streetcar Named Desire	163

Waiting for Godot **	164
Who's Afraid of Virginia Woolf? **	165
Narrative Poetry	166
Aeneid	166
Beowulf	167
Courtship of Miles Standish *	168
The Epic of Gilgamesh	169
Evangeline *	170
Idylls of the King	171
The Poem of the Cid: Dual Language Edition.	172
The Saga of the Volsungs	173
The Song of Roland	174
Troilus and Criseyde	175
Poetry, Collected Works	176
101 Great American Poems *	176
African-American Poetry: An Anthology, 1773-1927	177
American Primitive	178
Mr. Cogito	179
The Collected Songs of Cold Mountain	180
Great Love Poems	181
Holocaust Poetry	182
The Metamorphoses: Selected Stories in Verse	183
Metaphysical Poetry: An Anthology **	184
Poems and Songs	185
The Poetry of Arab Women	186
Selected Poems	187
Turtle Island	188

NONFICTION...	189
History / Biography / Social Science............	189
1831: Year of Eclipse............................……..	189
African Genesis: Folk Tales and Myths of Africa..	190
And Keep Your Powder Dry: An Anthropologist Looks at America **...........	191
Anne Frank: The Diary of a Young Girl *……	192
The Autobiography of Benjamin Franklin *....	193
Behind the Scenes in the Lincoln White House: Memoirs of an African-American Seamstress *…………...…………………	194
Black Elk Speaks: Being the Life Story of a Holy Man of the Oglala Sioux……………...	195
Black Gold of the Sun: Searching for Home in Africa and Beyond……………...……………	196
Black Hawk: An Autobiography…..…………	197
A Border Passage: From Cairo to America— A Woman's Journey………………………..	198
Confessions of Lady Nijo……………………..	199
The Conquest of Gaul………………………..…	200
Crossing Over: A Mexican Family on the Migrant Trail……………………...…………	201
The Cruelest Miles: The Heroic Story of Dogs and Men in a Race against an Epidemic…..	202
Crusades through Arab Eyes…………………	203
Curry: A Tale of Cooks and Conquerors……..	204
Days of Grace……………………...…………	205
Decisive Day: The Battle for Bunker Hill…….	206
The Declaration of Independence and Other Great Documents of American History 1775-1865…………...……………………..	207

Diary of an Early American Boy: Noah Blake 1805.. 208
Down on Parchman Farm: The Great Prison in the Mississippi Delta **............................ 209
Down These Mean Streets............................... 210
Einstein on Race and Racism.......................... 211
The Essential Gandhi: An Anthology of His Writings on His Life, Work, and Ideas........ 212
Execution by Hunger: The Hidden Holocaust.. 213
The Fall of Constantinople 1453..................... 214
Flu: The Story of the Great Influenza Pandemic of 1918 and the Search for the Virus That Caused It....................................... 215
For Cause and Comrades: Why Men Fought in the Civil War... 216
Founding Brothers: The Revolutionary Generation.. 217
Friday Night Lights: A Town, a Team, and a Dream.. 218
The Game.. 219
The Game They Played.................................... 220
Gauntlet: Five Friends, 20,000 Enemy Troops, & the Secret That Could Have Changed the Course of the Cold War.................................... 221
The Good Man of Nanking: The Diaries of John Rabe... 222
Having Our Say: The Delany Sisters' First 100 Years... 223
Here I Stand.. 224
Hip Hop Matters: Politics, Pop Culture, and the Struggle for the Soul of a Movement...... 225
Hiroshima... 226
How to Read Literature like a Professor: a Lively and Entertaining Guide to Reading Between the Lines **...................................... 227

I Know Why the Caged Bird Sings...............	228
I Never Had It Made: An Autobiography of Jackie Robinson....................................	229
I Write What I Like: Selected Writings..........	230
In the Heart of the Sea: The Tragedy of the Whaleship Essex.....................................	231
In These Girls, Hope is a Muscle *...............	232
Incidents in the Life of a Slave Girl..............	233
The Irish Famine: An Illustrated History.......	234
Johnstown Flood.......................................	235
Kaffir Boy: The True Story of a Black Youth's Coming-of-age in Apartheid South Africa...	236
The Lemon Tree: An Arab, a Jew, and the Heart of the Middle East........................	237
Life along the Silk Road............................	238
The Life of Olaudah Equiano......................	239
A Long Way Gone: Memoirs of a Boy Soldier..	240
The Lost German Slave Girl: The Extraordinary True Story of Sally Miller and Her Fight for Freedom in Old New Orleans...	241
A Love Supreme: The Making of John Coltrane's Masterpiece **.....................	242
Madness: A Brief History **.......................	243
The Man Who Would Be King: The First American in Afghanistan.......................	244
Man's Search for Meaning.........................	245
Marathon Woman: Running the Race to Revolutionize Women's Sports.................	246
Memoirs of Fray Servando Teresa de Mier......	247
My Land and My People: The Original Autobiography of His Holiness the Dalai Lama of Tibet...	248
My Journey to Lhasa.................................	249

Naked Economics: Undressing the Dismal Science **...............................	250
Narrative of my captivity among the Sioux Indians. By Fanny Kelly. With a brief account of General Sully's Indian expedition in 1864, bearing upon events occurring in my captivity *...................	251
Narrative of the Life of Frederick Douglass.....	252
Never Die Easy: The Autobiography of Walter Payton *...	253
News of a Kidnapping................................	254
The Only Girl in the Car............................	255
Ordinary Men: Reserve Police Battalion 101 and the Final Solution in Poland...............	256
The Pact *..	257
Polio: An American Story..........................	258
Red Legs and Black Sox: Edd Roush and the Untold Story of the 1919 World Series.......	259
The Right Stuff..	260
Rough Riders..	261
The Sixteenth Round: From Number 1 Contender To #45472...........................	262
Some Survived: An Eyewitness Account of the Bataan Death March and the Men Who Lived Through It *..................................	263
The Spirit Catches You and You Fall Down....	264
Stolen Harvest: The Hijacking of the Global Food Supply..	265
The Story of My Life *..............................	266
The Supreme Court..................................	267
The Sweet Science...................................	268
Tell Them Who I Am: The Lives of Homeless Women **...	269

There Are No Children Here: The Story of Two Boys Growing Up in Urban America	270
To Destroy You Is No Loss: The Odyssey of a Cambodian Family...............................	271
The True History of Chocolate.....................	272
The Twentieth Train: The True Story of the Ambush of the Death Train to Auschwitz....	273
Up from Slavery: An Autobiography.............	274
A Vietcong Memoir: An Inside Account of the Vietnam War and Its Aftermath................	275
We Took to the Wood.	276
We Wish to Inform You That Tomorrow We Will be Killed with Our Families: Stories from Rwanda....................................	277
Why Sinatra Matters	278
Winterdance: The Fine Madness of Running the Iditarod *	279
With Santa Anna in Texas: A Personal Narrative of the Revolution......................	280
The Woman Warrior: Memoirs of a Girlhood Among Ghosts..	281
Worse than Slavery: Parchman Farm and the Ordeal of Jim Crow Justice **................	282
Zimmermann Telegram.............................	283
Science / Math...	284
The Antibiotic Paradox: How the Misuse of Antibiotics Destroys Their Curative Powers **..	284
At the Fringes of Science: With a New Epilogue **..	285
Blue Frontier: Saving America's Living Seas...	286
The Botany of Desire: A Plant's-Eye View of the World...	287
A Briefer History of Time..........................	288
The Cartoon Guide to Genetics...................	289

Cats Are Not Peas: A Calico History of Genetics...	290
Complications: A Surgeon's Notes on an Imperfect Science.................................	291
Damned Lies and Statistics: Untangling Numbers from the Media, Politicians, and Activists...	292
The Double Helix: A Personal Account of the Discovery of the Structure of DNA...........	293
Dr. Tatiana's Sex Advice to All Creation: the Definitive Guide to the Evolutionary Biology of Sex......................................	294
Emotional Intelligence: 10th Anniversary Edition; Why It Can Matter More Than IQ **..	295
Five Quarts: A Personal and Natural History of Blood..	296
The Genie in the Bottle: 64 All New Commentaries on the Fascinating Chemistry of Everyday Life *...............	297
Gifted Hands: The Ben Carson Story *.........	298
Gorillas in the Mist..................................	299
Heart of the Sound: An Alaskan Paradise Found and Nearly Lost.......................	300
Hydrogen: The Essential Element **............	301
In the Shadow of Man................................	302
Innumeracy: Mathematical Illiteracy and Its Consequences.......................................	303
The Journey of Man: A Genetic Odyssey **....	304
Last Breath: The Limits of Adventure...........	305
The Lives of a Cell **................................	306
Looking for Earths: The Race to Find New Solar Systems...................................	307

Lords of the Harvest: Biotech, Big Money, and the Future of Food............	308
The Man Who Mistook His Wife for a Hat: And Other Clinical Tales............	309
Mathematics, Magic and Mystery (Cards, Coins, and Other Magic)............	310
The Naked Ape............	311
A Natural History of the Senses............	312
The New World of Mr. Tompkins **............	313
The Relaxation Response............	314
The Secret Life of Germs: What They Are, Why We Need Them, and How We Can Protect Ourselves Against Them............	315
The Selfish Gene **............	316
Silent Thunder: In the Presence of Elephants...	317
Stiff: The Curious Lives of Human Cadavers *	318
Waiting for Aphrodite: Journeys into the Time Before Bones............	319
Why Flip a Coin? The Art and Science of Good Decisions **............	320
Why We Love: The Nature and Chemistry of Romantic Love............	321
Zero: The Biography of a Dangerous Idea **..	322
Philosophy / Religion / Spirituality............	323
The Analects of Confucius **............	323
The Art of Loving............	324
Between Man and Man **............	325
Confessions............	326
The Essential Kabbalah: The Heart of Jewish Mysticism **............	327
The Essential Mystics: Selections from the World's Great Wisdom Traditions **............	328
Fakhruddin Iraqi: Divine Flashes............	329
Interior Castle............	330
Introduction to the Devout Life............	331

Islam: A Short History.....................................	332
New Seeds of Contemplation **...................	333
Pragmatism: A New Name for Some Old Ways of Thinking...	334
Shinto Norito - a Book of Prayers................	335
Teachings of the Hindu Mystics..................	336
Turning Points: Decisive Moments in the History of Christianity........................	337
LONG BOOKS...	338
The Autobiography of Malcolm X *..............	338
Before the Fallout: From Marie Curie to Hiroshima..	339
The Boys of Summer....................................	340
Bury My Heart at Wounded Knee: An Indian History of the American West................	341
Catch 22 **...	342
Doctor Zhivago...	343
The Good War: An Oral History of World War II..	344
The Grapes of Wrath.....................................	345
The Innocents Abroad...................................	347
Invisible Man..	348
The Kite Runner..	349
Les Miserables **...	350
The Magic Mountain.....................................	351
Main Street...	352
The Naked and the Dead...............................	353
Native Son...	354
The Octopus..	355
Schindler's List...	356
Silent Spring...	357
Sophie's World..	358
Two Years Before the Mast..........................	359
The World Is Flat: a Brief History of the Twenty-first Century............................	360

APPENDIX…………………………………..	361
INDICES……………………………………...	363
Author Index………....………………………	363
Authors by Country Index……………..…….	369
African Authors……..….……..………………	369
Asian Authors………………………………….	369
Australian & Pacific Island Authors………….	370
European Authors………………..…………...	370
Middle Eastern uthors……………………......	371
North American Authors……………...……..	372
South American & Caribbean Authors……..	375
African-American Authors Index……………	376
Women Authors Index……………………….	376
Date of First Publication Index…………….…	378
Keyword Index…………………..……………	389
'*'-Level Books (less challenging)……..…….	401
'**'-Level Books (challenging)…………..…...	404

Preface

"DEAR reader, I request you to read this Preface for your own satisfaction as well as mine." Francis de Sales penned those words in his *Introduction to a Devout Life* four centuries ago. No doubt every author feels the same sentiment, just as every reader may ask, "Do I really need to read the preface?" This preface is no exception to that request.

Your satisfaction will come from being better able to use this guide for your own benefit. Using it will bring great reading experiences to you. My satisfaction will come from knowing that your experience using this guide will be positive.

360° of Reading is a literature reference guide. It has an annotated bibliography of 360 books. That means it has all the information you need to find these books at libraries or bookstores. It is designed to be used as a supplement to required high school reading.

Why start an independent reading program? You can gain much from reading. It improves your reading comprehension. It increases your ability to focus your attention for long time periods. It expands your knowledge on diverse subjects. A long-term routine of independent reading is good preparation for the *SAT* and *ACT* exams.

How much independent reading should you do? That's a bit like asking, "How much physical exercise should you do?" It depends on your goals, the time you are able to commit and your motivation. Reading all 360 books in four years, though possible, is a Herculean task. A more reasonable goal, still very challenging, would be to read 100 books in four years. Even 12 books per year is a challenging goal for many students. However, any reading you do is helpful to you.

What is in this guide? Each of the books listed has its own reference page alphabetically ordered by book title within section. There are eight sections covering fiction and nonfiction. Each reference page includes bibliographic information (title, author, publication date, number of pages, and ISBN), date of first publication, a descriptive note, keywords and useful websites. Furthermore, the books are indexed by author, country of origin, date of publication, and keywords.

Standard Book

You may have noticed that the 360 books this guide lists range from 64 pages to over 1400 pages. (For the record, three-quarters of these books have less than 310 pages. Half have less than 256 pages. One-quarter have 188 pages or less. One-tenth—36 books—have fewer than 130 pages.) Reading a 64 page book is not the same as reading a 1400 page book! That means if we are setting a goal for reading a certain number of books per year, we need to define a standard book length.

The average length for these books is close to 260 pages, so that will be our standard book length. Now we can be more precise in defining goals. For example, your four-year goal could be to read the 'equivalent of 100 *standard books*'. That would be 26,000 pages (260 x 100). Reading a book that is 130 pages long would be 0.5 of a standard book equivalent. A book 520 pages long counts as 2 standard book equivalents.

This makes things fairer. If you and I each read ten books, but mine are each 26 pages while yours are each 260 pages, then you have read much more than me. I read the equivalent of 1 standard book while you read the equivalent of 10 standard books.

The 'standard book equivalent' for each book listed in this guide is given on its reference page.

Choosing a Book to Read

How should you choose which book to read? Just as they vary in length, these books vary in their level of difficulty. That is intentional. You will need to read more challenging books as a senior than as a freshman. Books that are more challenging to read are labeled with '**' (for example, *Naked Economics* ** and *Waiting for Godot* **). They require a greater amount of prerequisite learning than other books. They may require knowledge from upper level high school courses, or the vocabulary and language may be advanced. Books that are less challenging are marked with '*' (for example, *A Christmas Carol* * and *Anne Frank: the Diary of a Young Girl* *). However, labels of '**' or '*' are not absolute; they are suggestions. What is easy for one person might be difficult for another. Therefore, browse through a book before you decide to read it to see if it is right for you. There is a list of both '*' and '**' books at the end of the keyword index.

Each book reference has a 75 to 100 word descriptive note to help you decide if you want to read that book. Also, websites are listed for book reviews, study guides or author information for all of the books. (Sometimes a book is available free online. That website address is often given in the book reference.) All of this information should be used to decide which book to read.

You should strive to read books from each of the sections found in the table of contents. This will give you a well-rounded reading experience. You can further diversify your reading by selecting books published from varying time periods and authors from different countries.

You now have three things to do to improve your reading. First, if you haven't already started a routine of independent reading, do so now. Set a goal for the number of books you plan to read each year, keeping an eye on how long they are. You can use the log at the end of this book to record your progress. Second, be careful in your book selection. Reading material should be right for your ability and cover a broad range of subjects. Third, commit to a long-term program. Two years of following this routine will place you in a great position for academic success.

Literature Selection Criteria

So then, "What criteria were used to select books for this guide?" The criteria were based on the target audience. They are American high school students striving to get into the college of their choice. Students with that as a goal take challenging courses, are involved in extra-curricular school activities and need time for rest and recreation. Their time for independent reading is limited and often sporadic. Books suitable for that type of life-style need to be short, because students may not have the time to finish a long book. Therefore, an important criterion for this book list was short length.

A second criterion for making this list was to ensure diverse subject content. Many colleges interview students as part of the admissions process. They are looking for information about applicants beyond what is found in a standardized test score, or GPA. They hope to find interesting and mature students. That means students who have an awareness of the world around them. All of the students they interview have roughly the same core set of knowledge obtained from the same standard courses. Students can stand out from the crowd by the independent learning they do. Reading literature is a great way to expand your knowledge of the world.

Accordingly, this guide includes both fiction and nonfiction. The fiction part consists of four sections: novels, drama, narrative poetry, and collective works of poetry. The nonfiction part has three sections. They are history/biography/sociology, science/mathematics, and philosophy/religion/spirituality. This criterion ensured books of varied genre and subject matter were included in the list.

A third set of criteria included books from a broad range of countries and publication dates. This further diversified the list. The countries of origin and publication date indices aid the reader in examining this diversity.

A fourth set of criteria often worked at cross-purposes to each other. The books should be widely read and acknowledged for being of high quality. After all, much of the value from reading comes from discussing with others the meaning of what the author has written. However, the list also should guide you to great books you otherwise likely would miss. If not, you might as well simply go to lists such as those for Pulitzer Prize, or National Book Award winners. So, you will find both well-known books (e.g., *1984*, and *The Old Man and the Sea*) and less widely known books (e.g., *Brighter Sun*, and *Where We Once Belonged*) in this guide.

Lastly, I tried to include as many well-known authors as possible. Often, a famous author has a better-known book than is listed here. This is the case for authors such as Barbara Tuchman whose better-known books are longer than what is suitable for this guide.

The final list is the result of applying all five criteria. A section of 22 'long' books (i.e., at least 400 pages) is included as a sample of longer literature. The appendix points you to an additional forty excellent books.

Rating Books

You can exercise some of your critical thinking skills by rating the books you read. Each reference page includes a scale, ranging from 1 to 9, for rating books. Record your opinion about the books you read by circling a number on that scale.

The rating you give a book is not as important as the reasoning process you went through in giving it. You can develop your reasoning skills by taking high school English courses and reading published book reviews. English courses that analyze literature are especially helpful. You can find reviews in periodicals such as the *New York Review of Books* and the *Library Journal*. You also can find published book reviews online. (A good place to look is www.reviewsofbooks.com).

Careful reading does increase your knowledge and reasoning skills. That makes you a better student and improves your chances for a happy college experience. It also can connect you to the thoughts and experiences of earlier generations. Reading can unite you with your cultural heritage. It also can raise your awareness of other cultures.

360° of Reading guides you through a diverse literature. These books suit a wide variety of tastes and abilities. Use this guide to begin your journey towards a greater understanding of yourself and the universe.

Book References

FICTION

Novels / Short Stories

Fiction
Novels / Short Stories

18 Best Stories by Edgar Allan Poe *
by Edgar Allan Poe, Vincent Price (editor), Chandler Brossard (editor) (1965) 288p, ISBN-13: 978-0440322276

Standard book equivalent: 1.1
First published: early 19th century

Poe (1809 – 1849) was an American author noted for his macabre themes. This collection includes: 'The Black Cat'; 'The Fall of the House of Usher'; 'The Masque of the Red Death'; 'The Facts in the Case of M. Valdemar'; 'The Premature Burial'; 'Ms. Found in a Bottle'; 'A Tale of the Ragged Mountains'; 'The Sphinx'; 'The Murders in the Rue Morgue'; 'The Tell-Tale Heart'; 'The Gold-Bug'; 'The System of Dr. Tarr and Prof. Fether'; 'The Man That Was Used Up'; 'The Balloon Hoax'; 'A Descent Into the Maelstrom'; 'The Purloined Letter'; 'The Pit and The Pendulum'; 'The Cask of Amontillado'.

Keywords: American author, horror, short-stories

Websites:
http://www.sparknotes.com/lit/poestories/
http://www.poemuseum.org/
http://www.online-literature.com/poe/

Rate this book: 1 – 2 – 3   4 – 5 – 6   7 – 8 – 9

Fiction
Novels / Short Stories

1984
by George Orwell (1950) 336p, ISBN-13: 978-0451524935

Standard book equivalent: 1.3
First published: 1949

Nineteen Eighty-Four is a political novel written by British author George Orwell (1903 – 1950) in opposition to totalitarianism. The book depicts a negative utopia, or dystopia, in which an omnipresent state wields total control. Its central theme is the danger of totalitarianism, especially Stalinism, and the role language plays in shaping thought. The main character is Winston Smith, a middle-aged member of the ruling party whose thoughts turn to revolution. The plot traces Winston's frustration and reaction to the State's oppression.

Keywords: British author, dictatorship, dystopia, politics, Stalinism, totalitarianism

Websites:
http://www.sparknotes.com/lit/1984/index.html
http://www.gradesaver.com/classicnotes/titles/1984/
http://www.online-literature.com/orwell/1984/

Rate this book: 1 – 2 – 3   4 – 5 – 6   7 – 8 – 9

Fiction
Novels / Short Stories

The Adventures of Huckleberry Finn *
by Mark Twain (1981) 320p, ISBN-13: 978-0553210798

Standard book equivalent: 1.2
First published: 1884

Mark Twain (1835 – 1910) is a pseudonym for American author Samuel Clemens. The novel's setting is 1830s Missouri. Huck Finn is the narrator—a 13 year old, semi-literate boy. He's been raised to understand blacks as property. His attitude changes as he gets to know Jim on their flight to freedom. Jim is escaping slavery and Huck is escaping his abusive father. Huck's dilemma is to decide whether or not to rescue Jim when he is captured and held for return to slavery. In Huck's society, stealing a slave is the basest of crimes.

Keywords: American author, abuse, adventure, Missouri, racism

Websites:
http://www.sparknotes.com/lit/huckfinn/index.html
http://www.gradesaver.com/classicnotes/titles/huckfinn/
http://etext.virginia.edu/twain/huckfinn.html

Rate this book: 1 – 2 – 3   4 – 5 – 6   7 – 8 – 9

Fiction
Novels / Short Stories

The Alchemist: A Fable About Following Your Dream *
by Paulo Coelho (1995) 176p, ISBN-13: 978-0062502186

Standard book equivalent: 0.7
First published: 1988

Coelho (b. 1947) is a Brazilian writer strongly influenced by his Catholic faith. *The Alchemist* is a fable about Santiago, an Andalusian shepherd boy. Acting on his dream of distant treasure he leaves Spain for a quest through North Africa. The plot loosely follows that of the English legend, *The Pedlar of Swaffham*. Major themes of the novel include the importance of following one's dreams, searching for one's true mission in life, and that good deeds are eventually rewarded.

Keywords: Brazilian author, adventure, Egypt, fable, inspirational, Spain

Websites:
http://www.paulocoelho.com.br/engl/
http://www.worldmind.com/Cannon/Culture/Interviews/coelho.html
http://bookreviews.nabou.com/reviews/thealchemist.html

Rate this book: 1 – 2 – 3   4 – 5 – 6   7 – 8 – 9

Fiction
Novels / Short Stories

Alfred and Guinevere *
by James Schuyler, John Ashbery (Introduction) (2002)
160p, ISBN-13: 978-0940322493

Standard book equivalent: 0.6
First published: 1958

James Schuyler (1923 – 1991) was an American poet and novelist. This novel is about Alfred and Guinevere, who are children sent to live in the country with their uncle and grandmother. It is not clear to them why they have been sent to the country and their attempts to piece together the goings-on of their environs and the intentions of the adults around them is portrayed through dialogue, letters, and diary entries. The story derives much humor from their growing awareness of how the world works and the role their innocence plays in impeding their often comical search for knowledge.

Keywords: American author, children, family, mystery

Websites:
http://www.poets.org/poet.php/prmPID/1120
http://www.famouspoetsandpoems.com/poets/james_schuyl
   er
http://www.litencyc.com/php/speople.php?rec=true&UID=
   5909

Rate this book: 1 – 2 – 3   4 – 5 – 6   7 – 8 – 9

Fiction
Novels / Short Stories

All Quiet on the Western Front *
by Erich Maria Remarque (1996) 304p, ISBN-13: 978-0449911495

Standard book equivalent: 1.2
First published: 1929

Remarque (1898 – 1970) was a German author whose works were banned by the Nazis. *All Quiet* follows the life of nineteen-year old German soldier Paul Bäumer during World War I. He serves as the narrator for the novel, which is noted for its depiction of the monotony, horror and cruelty soldiers face in war. Paul joins the army, along with his friends, after hearing romantic tales of war from their school teachers. However, they quickly learn the realities of army-life as they never see any evidence of glory or romanticism in anything they experience.

Keywords: German author, coming-of-age, WWI, war

Websites:
http://www.sparknotes.com/lit/allquiet/index.html
http://www.bookrags.com/notes/aq/
http://www.gradesaver.com/classicnotes/titles/western/

Rate this book: 1 – 2 – 3   4 – 5 – 6   7 – 8 – 9

Fiction
Novels / Short Stories

Animal Farm *
by George Orwell (2003) 128p, ISBN-13: 978-0452284241

Standard book equivalent: 0.4
First published: 1945

Animal Farm is British author Orwell's (1903 - 1950) satire about communism and totalitarianism. The allegory begins with Old Major the Boar telling fellow animals about his dream in which all animals share equally and have no humans to oppress them. The animals on the farm stage an uprising, get rid of the farmer, and take over the running of the farm. However, the pigs eventually assume complete control over the other farm animals and become indistinguishable from the humans they ousted.

Keywords: British author, dictatorship, fable, satire

Websites:
http://www.sparknotes.com/lit/animalfarm/index.html
http://www.online-literature.com/orwell/animalfarm/
http://www.gradesaver.com/classicnotes/titles/animalfarm/

Rate this book: 1 – 2 – 3   4 – 5 – 6   7 – 8 – 9

Fiction
Novels / Short Stories

April Morning *
by Howard Fast (1983) 208p, ISBN-13: 978-0553273229

Standard book equivalent: 0.8
First published: 1961

Howard Fast (1914 – 2003) was an American novelist and television writer. *April Morning* is a coming-of-age story about Adam Cooper, a 15-year-old who gets caught up in the Battle of Lexington and Concord during the American Revolution. The novel starts with Adam being scolded by his father for laziness. However, the day's events soon change their lives as Adam's father is called to a town meeting—the British are marching out of Boston to seize the colonists' arsenal. By the end of the day Adam learns the meaning of responsibility.

Keywords: American author, American Revolution, coming-of-age, war

Websites:
http://en.wikipedia.org/wiki/April_Morning
http://www.spartacus.schoolnet.co.uk/USAfast.htm
http://www.nndb.com/people/716/000115371/

Rate this book: 1 – 2 – 3   4 – 5 – 6   7 – 8 – 9

Fiction
Novels / Short Stories

Arabian Nights and Days
by Naguib Mahfouz (1995) 240p, ISBN-13: 978-0385469012

Standard book equivalent: 0.9
First published: 1979

Egyptian author Mahfouz (1911 – 2006) was the winner of the 1988 Nobel Prize in Literature and the first Arabic author to be so honored. *Arabian Nights* tells a story that begins on the day following the "Thousand and One Nights", when the vizier of Dandan learns that his daughter, Shahrzad, has succeeded in saving her life by enchanting the sultan with wondrous tales. However, Shahrzad is still miserable because she distrusts her husband, whom she realizes continues to be capable of causing her great harm.

Keywords: Egyptian author, Arab experience, fable, marriage, Nobel Prize (Literature)

Websites:
http://www.kirjasto.sci.fi/mahfouz.htm
http://www.sis.gov.eg/En/Arts&Culture/EFiguers/0715000
    00000000003.htm
http://www.compulsivereader.com/html/modules.php?op=
    modload&name=News&file=article&sid=180&mode=
    thread&order=0&thold=0

Rate this book: 1 – 2 – 3   4 – 5 – 6   7 – 8 – 9

Fiction
Novels / Short Stories

As I Lay Dying **
by William Faulkner (1991) 288p, ISBN-13: 978-0679732259

Standard book equivalent: 1.1
First published: 1930

American author Faulkner (1897 - 1962) won the Nobel Prize in Literature in 1949. He is noted for his depiction of life in the American South and his stream of consciousness writing style. This novel follows the Bundren family as they take the ripening corpse of Addie, wife and mother, on a hideously comic journey. Addie was the wife of a poor Mississippi hill farmer, and her family is honoring her wish to be buried with "her people" in the town of Jefferson. During the journey the thoughts of each of the family members are revealed.

Keywords: American author, death, Nobel Prize (Literature), the South

Websites:
http://www.sparknotes.com/lit/asilay/
http://www.gradesaver.com/classicnotes/titles/dying/
http://en.wikipedia.org/wiki/As_I_Lay_Dying

Rate this book: 1 – 2 – 3   4 – 5 – 6   7 – 8 – 9

Fiction
Novels / Short Stories

At Swim-Two-Birds **
by Flann O'Brien, William H. Gass (Introduction) (1998)
336p, ISBN-13: 978-1564781819

Standard book equivalent: 1.3
First published: 1939

O'Brien (1911 – 1966) was an Irish author. This novel is narrated by a college student who never goes to class. Instead, he spends his time carousing with friends. The student begins to write a manuscript about an Irish novelist, Dermott Trellis, who is writing a morality tale about sin. The manuscript takes up the greater portion of the novel with the student's reminiscences periodically interrupting. The characters Trellis has created resent the roles he created for them and get revenge by rewriting his manuscript when he goes to sleep. Compare to *The Crying of Lot 49*.

Keywords: Irish author, Ireland

Websites:
http://www.litencyc.com/php/sworks.php?rec=true&UID=6483
http://findarticles.com/p/articles/mi_m0403/is_n2_v39/ai_14773411
http://en.wikipedia.org/wiki/At_Swim-Two-Birds

Rate this book: 1 – 2 – 3   4 – 5 – 6   7 – 8 – 9

Fiction
Novels / Short Stories

Atticus
by Ron Hansen (1997) 256p, ISBN-13: 978-0060927868

Standard book equivalent: 1.0
First published: 1995

American author Hansen (b. 1947) was nominated for the 1996 National Book Award for *Atticus*. This story is about Atticus Cody, a 67-year-old Colorado cattle man. He goes to Mexico to retrieve the body of his younger son, an artist and alcoholic who committed suicide. The grieving father meets Scott's friends and is forced to cope with a culture alien to him, while he begins to suspect that his son was actually murdered. A primary theme of the novel is the great depth of love the father has for his son.

Keywords: American author, alcoholism, loss, love, Mexico, mystery, suicide

Websites:
http://en.wikipedia.org/wiki/Ron_Hansen_%28novelist%29
http://www.sacbee.com/static/live/lifestyle/bookclub/archives/hansen.html
http://www.harpercollins.com/author/authorExtra.aspx?authorID=4172&isbn13=9780060927868&displayType=readingGuide

Rate this book: 1 – 2 – 3   4 – 5 – 6   7 – 8 – 9

Fiction
Novels / Short Stories

The Autobiography of an Ex-Colored Man
by James Weldon Johnson (1995) 112p, ISBN-13: 978-0486285122

Standard book equivalent: 0.4
First published: 1912

Johnson (1871 – 1938) was the author of the lyrics to the Black National Anthem, "Lift Ev'ry Voice and Sing". *The Autobiography of an Ex-Colored Man* explores the meaning of race. Its theme of moral cowardice is a backdrop to the tragic story of the unnamed narrator, the light-skinned child of a black mother and white father, who comes-of-age in early 20th century America. The narrator is born in Georgia and raised in Connecticut where he experiences little discrimination until he is identified as "colored".

Keywords: African-American author, American author African American experience, coming-of-age, racism

Websites:
http://www.litencyc.com/php/sworks.php?rec=true&UID=1546
http://www.gutenberg.org/etext/11012
http://www.poets.org/poet.php/prmPID/72

Rate this book: 1 – 2 – 3   4 – 5 – 6   7 – 8 – 9

Fiction
Novels / Short Stories

The Awakening
by Kate Chopin (1993) 128p, ISBN-13: 978-0486277868

Standard book equivalent: 0.5
First published: 1899

American author Chopin (1851 – 1904) grew up in St Louis, Missouri. *The Awakening* is a story about a New Orleans woman, 28-year old Edna Pontellier, who becomes dissatisfied with her marriage. She abandons her husband and children to search for love and self-understanding after visiting a resort island one summer. The scenes of infidelity and lust caused a scandal in early twentieth century America, based on moral rather than literary grounds, and followed Chopin for the rest of her life.

Keywords: American Author, woman author, feminism, love, marriage, New Orleans

Websites:
http://www.pagebypagebooks.com/Kate_Chopin/The_Awakening_and_Selected_Short_Stories/
http://www.vcu.edu/engweb/eng384/awake.htm
http://docsouth.unc.edu/chopinawake/menu.html
http://www.pbs.org/katechopin/

Rate this book: 1 – 2 – 3   4 – 5 – 6   7 – 8 – 9

Fiction
Novels / Short Stories

Balzac and the Little Chinese Seamstress
by Dai Sijie (2002) 192p, ISBN-13: 978-0385722209

Standard book equivalent: 0.7
First published: 2000

Sijie (b. 1954) is a Chinese author and film maker; he is now a French citizen. *Balzac and the Little Chinese Seamstress* follows the lives of two middle-class teens that have been sent to a Chinese village for "re-education" during Mao's Cultural Revolution. They steal a suitcase filled with classic Western literature and decide to use them to re-educate the peasant seamstress to Western thought. The cultural universality of great literature and its role in raising one's consciousness are explored. See also, *Becoming Madame Mao*.

Keywords: Chinese author, coming-of-age, China, love, Mao

Websites:
http://www.readinggroupguides.com/guides3/balzac_and_the_seamstress1.asp
http://www.complete-review.com/reviews/china/daisijie.htm
http://booksiloved.com/3/Balzac_and_the_Little_Chinese_Seamstress.html

Rate this book: 1 – 2 – 3   4 – 5 – 6   7 – 8 – 9

Fiction
Novels / Short Stories

The Baron in the Trees
by Italo Calvino (1977) 228p, ISBN-13: 978-0156106801

Standard book equivalent: 0.9
First published: 1957

Calvino (1923 – 1985) was an Italian author who was a communist until his abrupt break with the party in 1957. *The Baron in the Trees* is an example of magical realism. Cosimo, a young eighteenth-century Italian nobleman, rebels against his parents by climbing into the trees to remain there for the rest of his life. He quickly adapts to his arboreal existence leading a full life, including love affairs. The novel's supporting characters also are eccentric and include his dog, domineering mother, disaster prone sister, and even Napoleon Bonaparte.

Keywords: Italian author, fable, Italy, magical realism

Websites:
http://www.geocities.com/Athens/Forum/7504/calvino.html
http://www.des.emory.edu/mfp/calvino/
http://greatsfandf.com/AUTHORS/ItaloCalvino.php

Rate this book: 1 – 2 – 3   4 – 5 – 6   7 – 8 – 9

Fiction
Novels / Short Stories

Becoming Madame Mao
by Anchee Min (2001) 330p, ISBN-13: 978-0618127009

Standard book equivalent: 1.3
First published: 2001

Min (b. 1957) was born in Shanghai and immigrated to the United States in 1984. This is a historical novel that portrays Madame Mao's poor background, rise to power and insatiable thirst for power. Yunhe was born to a rural concubine in 1919. She renamed herself Lan Ping after running away to Shanghai in 1934 with ambitions to be an actress. Lan Ping joined the Red Army where she met and married Mao Zedong who changed her name to Jiang Ching. Suggested companion book: *Balzac and the Little Chinese Seamstress.*

Keywords: Chinese-American author, Woman author, China, coming-of-age, dictatorship, Mao, marriage

Websites:
http://www.houghtonmifflinbooks.com/readers_guides/min
    /bookinfo.shtml
http://www.theconnection.org/shows/2000/06/20000626_b
    _main.asp
http://www.barclayagency.com/min.html

Rate this book: 1 – 2 – 3   4 – 5 – 6   7 – 8 – 9

Fiction
Novels / Short Stories

Bel Canto
by Ann Patchett (2002) 336p, ISBN-13: 978-0060934415

Standard book equivalent: 1.3
First published: 2001

American author Patchett (b. 1963) was born in Los Angeles. She won the Orange Prize for Fiction and PEN/Faulkner Award for Fiction in 2002 for *Bel Canto*. It is the story of a hostage crisis in an unnamed South American country. A birthday party, with an international guest list, is held at the home of the country's vice president. It is invaded by terrorists and the story traces the bonds that develop between people of different nationalities and political persuasions during the ordeal.

Keywords: Woman author, American author, PEN/Faulkner Award, South America, terrorism

Websites:
http://www.annpatchett.com/aboutann.html
http://www.bookreporter.com/authors/au-patchett-ann.asp
http://www.pbs.org/newshour/conversation/july-dec02/patchett_7-02.html

Rate this book: 1 – 2 – 3   4 – 5 – 6   7 – 8 – 9

Fiction
Novels / Short Stories

The Bell Jar **
by Sylvia Plath (2000) 288p, ISBN-13: 978-0060930189

Standard book equivalent: 1.1
First published: 1963

Sylvia Plath (1932 – 1963) was an American author and poet who suffered from clinical depression. *The Bell Jar* is a semi-autobiographical novel that traces the story of a talented young woman's descent into madness. Esther Greenwood, the main character, gets an internship at a prominent magazine in New York City and finds life in New York to be both exhilarating and frightening. She gradually slips into an ever deeper depression and becomes institutionalized. The title refers to both a bell jar—that suffocates and places specimens in plain view— and to the famous Belleview psychiatric hospital in New York.

Keywords: Woman author, American author, mental illness, New York City

Websites:
http://www.sylviaplath.info/belljar.html
http://www.gradesaver.com/classicnotes/titles/belljar/
http://www.sparknotes.com/lit/belljar/

Rate this book: 1 – 2 – 3   4 – 5 – 6   7 – 8 – 9

Fiction
Novels / Short Stories

A Bend in the River
by V.S. Naipaul (1989) 288p, ISBN-13: 978-0679722021

Standard book equivalent: 1.1
First published: 1979

Naipaul (b. 1932) is a British author of Trinidadian and Indian ancestry, and 2001 Nobel Prize in Literature winner. The novel's setting is the city of Kisangani, on the Congo River. It takes place after Congo's freedom from Belgium and tells the story of the early days of Zaire's independence. The protagonist is a young Indian businessman who has purchased a small shop. The fortunes of both the country and the shopkeeper spiral downwards. Naipaul's depictions of Africa, colonialism, and life in newly independent African nations have been widely acclaimed for their accuracy and sensitivity.

Keywords: British author, Trinidadian author, Africa, colonialism, cross-cultural, Nobel Prize (Literature)

Websites:
http://www.postcolonialweb.org/caribbean/naipaul/naipaulov.html
http://www.pbs.org/newshour/gergen/jan-june00/naipaul_3-3.html
http://www.english.emory.edu/Bahri/Naipaul.html

Rate this book: 1 – 2 – 3   4 – 5 – 6   7 – 8 – 9

Fiction
Novels / Short Stories

Brave New World
by Aldous Huxley (1998) 288p, ISBN-13: 978-0060929879

Standard book equivalent: 1.1
First published: 1932

Huxley (1894 – 1963) was a British author of novels and essays. *Brave New World* is a classic science fiction work set in London during the 26th century. It describes an earth that is unified under The World State, which is planned around the principles of Henry Ford. The novel serves as a warning to the dangers of governments that grow increasingly powerful and invasive of its citizen's liberties. It is often compared to Orwell's *1984*. *Brave New World* anticipates many developments in reproductive technology and eugenics that combine to affect society's character.

Keywords: British author, dystopia, politics, science fiction, totalitarianism

Websites:
http://www.hedweb.com/huxley/bnw/
http://www.sparknotes.com/lit/bravenew/
http://www.cliffsnotes.com/WileyCDA/LitNote/id-45.html

Rate this book: 1 – 2 – 3   4 – 5 – 6   7 – 8 – 9

Fiction
Novels / Short Stories

Bridge of San Luis Rey
by Thornton Wilder (2003) 160p, ISBN-13: 978-0060088873

Standard book equivalent: 0.6
First published 1927

American author Wilder (1897 – 1975) won the 1928 Pulitzer Prize for *Bridge of San Luis Rey*. The novel tells the story of a bridge collapse in eighteenth-century Peru, causing the deaths of five people. A friar witnessing the event sets out to learn about the victims. The novel explores philosophical questions of evil and why bad things happen to good people. It is noted for its simplicity, beauty and melancholy style. The book is often cited as the prototype for modern day disaster literature using flashbacks to examine the lives of characters affected by a great calamity.

Keywords: American author, disaster, Pulitzer Prize, South America

Websites:
http://www.harpercollins.com/author/authorExtra.aspx?authorID=10563&isbn13=9780060088873&displayType=readingGuide
http://www.tcnj.edu/~wilder/
http://en.wikipedia.org/wiki/Thornton_Wilder

Rate this book: 1 – 2 – 3   4 – 5 – 6   7 – 8 – 9

Fiction
Novels / Short Stories

The Bridges at Toko-Ri *
by James A. Michener (1984) 128p, ISBN-13: 978-0449206515

Standard book equivalent: 0.5
First published: 1953

Michener (1907 – 1997) was an American author of many sweeping novels that often covered multiple generations within a particular geographical setting. *The Bridges of Toko-Ri* is atypical among his novels; it is short and focused on the lives of a few U.S. Navy fighter pilots taking part in the Korean conflict. The plot of the book is driven by a plan to destroy the strategic bridges of the title. The main character is Brubaker a former pilot of World War II who leaves civilian life to return to military service in the Korean War.

Keywords: American author, aviation, Korea, Korean War, pilots, war

Websites:
http://www.findarticles.com/p/articles/mi_m0IAX/is_3_84/ai_108548248
http://www.allreaders.com/Topics/info_25679.asp
http://www.achievement.org/autodoc/page/mic0bio-1

Rate this book: 1 – 2 – 3   4 – 5 – 6   7 – 8 – 9

Fiction
Novels / Short Stories

Brighter Sun *
by Samuel Selvon (1987) 224p, ISBN-13: 978-0582642652

Standard book equivalent: 0.9
First published: 1952

Selvon (1923 – 1994) was a Caribbean author born in Trinidad. His writing is often praised for its realism and great attention to dialect. *Brighter Sun* is set in Trinidad and explores peasant experience during a time of socio-economic change. It focuses on the everyday experiences of islanders in Trinidad through the main characters of Tiger and Urmilla who are newly married and growing into adulthood. Immigration, the lure of London and the impact of "Yankee" culture on the Island are portrayed.

Keywords: Caribbean author, immigrants, London, marriage, short-stories, Trinidad

Websites:
http://www.hrc.utexas.edu/research/fa/selvon.html
http://www.peepaltreepress.com/author_display.asp?au_id=84
http://www.eng.fju.edu.tw/worldlit/caribbean/Selvon.htm

Rate this book: 1 – 2 – 3   4 – 5 – 6   7 – 8 – 9

Fiction
Novels / Short Stories

Candide **
by Voltaire, (1991) 112p, ISBN-13: 978-0486266893

Standard book equivalent: 0.4
First published: 1759

Francois-Marie Arouet (1694 – 1778) was a French philosopher who is better known by his pseudonym Voltaire. Voltaire never publicly admitted to being the author of *Candide*. The work is signed with the pseudonym Monsieur le docteur Ralph. *Candide* is the story of an optimistic and naïve young man who travels the world seeking to be reunited with his lost love. It is often thought to be a satire attacking the philosophy of Gottfried Leibniz who is portrayed by the character Pangloss.

Keywords: French author, absurdism, fable, optimism

Websites:
http://www.literature.org/authors/voltaire/candide/
http://www.sparknotes.com/lit/candide/
http://humanities.uchicago.edu/homes/VSA/Candide/

Rate this book: 1 – 2 – 3   4 – 5 – 6   7 – 8 – 9

Fiction
Novels / Short Stories

A Canticle for Leibowitz **
by Walter M. Miller, (2006) 352p, ISBN-13: 978-0060892999

Standard book equivalent: 1.4
First published: 1959

Miller (1923 – 1996) was an American science fiction writer whose novel won the Hugo Award in 1961. The setting is many centuries in the future after an apocalyptic nuclear war. It opens with the accidental excavation of what becomes a holy artifact, a memo scrawled by the hand of Saint Leibowitz, which reads "Pound pastrami, can kraut, six bagels—bring home for Emma." To the Brothers of Saint Leibowitz, it is a symbol of hope from the distant past. *A Canticle for Leibowitz* tackles the sociological and religious implications of the cyclical rise and fall of civilizations.

Keywords: American author, dystopia, nuclear war, religion, science fiction

Websites:
https://www.wsu.edu/~brians/science_fiction/canticle.html
http://www.imaginedat.net/miller.htm
http://www.sfsite.com/10b/cant19.htm

Rate this book: 1 – 2 – 3   4 – 5 – 6   7 – 8 – 9

Fiction
Novels / Short Stories

The Catcher in the Rye
by J.D. Salinger (2001) 288p, ISBN-13: 978-0316769174

Standard book equivalent: 1.1
First published: 1951

American author Salinger (b. 1919) is the author of a novel and several short stories. The widely acclaimed *The Catcher in the Rye* is a coming-of-age novel about Holden Caulfield, a seventeen year old prep school adolescent. It relates his lonely, life-changing twenty-four hour stay in New York City. He experiences the phoniness of the adult world while attempting to deal with the death of his younger brother, an overwhelming compulsion to lie and troubling sexual experiences. It is frequently found on high school required reading lists.

Keywords: American author, coming-of-age, mental illness, New York City

Websites:
http://www.sparknotes.com/lit/catcher/
http://www.gradesaver.com/classicnotes/titles/catcherrye/
http://www.homework-online.com/tcitr/index.asp

Rate this book: 1 – 2 – 3   4 – 5 – 6   7 – 8 – 9

Fiction
Novels / Short Stories

Cat's Cradle
by Kurt Vonnegut Jr. (1998) 304p, ISBN-13: 978-0385333481

Standard book equivalent: 1.2
First published: 1963

Vonnegut (1922 – 2007) was an American author and satirist. *Cat's Cradle* is a science fiction novel and satire that examines religion, science and technology. The narrator is John, a man researching a novel on Hiroshima. He discovers that someone has developed a chemical (ice-nine) that could destroy the world. Ice-nine is a form of water that is solid at room temperature. When it comes in contact with normal water ice-nine catalyzes water's change to ice-nine. The novel's title refers to the string game the fictional creator of the atomic bomb was playing when the Hiroshima bomb was dropped.

Keywords: American author, atomic bomb, Hiroshima, ice-nine, politics, science fiction, technology

Websites:
http://www.sparknotes.com/lit/catscradle/
http://www.gradesaver.com/classicnotes/titles/cradle/
http://www.vonnegut.com/

Rate this book: 1 – 2 – 3   4 – 5 – 6   7 – 8 – 9

Fiction
Novels / Short Stories

Changes: A Love Story
by Ama Ata Aidoo (1993) 208p, ISBN-13: 978-1558610651

Standard book equivalent: 0.8
First published: 1991

Ghanaian author Aidoo (b. 1942) is a Visiting Professor of Africana Studies at Brown University. *Changes*, her second novel, is the story of a woman discovering herself while trying to balance her need for independence with her need for attention and love within the context of Ghanaian culture. She learns to appreciate the truth and richness of her culture. *Changes* highlights the tension between Western and Ghanaian culture. The novel depicts the clutter of the zongo, the frustrations of working life in Accra, and the disillusionment of love.

Keywords: Ghanaian author, woman author, Africa, feminism, Ghana, love, marriage

Websites:
http://www.findarticles.com/p/articles/mi_m1264/is_n10_v24/ai_14804594
http://www.kirjasto.sci.fi/aidoo.htm
http://www.postcolonialweb.org/africa/ghana/aidoo/aidoov.html

Rate this book: 1 – 2 – 3   4 – 5 – 6   7 – 8 – 9

Fiction
Novels / Short Stories

Chocolat
by Joanne Harris (2000) 319p, ISBN-13: 978-0552998482

Standard book equivalent: 1.2
First published: 1999

Harris (b. 1964) is a British author. Her novel, *Chocolat*, takes place in a small fictional French town. There are two main characters. Vianne Rocher, an outsider and mother of a 6-year old girl, opens a chocolate shop when she arrives in town. Francis Reynaud is a priest of the local parish and fears the shop will tempt church-goers to forget their Lenten vows and over-indulge. The story is told in first person from the point of view of the two main characters in alternating chapters. It covers themes about compassion, tolerance, understanding, bigotry, greed, and hatred.

Keywords: British author, woman author, chocolate, France, prejudice, tolerance

Websites:
http://www.joanne-harris.co.uk/
http://news.bbc.co.uk/1/hi/talking_point/forum/1238295.stm
http://www.calitreview.com/Interviews/harris_8023.htm

Rate this book: 1 – 2 – 3   4 – 5 – 6   7 – 8 – 9

Fiction
Novels / Short Stories

A Christmas Carol *
by Charles Dickens (1991) 80p, ISBN-13: 978-0486268651

Standard book equivalent: 0.3
First published: 1843

British author Charles Dickens (1812 – 1870), the author of *Oliver Twist* and *A Tale of Two Cities*, invented the modern concept of Christmas Spirit with *A Christmas Carol*. It was written at a time when the holiday's popularity was waning and is credited with renewing Christmas' status as an important cultural holiday. It is about the relationship between mean-spirited Scrooge and his mild-mannered clerk, Bob Cratchit. Scrooge becomes aware of his own miserly ways after being visited by three ghosts.

Keywords: British author, business, Christmas, England, greed, Scrooge

Websites:
http://www.sparknotes.com/lit/christmascarol/
http://www.stormfax.com/dickens.htm
http://www.victorianweb.org/authors/dickens/pva13.html

Rate this book: 1 – 2 – 3   4 – 5 – 6   7 – 8 – 9

Fiction
Novels / Short Stories

Chronicle of a Death Foretold
by Gabriel Garcia Marquez (2003) 128p, ISBN-13: 978-1400034710

Standard book equivalent: 0.5
First published: 1981

Marquez (b. 1928) is a Colombian author and winner of the 1982 Nobel Prize in Literature. This novel is based on a true story. It tells the tale of a revenge killing recorded in the newspapers. A young girl in a South American village is newly married, but she is found to have already lost her virginity. Her brothers are honor-bound to kill the man responsible. Although they have no interest in taking action, they nonetheless act because no one will stop them.

Keywords: Colombian author, love, Nobel Prize (Literature), South America

Websites:
http://www.sparknotes.com/lit/chrondeath/
http://www.themodernword.com/gabo/gabo_biography.html
http://en.wikipedia.org/wiki/Chronicle_of_a_Death_Foretold

Rate this book: 1 – 2 – 3   4 – 5 – 6   7 – 8 – 9

Fiction
Novels / Short Stories

The Color Purple
by Alice Walker (1990) 304p, ISBN-13: 978-0671727796

Standard book equivalent: 1.2
First published: 1982

Alice Walker (b. 1944) is an American author and feminist. She was awarded a 1983 Pulitzer Prize for *The Color Purple*. This novel is the story of a young woman who sees herself as property until another woman teaches her to value herself. The main character is Celie, a 14-year old uneducated African American woman in early twentieth century Macon, Georgia. It is written as a series of letters by Celie to God. Celie writes the letters because of the treatment she receives from her abusive father.

Keywords: African American author, woman author, abuse, African American experience, coming-of-age, epistolary novel, feminism, Georgia, inspirational, Pulitzer Prize, the South

Websites:
http://www.sparknotes.com/lit/purple/
http://www.luminarium.org/contemporary/alicew/
http://thebestnotes.com/booknotes/Color_Purple/Color_Purple02.html

Rate this book: 1 – 2 – 3   4 – 5 – 6   7 – 8 – 9

Fiction
Novels / Short Stories

Cry, the Beloved Country
by Alan Paton (2003) 320p, ISBN-13: 978-0743262170

Standard book equivalent: 1.2
First published: 1948

Paton (1903 – 1988) was a South African author and founder of the Liberal Party. He wrote *Cry, the Beloved Country* while on an overseas trip and finished it in San Francisco on Christmas Eve, 1946. It takes place in 1940s South Africa and is the story of Zulu Methodist pastor Stephen Kumalo, who searches for his sick sister in Johannesburg. There, he discovers that she has become a prostitute and his son a murderer. The novel is a protest against social behavior that was soon to be officially established as apartheid.

Keywords: South African author, Africa, apartheid, racism, South Africa

Websites:
http://www.sparknotes.com/lit/cry/
http://www.gradesaver.com/classicnotes/titles/cry/
http://www.bookrags.com/notes/cbc/

Rate this book: 1 – 2 – 3   4 – 5 – 6   7 – 8 – 9

Fiction
Novels / Short Stories

The Crying of Lot 49 **
by Thomas Pynchon (1999) 160p, ISBN-13: 978-0060931674

Standard book equivalent: 0.6
First published: 1966

Pynchon (b. 1937) is the American author of *V* and *Gravity's Rainbow*, and a MacArthur Fellow (1988). He is known for his avoidance of publicity. *The Crying of Lot 49* is his shortest novel. It is steeped in symbolism, puns, dry humor and conspiracies. The plot revolves around a centuries-old conflict—discovered by the protagonist, Oedipa Maas—between two mail distribution companies. A play within the story, *The Courier's Tragedy*, occupies much of the novel.

Keywords: American author, California

Websites:
http://www.sparknotes.com/lit/lot49/
http://www.gradesaver.com/classicnotes/titles/crying/
http://www.harpercollins.com/author/authorExtra.aspx?isbn13=9780060931674&displayType=readingGuide

Rate this book: 1 – 2 – 3   4 – 5 – 6   7 – 8 – 9

Fiction
Novels / Short Stories

The Curious Incident of the Dog in the Night-Time
by Mark Haddon (2004) 240p, ISBN-13: 978-1400032716

Standard book equivalent: 0.9
First published: 2003

Haddon (b. 1962) is a British novelist awarded the 2004 Commonwealth Writers' Prize Overall Best First Book for *The Curious Incident*. It is an unusual murder mystery narrated by autistic fifteen-year-old Christopher, who must prove his innocence when a neighborhood dog is killed. It soon becomes evident to the reader that the plot is secondary to the main character. The reader is invited to observe how Christopher reacts to the events unfolding around him. Having some knowledge about autism will be beneficial to understanding the subtleties of Christopher's behavior.

Keywords: British author, autism, crime, mental illness

Websites:
http://www.markhaddon.com/
http://www.npr.org/templates/story/story.php?storyId=4707767
http://www.timesonline.co.uk/article/0,,2101-2315884,00.html

Rate this book: 1 – 2 – 3   4 – 5 – 6   7 – 8 – 9

Fiction
Novels / Short Stories

Darkness at Noon **
by Arthur Koestler (1984) 224p, ISBN-13: 978-0099424918

Standard book equivalent: 0.9
First published: 1940

Koestler (1905 – 1983) was a Hungarian author. *Darkness at Noon* is a chilling look at Stalin's Russia during the late 1930s. The novel is based on the Moscow trials of 1936-38 in which Stalin arrested and executed almost every major Bolshevik surviving from the Revolution. The main character, Rubashov, is a government official who is arrested, imprisoned, tortured and forced to confess to crimes he did not commit. Having some background in the history of Stalin's purges will enable the reader to get more out of the novel.

Keywords: Hungarian author, dictatorship, Russia, Stalinism, totalitarianism

Websites:
http://www.bookrags.com/studyguide-darkn/?ref=fbn
http://www.kirjasto.sci.fi/koestler.htm
http://www.politicalusa.com/columnists/giardiello/giardiello_review_007.htm

Rate this book: 1 – 2 – 3   4 – 5 – 6   7 – 8 – 9

Fiction
Novels / Short Stories

The Day of the Locust
by Nathanael West (1983) 208p, ISBN-13: 978-0451523488

Standard book equivalent: 0.8
First published: 1939

American author West (1903 – 1940) was both a screenwriter and novelist. The setting for *The Day of the Locust* is Hollywood, California, during the Great Depression. The main character, Tod Hackett, is a set designer who becomes involved in the lives of several individuals perverted by the artificial and decadent Hollywood lifestyle. Hackett's completion of his painting "The Burning of Los Angeles" coincides with the explosion of the other characters' unfulfilled dreams in riot and murder. One of the novel's characters coincidentally is named Homer Simpson.

Keywords: American author, California, decadence, Great Depression, Hollywood

Websites:
http://www.sparknotes.com/lit/locust/
http://www.litencyc.com/php/speople.php?rec=true&UID=4670
http://www.webster.edu/~corbetre/personal/reading/west-locust.html

Rate this book: 1 – 2 – 3   4 – 5 – 6   7 – 8 – 9

Fiction
Novels / Short Stories

Death Comes for the Archbishop
by Willa Cather (1990) 304p, ISBN-13: 978-0679728894

Standard book equivalent: 1.2
First published: 1927

Willa Cather (1873 – 1947) is the American author of *O Pioneers*, and *My Antonia*. *Death Comes for the Archbishop* is based on two real life French Catholic priests who were sent to the American Southwest in 1851. The novel reads like a series of short stories with the priests traveling throughout the area and meeting a wide variety of people along the way. Their adventures typically have religious undertones. For example, when one of them gets lost in the desert he sees a juniper tree in the shape of a cross that leads him to food and shelter.

Keywords: American author, woman author, death, religion, Southwest

Websites:
http://www.cliffsnotes.com/WileyCDA/LitNote/id-170,pageNum-86.html
http://education.yahoo.com/homework_help/cliffsnotes/death_comes_for_the_archbishop/
http://www.bookrags.com/Death_Comes_for_the_Archbishop

Rate this book: 1 – 2 – 3   4 – 5 – 6   7 – 8 – 9

Fiction
Novels / Short Stories

A Death in the Family
by James Agee (1998) 320p, ISBN-13: 978-0375701238

Standard book equivalent: 1.2
First published: 1957

James Agee (1909 – 1955) was an American author who won a 1958 Pulitzer Prize for *A Death in the Family*. The novel is autobiographical of his boyhood in that it mirrors the loss his family felt at his father's death. One of the novel's themes concerns the dual roots many families of the day had in both rural and urban America and the tensions that often arose because of that duality. This novel was published posthumously. It is soon to be revised on the basis of new research that provides for a different editing of the original incomplete manuscript.

Keywords: American author, death, family, Pulitzer Prize

Websites:
http://www.sparknotes.com/lit/deathinthefamily/
http://www.literarydictionary.com/php/sworks.php?rec=true&UID=7198
http://www.pbs.org/wnet/ihas/poet/agee.html

Rate this book: 1 – 2 – 3   4 – 5 – 6   7 – 8 – 9

Fiction
Novels / Short Stories

Dinner at the Homesick Restaurant
by Anne Tyler (1996) 336p, ISBN-13: 978-0449911594

Standard book equivalent: 1.3
First published: 1982

Tyler (b. 1941) is an American author of short stories and novels. *Dinner at the Homesick Restaurant* is set in 1960s Baltimore, Maryland. It examines the importance of family and the imperfections they inevitably experience through the lives of the dysfunctional Tull family. The main characters are single mother Pearl, and her children: Cody, Ezra, and Jenny. The novel follows their lives and the issues they face, which can be traced back to the father who deserted them. The title refers to the annual family dinners, which are always accompanied with conflict.

Keywords: American author, woman author, Baltimore, family

Websites:
http://www.litencyc.com/php/sworks.php?rec=true&UID=5607
http://www.bookrags.com/Dinner_at_the_Homesick_Restaurant
http://puthagam.blogspot.com/2006/04/dinner-at-homesick-restaurant-by-anne.html

Rate this book: 1 – 2 – 3   4 – 5 – 6   7 – 8 – 9

Fiction
Novels / Short Stories

Dracula
by Bram Stoker (2000) 320p, ISBN-13: 978-0486411095

Standard book equivalent: 1.2
First published: 1897

Stoker (1847 – 1912) was an Irish author of several novels and short stories, though best known as the author of *Dracula*. It is the story of a naive young Englishman who travels to Transylvania to do business with a client, Count Dracula. After resorting to his true nature and dealing with the Englishman, Dracula boards a ship for England in search of fresh blood. *Dracula*, like *The Color Purple*, is written as a series of letters or diary entries (i.e., it is an epistolary novel).

Keywords: Irish author, epistolary novel, horror, Transylvania

Websites:
http://www.sparknotes.com/lit/dracula/
http://www.cliffsnotes.com/WileyCDA/LitNote/id-91.html
http://www.online-literature.com/stoker/

Rate this book: 1 – 2 – 3   4 – 5 – 6   7 – 8 – 9

Fiction
Novels / Short Stories

Elbow Room
by James Alan McPherson (1986) 288p, ISBN-13: 978-0449213575

Standard book equivalent: 1.1
First published: 1977

McPherson (b. 1943) is an American short-story writer and winner of a 1978 Pulitzer Prize for *Elbow Room*. He was awarded a Guggenheim Fellowship in 1973 and a MacArthur Fellowship in 1981. *Elbow Room* is a collection of twelve stories that deal with the families, relationships, and experiences of people as a part of African American society. His characters are trapped by assumptions and misled by appearances as they attempt to rely on their misunderstood experiences to navigate their lives.

Keywords: American author, African American author, African American experience, Pulitzer Prize, short-stories

Websites:
http://sprg.ssl.berkeley.edu/~jmcd/book/revs3/elrm.html
http://www.fringemagazine.org/issue_02_criticism.htm
http://www.georgetown.edu/tamlit/newsletter/7/Profiles.htm

Rate this book: 1 – 2 – 3   4 – 5 – 6   7 – 8 – 9

Fiction
Novels / Short Stories

A Farewell to Arms
by Ernest Hemingway (1994) 304p, ISBN-13: 978-0684801469

Standard book equivalent: 1.2
First published 1929

Hemingway (1899 – 1961) was an American author and winner of both a Pulitzer Prize and the 1954 Nobel Prize in Literature. He is noted for his economical writing style and characters that exude grace under pressure. *A Farewell to Arms* is a love story that draws heavily on Hemingway's experiences as a young soldier in Italy. It tells the story of Lieutenant Frederic Henry, a young American ambulance driver serving in the Italian army during World War I. Henry falls in love with the English nurse Catherine Barkley.

Keywords: American author, Italy, love, Nobel Prize (Literature), Pulitzer Prize, WWI, war

Websites:
http://www.sparknotes.com/lit/farewell/
http://www.ernest.hemingway.com/
http://www.gradesaver.com/classicnotes/titles/farewelltoarms/

Rate this book: 1 – 2 – 3   4 – 5 – 6   7 – 8 – 9

Fiction
Novels / Short Stories

Ficciones
by Jorge Luis Borges (1969) 174p, ISBN-13: 978-0802130303

Standard book equivalent: 0.7
First published: 1944

Jorge Luis Borges (1899 – 1986) was one of Argentina's best-known writers and has a worldwide audience. Borges is also noted for his reviews of imaginary literary works. He is often compared with Vladimir Nabokov and James Joyce. This is an English translation of *Ficcones*. The seventeen imaginative, whimsical, fantastic and often bizarre short-stories collected in *Ficciones* explore the themes of mirrors, cults, plots, and history. The book is divided into two parts, 'The Garden of Forking Paths' and 'Artifices', each introduced by a prologue written by Borges.

Keywords: Argentinean author, short-stories

Websites:
http://www.themodernword.com/borges/
http://www.complete-review.com/reviews/borgesjl/ficciones.htm
http://www.smu.edu/bridwell/exhibits/ficcionescharacteristics.htm

Rate this book: 1 – 2 – 3   4 – 5 – 6   7 – 8 – 9

Fiction
Novels / Short Stories

The Fixer
by Bernard Malamud (1994) 304p, ISBN-13: 978-0140185157

Standard book equivalent: 1.2
First published: 1966

Malamud (1914 – 1986) was an American author. *The Fixer* won both the National Book Award and a Pulitzer Prize in 1967. It is about Yakov Bok, a humble Jewish fixer (handyman) in Russia in 1910. He leaves his village and moves to Kiev looking for work and a better life. Life is dangerous because government sanctioned pogroms are widespread. Bok, pretending to be gentile, finds work with an anti-Semite at a brickyard. Things go well until a young Christian boy is killed and Bok is framed for the murder though there is no evidence against him.

Keywords: American author, Jewish experience, pogrom, Pulitzer Prize, Russia, tolerance

Websites:
http://www.bookrags.com/studyguide-fixer/?ref=fbn
http://www2.dokkyo.ac.jp/~esemi006/malamud/art/novels01.htm#tf
http://www.myjewishlearning.com/culture/literature/Overview_Jewish_American_Literature/Into_The_Literary_Mainstream/Literature_Malamud_Norton.htm

Rate this book: 1 – 2 – 3   4 – 5 – 6   7 – 8 – 9

Fiction
Novels / Short Stories

Flatland: A Romance of Many Dimensions **
by Edwin A. Abbott (1992) 96p, ISBN-13: 978-0486272634

Standard book equivalent: 0.4
First published: 1884

British author Abbott (1838 – 1926) was a schoolmaster and theologian. *Flatland* is a fable about a two dimensional world. The narrator, Square, guides the reader through life in two dimensions. Square dreams of a visit to Lineland, and tries to convince that realm's monarch of a second dimension. Next, Square is visited by a sphere, which he cannot comprehend until he sees the third dimension for himself. He then dreams of visiting Pointland (a self-aware point that occupies all space and knows nothing but itself) and learns that he cannot "rescue [the point] from his self-satisfaction".

Keywords: British author, fable, math

Websites:
http://abbott.thefreelibrary.com/
http://www.mathaware.org/mam/00/master/people/abbott/index.html
http://www.newmanu.edu/fs/pages/burgesonj/FlatlandWS.htm

Rate this book: 1 – 2 – 3   4 – 5 – 6   7 – 8 – 9

Fiction
Novels / Short Stories

Flowers for Algernon
by Daniel Keyes (2000) 224p, ISBN-13: 978-1857989380

Standard book equivalent: 0.9
First published: 1966

Keyes (b. 1927) is an American author of science fiction. *Flowers of Algernon* was originally published as a short story in 1959 and then expanded into a novel in 1966. It is about Charlie Gordon, a mentally retarded adult who becomes a genius after undergoing an experimental brain operation. The depth of the Charlie Gordon character both before and after the operation is a major strength of the novel. Intolerance and discrimination of society toward the mentally disadvantaged is a central theme of the novel.

Keywords: American author, coming-of-age, love, science fiction, prejudice, science fiction, tolerance

Websites:
http://www.sparknotes.com/lit/algernon/
http://www.danielkeyesauthor.com/
http://www.scifi.com/sfw/issue76/classic.html

Rate this book: 1 – 2 – 3   4 – 5 – 6   7 – 8 – 9

Fiction
Novels / Short Stories

The Following Story **
by Cees Nooteboom (2006) 128p, ISBN-13: 978-0156002547

Standard book equivalent: 0.5
First published: 1991

Nooteboom (b. 1933) is a Dutch author whose works often examine the relationship between reality and imagination. This is a story about a man traveling through space who tells a story about traveling through time. From the Harcourt publicity page, "Herman Mussert went to bed last night in Amsterdam and wakes in Lisbon in a hotel room where he slept with another man's wife more than twenty years ago." We follow Mussert's soul as it moves on, eventually leaving life and finding meaning: endless death, endless transformations, and endless love. The subjects of immortality and time feature prominently.

Keywords: Dutch author, adventure, immortality, time

Websites:
http://www.complete-review.com/reviews/nootec/following.htm
http://www.kirjasto.sci.fi/nooteb.htm
http://nl.wikipedia.org/wiki/Cees_Nooteboom

Rate this book: 1 – 2 – 3   4 – 5 – 6   7 – 8 – 9

Fiction
Novels / Short Stories

Fools and Other Stories
by Njabulo Ndebele (1986) 280p, ISBN-13: 978-0930523206

Standard book equivalent: 1.1
First published: 1984

Ndebele (b. 1913) is a South African author and Vice-Chancellor of the University of Cape Town. This is a collection of five of his short-stories: The Test, The Prophetess, Uncle, The Music of the Violin, and Fools. They all are set in the black South African township of Charterston near Nigel, which is approximately 30 miles southeast of Johannesburg. The daily struggle of ordinary people living under apartheid is a common theme of these stories. Each story has religious undertones. The South African film *Fools* (1997) directed by Ramadan Suleman is based on the title story.

Keywords: South African author, Africaapartheid, short-stories, South Africa

Websites:
http://www2.univ-reunion.fr/~ageof/text/74c21e88-302.html
http://users.iafrica.com/h/ho/hornpet/Ndebele.htm
http://spot.pcc.edu/~mdembrow/fools.htm

Rate this book: 1 – 2 – 3   4 – 5 – 6   7 – 8 – 9

Fiction
Novels / Short Stories

Frankenstein
by Mary Shelley (1994) 176p, ISBN-13: 978-0486282114

Standard book equivalent: 0.3
Written between 1816 and 1818

Shelley (1797 – 1851) was a British author married to poet Percy Shelley. The setting for *Frankenstein* is eighteenth century Europe and shifts among Geneva, the Alps, England and Scotland. It is the story of a brilliant scientist, Dr. Victor Frankenstein, who is obsessed with playing God by creating a living human being. God punishes him by turning the creature into a horrible monster. Terrified, Frankenstein rejects his creation. The novel explores the danger of a pursuit of science and technology that does not consider and heed potential hazards.

Keywords: English author, woman author, horror, science fiction, technology

Websites:
http://www.sparknotes.com/lit/frankenstein/index.html
http://www.georgetown.edu/faculty/irvinem/english016/franken/franken.htm
http://www.bookrags.com/notes/frk/

Rate this book: 1 – 2 – 3   4 – 5 – 6   7 – 8 – 9

Fiction
Novels / Short Stories

From a Crooked Rib
by Nuruddin Farah (2006) 176p, ISBN-13: 978-0143037262

Standard book equivalent: 0.7
First published: 1970

Somali author Farah's (b. 1945) writings are often about Somali women's liberation. *From a Crooked Rib* is about Ebla, an eighteen year old Somali orphan who discovers that her grandfather has promised her hand to an older man. However, her escape to Mogadishu finds her as powerless and dependent on men as she was out in the bush. As she experiences servitude, marriage, poverty, and violence, Ebla fights to keep her identity in an unsympathetic society.

Keywords: Somalia author, Africafeminism, love, poverty, Somalia

Websites:
http://www.kirjasto.sci.fi/farah.htm
http://www.africultures.com/anglais/articles_anglais/35wabe.htm
http://people.africadatabase.org/en/profile/2472.html

Rate this book: 1 – 2 – 3   4 – 5 – 6   7 – 8 – 9

Fiction
Novels / Short Stories

Girl with a Pearl Earring *
by Tracy Chevalier (2001) 248p, ISBN-13: 978-0452282155

Standard book equivalent: 1.0
First published: 1998

Chevalier (b. 1962) is an American author of historical fiction. The *Girl with a Pearl Earring* tells the story of sixteen-year-old Griet, whose life is changed by her brief encounter as a model for the famous painter Vermeer. She was sent by her family to work in the Vermeer household and must learn how to fit in with the Vermeer family. The tranquility of her stay in the household is threatened when a patron requests that Griet be the subject of Vermeer's next painting.

Keywords: American author, woman author, The Netherlands, Vermeer

Websites:
http://www.tchevalier.com/
http://www.hirohurl.net/chevalier.html
http://essentialvermeer.20m.com/interviews_newsletters/chevalier_interview.htm

Rate this book: 1 – 2 – 3   4 – 5 – 6   7 – 8 – 9

Fiction
Novels / Short Stories

Go Tell It on the Mountain *
by James Baldwin (2000) 240p, ISBN-13: 978-0385334570

Standard book equivalent: 0.9
First published: 1953

Baldwin (1924 – 1987) was an American author noted for his stories about personal identity and the African American experience. *Go Tell It on the Mountain* is his first novel. It is about the struggles a fourteen-year old faces in coming to terms with his identity as an African-American in 1950s New York. The story examines the positive and negative roles of the Christian church in the lives of African Americans. The biblical story of Ham and his father, Noah, is heavily referenced in the novel.

Keywords: American author, African-American author, African American experience, New York City, racism, religion

Websites:
http://www.sparknotes.com/lit/gotellit/
http://www.cliffsnotes.com/WileyCDA/LitNote/id-116.html
http://www.kirjasto.sci.fi/jbaldwin.htm

Rate this book: 1 – 2 – 3   4 – 5 – 6   7 – 8 – 9

Fiction
Novels / Short Stories

Going After Cacciato
by Tim O'Brien (1999) 352p, ISBN-13: 978-0767904421

Standard book equivalent: 1.4
First published: 1978

American author O'Brien (b. 1946) won the 1979 National Book Award for *Going After Cacciato*. Reality and fantasy merge in this fictional tale of a private's decision to lay down his rifle during the Vietnam War and begin a bizarre journey from the jungles of Indochina to Paris, France. All the while, he is pursued by the platoon he deserted. It is a cat and mouse game that describes how fear and heroism vie for control of our hearts.

Keywords: American Author, France, National Book Award, Vietnam, war

Websites:
http://www.stfrancis.edu/en/student/O'Brien/cacciato.htm
http://www.sparknotes.com/lit/thingscarried/context.html
http://www.illyria.com/tobhp.html

Rate this book: 1 – 2 – 3   4 – 5 – 6   7 – 8 – 9

Fiction
Novels / Short Stories

The Good Earth *
by Pearl Buck (1987) 260p, ISBN-13: 978-0671623937

Standard book equivalent: 1.0
First published: 1931

Buck (1892 – 1973) was an American author who won the 1938 Nobel Prize in Literature, and a 1932 Pulitzer Prize for *The Good Earth*. *The Good Earth* follows a Chinese peasant family through famine and floods to prosperity. A major theme of the novel is the goodness of the earth. Connection to the land is associated with piety and respect for nature, while alienation from it is associated with decadence. Buck shows this through the main character, Wang Lung, who becomes more decadent as his fortunes increase and his ties to the land are lessened.

Keywords: American Author, woman author, agriculture, China, decadence, Nobel Prize (Literature), Pulitzer Prize

Websites:
http://www.bookrags.com/notes/ge/
http://www.sparknotes.com/lit/goodearth/
http://www.cliffsnotes.com/WileyCDA/LitNote/id-184.html

Rate this book: 1 – 2 – 3   4 – 5 – 6   7 – 8 – 9

Fiction
Novels / Short Stories

A Good Man is Hard to Find *
by Flannery O' Connor (2001) 256p, ISBN-13: 978-0704346963

Standard book equivalent: 1.0
First published: 1955

O' Connor (1925 – 1964) was an American author from Milledgeville, Georgia. *A Good Man is Hard to Find* is a collection of eleven of her short stories. The subjects of the stories range from baptism to serial killers to human greed and exploitation. It contains the stories: 'A Good Man is Hard to Find', 'The River', 'The Life You Save May Be Your Own', 'A Stroke of Good Fortune', 'A Temple of the Holy Ghost', 'The Artificial Nigger', 'A Circle in the Fire', 'A Late Encounter with the Enemy', 'Good Country People', 'The Displaced Person', and 'Around the Hedges'.

Keywords: American author, woman author, short-stories

Websites:
http://www.litencyc.com/php/speople.php?rec=true&UID=3373
http://english.tyler.cc.tx.us/engl2333nbyr/o'connor.htm
http://www.literarytraveler.com/literary_articles/flannery_oconnor.aspx

Rate this book: 1 – 2 – 3   4 – 5 – 6   7 – 8 – 9

Fiction
Novels / Short Stories

Goodbye, Columbus
by Philip Roth (1994) 320p, ISBN-13: 978-0679748267

Standard book equivalent: 1.2
First published: 1959

Roth (b. 1933) is a Jewish American author. *Goodbye Columbus*, the 1960 National Book Award winner, is a novella and five short stories. Each story is about the assimilation of second or third generation Jews into American society. The title story is about Neil Klugman, a hard luck college graduate. Neil is a poor Jewish boy from Newark, which mirrors Roth's own background. His first great love affair is with Brenda Patimkin, a rich girl from Short Hills. Brenda is all he could ever want in a woman, except she is upper-class and he is not.

Keywords: American author, Jewish author, assimilation, Jewish experience, love, short-stories

Websites:
http://www.bookrags.com/studyguide-goodbyecolumbus/
http://orgs.tamu-commerce.edu/rothsoc/
http://www.kirjasto.sci.fi/proth.htm

Rate this book: 1 – 2 – 3   4 – 5 – 6   7 – 8 – 9

Fiction
Novels / Short Stories

The Great Gatsby
by F. Scott Fitzgerald (1995) 240p, ISBN-13: 978-0684801520

Standard book equivalent: 0.9
First published: 1925

Fitzgerald (1896 – 1940) was an American author of novels and short-stories. *The Great Gatsby* is set in decadent 1920's Long Island, New York during a time when bootleggers became rich because of Prohibition. The novel paints the era as a time of moral decay governed by the empty pursuit of pleasure. The title character is Jay Gatsby. His rise to glory and eventual fall from grace is a cautionary tale about the American Dream. The friends he makes during his climb up the social ladder all desert him when he is no longer in a position to help them.

Keywords: American author, decadence, Long Island

Websites:
http://www.sparknotes.com/lit/gatsby/
http://www.gradesaver.com/classicnotes/titles/gatsby/
http://www.bookrags.com/notes/gat/

Rate this book: 1 – 2 – 3   4 – 5 – 6   7 – 8 – 9

Fiction
Novels / Short Stories

Heart of Darkness
by Joseph Conrad (1990) 80p, ISBN-13: 978-0486264646

Standard book equivalent: 0.3
First published: 1899

Conrad (1857 – 1927) was a Polish-born British novelist. *Heart of Darkness* was originally published as a three part serial in *Blackwood's Magazine*. The novel, set in the Belgian colony of Congo, is structured as a story within a story as the narrator recounts Marlow—a ship's captain—telling a story. His story is about Marlow's journey up the Congo River to find the morally deprived ivory agent Kurtz. The novel depicts a colonial mentality of Africa when Europeans thought it was morally correct to plunder the riches of Africa.

Keywords: British author, Africa, colonialism, Congo

Websites:
http://www.sparknotes.com/lit/heart/
http://www.online-literature.com/conrad/heart_of_darkness/
http://www.cx.unibe.ch/ens/cg/africanfiction/conrad/bradley/bradley.html

Rate this book: 1 – 2 – 3   4 – 5 – 6   7 – 8 – 9

Fiction
Novels / Short Stories

Hound of the Baskervilles *
by Sir Arthur Conan Doyle (1994) 128p, ISBN-13: 978-0486282145

Standard book equivalent: 1.0
First published: 1902

Doyle (1859 – 1930) was a Scottish author best known for his Sherlock Holmes stories. *The Hound of the Baskervilles* was inspired from the local legends told to Doyle by his friend Fletcher Robinson on a visit to some eerie English moors. The legends were about escaped prisoners and a 17th-century aristocrat who fell afoul of the family dog. The novel's setting is Dartmoor, England in 1899. It begins with a request that Holmes investigate a supposed curse on the House of the Baskervilles. A demonic dog has been attacking and killing members of the Baskerville family.

Keywords: British author, crime, England, mystery, Sherlock Holmes

Websites:
http://www.sparknotes.com/lit/hound/
http://www.online-literature.com/doyle/baskervilles/
http://www.pbs.org/wgbh/masterpiece/hound/tguide.html

Rate this book: 1 – 2 – 3   4 – 5 – 6   7 – 8 – 9

Fiction
Novels / Short Stories

Housekeeping
by Marilynne Robinson (2004) 224p, ISBN-13: 978-0312424091

Standard book equivalent: 0.9
First published: 1980

Robinson (b. 1947) is an American author. Her novel, *Housekeeping*, won the 1981 PEN/Hemingway Award. It is the story of Ruth, her sister Lucille, and the loss and longing they feel at being uprooted from the city. Ruth and Lucille are being raised in rural Fingerbone, Idaho by their grandmother because the pressures of family life in the city have destroyed their mother. An important theme of the novel is the impermanence of life and happiness, shown as the sisters struggle to adapt to their ever changing situation.

Keywords: American author, woman author, coming-of-age, family, Idaho, PEN/Hemingway Award

Websites:
http://www.lectures.org/robinson.html
http://www.powells.com/interviews/robinson.html
http://www.ncteamericancollection.org/litmap/robinson_marilynne_id.htm

Rate this book: 1 – 2 – 3   4 – 5 – 6   7 – 8 – 9

Fiction
Novels / Short Stories

How the Garcia Girls Lost Their Accents *
by Julia Alvarez (1992) 304p, ISBN-13: 978-0452268067

Standard book equivalent: 1.2
First published: 1991

Alvarez (b. 1950) is an American poet, novelist and essayist. *How the Garcia Girls Lost Their Accents* is a collection of fifteen tales that chronicle a Dominican family's exile to the Bronx. A common thread running through the stories is the four Garcia daughters' rebellion against their immigrant elders. The stories deal with coming-of-age issues and the difficulties immigrant youth face when assimilating into an alien culture. They highlight the tensions families undergo as younger members look to the foreign culture and leave their traditions behind.

Keywords: American author, woman author, assimilation, coming-of-age, cross-cultural, Dominican Republic, immigrants, New York City, short-stories

Websites:
http://www.sparknotes.com/lit/garciagirls/
http://us.penguingroup.com/static/rguides/us/garcia_girls.html
http://www.alvarezjulia.com/

Rate this book: 1 – 2 – 3   4 – 5 – 6   7 – 8 – 9

Fiction
Novels / Short Stories

Howards End
by E. M. Forster (2002) 256p, ISBN-13: 978-0486424545

Standard book equivalent: 1.0
First published: 1910

Forster (1879 – 1970) was a British author. *Howards End* is about class struggle in turn-of-the-century England. The main characters represent three different groups within the Edwardian middle classes: the Schlegels (intellectuals), the Wilcoxes (thoughtless tycoons) and the Basts (the struggling lower-middle-class). Its main theme is the difficulty of relationships between members of different social classes. Howards End is the home about which most of the action centers. Ruth Wilcox wants to will it to Martha Schlegel, but the rest of the Wilcoxes are against it to the point of destroying the will when Ruth dies.

Keywords: British author, England, social class

Websites:
http://www.online-literature.com/forster/howards_end/
http://www.sparknotes.com/lit/howardsend/
http://books.guardian.co.uk/reviews/classics/0,,99912,00.html

Rate this book: 1 – 2 – 3   4 – 5 – 6   7 – 8 – 9

Fiction
Novels / Short Stories

The Human Comedy *
by William Saroyan (1966) 192p, ISBN-13: 978-0440339335

Standard book equivalent: 0.7
First published: 1943

Saroyan (1908 – 1981) was an American author from Fresno, California. The main character of the *Human Comedy* is Homer McCauley, a fourteen year-old boy growing up fatherless in California during World War II. He attempts to assume the role of father-figure in his family and earns money delivering telegrams. The story presents American family life during the difficult war years and has a quality of "everything will be all right" about it. It is a story in which the plot is secondary to character development.

Keywords: American author, California, coming-of-age, war, WWII

Websites:
http://www.kirjasto.sci.fi/saroyan.htm
http://www.pbs.org/newshour/essays/rodriguez_5-26.html
http://www.williamsaroyansociety.org/

Rate this book: 1 – 2 – 3   4 – 5 – 6   7 – 8 – 9

Fiction
Novels / Short Stories

The Illustrated Man *
by Ray Bradbury (1983) 192p, ISBN-13: 978-0553274493

Standard book equivalent: 1.1
First published: 1951

Bradbury (b. 1920) is an American author noted for his science fiction novels, short-stories and screenplays. *The Illustrated Man* is a collection of eighteen science fiction stories that has remained in print since first being published. The stories are introduced through a mysterious man covered in tattoos whom the narrator meets. Each tattoo comes to life in turn, revealing the future and a new story. Most of the stories carry a theme warning of the dangers of technology.

Keywords: American author, science fiction, short-stories

Websites:
http://www.raybradbury.com/
http://www.greenmanreview.com/book/book_bradbury_illustratedman.html
http://www.edhelper.com/books/The_Illustrated_Man.htm

Rate this book: 1 – 2 – 3   4 – 5 – 6   7 – 8 – 9

Fiction
Novels / Short Stories

Interpreter of Maladies
by Jhumpa Lahiri (1999) 160p, ISBN-13: 978-0395927205

Standard book equivalent: 0.6
First published: 1999

Lahiri (b. 1967) is an American author of Bengali decent and since 2005, vice president of the PEN American Center in New York. Her fiction typically is about the lives of Indian-Americans, particularly Bengalis. *Interpreter of Maladies* is a collection of nine short-stories that won a Pulitzer Prize in 2000. It is about Indians living in the Boston area (though two of the stories are set in India) and the cross-cultural issues they must face as immigrants in a foreign culture.

Keywords: American author, woman author, assimilation, Boston, cross-cultural, immigrants, India, Pulitzer Prize, short-stories

Websites:
http://www.houghtonmifflinbooks.com/catalog/authordetail.cfm?authorID=4768
http://www.houghtonmifflinbooks.com/readers_guides/interpreter_maladies.shtml
http://www.bookreporter.com/reviews/039592720X.asp

Rate this book: 1 – 2 – 3   4 – 5 – 6   7 – 8 – 9

Fiction
Novels / Short Stories

The Joy Luck Club
by Amy Tan (2006) 288p, ISBN-13: 978-0143038092

Standard book equivalent: 1.1
First published: 1989

Tan (b. 1952) is an American author who often writes about the Asian American experience and mother-daughter relationships. *The Joy Luck Club* tells the story of four Chinese women as they and their children are assimilated into American culture. In 1949, they begin meeting in San Francisco to play mah jong, invest in stocks and tell "say" stories, as their relationships persist through the years. *The Joy Luck Club* was adapted into a feature film in 1994.

Keywords: American author, woman author, assimilation, California, China, cross-cultural, family, feminism, immigrants

Websites:
http://www.sparknotes.com/lit/joyluck/
http://www.bookrags.com/notes/jlc/
http://www.amytan.net/

Rate this book: 1 – 2 – 3   4 – 5 – 6   7 – 8 – 9

Fiction
Novels / Short Stories

Joys of Motherhood
by Buchi Emecheta (1980) 224p, ISBN-13: 978-0807609507

Standard book equivalent: 0.9
First published: 1979

Emecheta (b. 1944) is a Nigerian author whose works examine the roles of women, particularly motherhood, in African society. This story of a young mother's struggles in 1950s Lagos is a study of how polygamy and patriarchy affect the changing roles of women in urban Nigeria. The main character is Nnu Ego, a mother who derives her sense of worth from the success of her children. When they fail to meet her expectations her own self-esteem is threatened.

Keywords: Nigerian author, woman author, Africa, family, feminism, motherhood, Nigeria

Websites:
http://www.english.emory.edu/Bahri/Emech.html
http://www.wsu.edu/~brians/anglophone/emecheta.html
http://emeagwali.com/nigeria/biography/buchi-emecheta-voice-09jul96.html

Rate this book: 1 – 2 – 3   4 – 5 – 6   7 – 8 – 9

Fiction
Novels / Short Stories

The Jungle
by Upton Sinclair (2001) 320p, ISBN-13: 978-0486419237

Standard book equivalent: 1.2
First published: 1906

Sinclair (1878 – 1968) was an American author and staunch Socialist. He won a 1942 Pulitzer Prize for *Dragon's Teeth*. *The Jungle* is a best-selling novel that reveals the grossly unfair labor practices and unsanitary working conditions in the Chicago stockyards at the end of the nineteenth century. It tells the grim story of an immigrant Lithuanian family who arrive full of optimism but soon descend into abject poverty, and moral and psychological depression. Publication of this book is often cited as causing a significant drop in foreign sales of American meat.

Keywords: American author, Chicago, food, immigrants, Pulitzer Prize, work

Websites:
http://www.spartacus.schoolnet.co.uk/Jupton.htm
http://www.online-literature.com/upton_sinclair/jungle/
http://www.sparknotes.com/lit/jungle/

Rate this book: 1 – 2 – 3   4 – 5 – 6   7 – 8 – 9

Fiction
Novels / Short Stories

The Kingdom of This World
by Alejo Carpentier, Harriet de Onis (translator) (2006)
190p, ISBN-13: 978-0374530112

Standard book equivalent: 0.7
First published: 1949

Carpentier (1904 – 1980) was a Cuban novelist of Russian and French parentage. *The Kingdom of This World* is a novel that describes the atmosphere of superstition and social upheaval in Haiti after its revolution in the early nineteenth century. This book chronicles the era of King Henri-Christophe through the narrative of the slave Ti-Noel. He reigned through an era of chaos, violence, superstition and socio-political upheaval. *The Kingdom of This World* is often cited as a representative example of magical realism.

Keywords: Cuban author, Haiti, magical realism, politics, slavery, war

Websites:
http://www.webster.edu/~corbetre/haiti/bookreviews/carpentier.htm
http://www.google.com/search?sourceid=navclient&ie=UTF-8&rls=GWYA,GWYA:2005-30,GWYA:en&q=%22Henri%2DChristophe%27s
http://www.curledup.com/kingthis.htm

Rate this book: 1 – 2 – 3   4 – 5 – 6   7 – 8 – 9

Fiction
Novels / Short Stories

Kokoro **
by Natsume Soseki (1957) 248p, ISBN-13: 978-0895267153

Standard book equivalent: 1.0
First published: 1914

Soseki (1867 – 1916) was a famous Japanese author whose likeness has appeared on Japanese currency. *Kokoro* can be translated as "the heart of things". The novel deals with the transition of Japan into the modern era and chronicles the friendship between a young man and an older man. Suicide is examined in the light of social isolation brought on by the passing of traditional culture and the failure of modern culture to adequately serve as a substitute. Compare with *Things Fall Apart*.

Keywords: Japanese author, family, friendship, Japan, suicide

Websites:
http://www.ibiblio.org/eldritch/ns/soseki.html
http://www.kirjasto.sci.fi/natsume.htm
http://en.wikipedia.org/wiki/Natsume_Soseki

Rate this book: 1 – 2 – 3   4 – 5 – 6   7 – 8 – 9

Fiction
Novels / Short Stories

Life of Pi
by Yann Martel, Grace Laciste (2003) 336p, ISBN-13: 978-0156027328

Standard book equivalent: 1.3
First published: 2001

Martel (b. 1963) is a Canadian author. *Life of Pi* is a fable about an Indian boy, Pi, who is the son of a zookeeper. Philosophical thoughts about Hinduism, Christianity and Islam are woven into the fable. Pi's family plans to move to Canada with their animals. Along the way they are shipwrecked in the Pacific Ocean and Pi finds himself aboard a life boat with a group of animals including a Bengal tiger. Pi is now faced with surviving aboard the boat with the tiger for what turns out to be 227 days.

Keywords: Canadian author, adventure, fable, India, Man Booker Award, Pacific Ocean, religion

Websites:
http://www.powells.com/fromtheauthor/martel.html
http://books.guardian.co.uk/reviews/generalfiction/0,6121,721434,00.html
http://www.januarymagazine.com/fiction/lifeofpi.html

Rate this book: 1 – 2 – 3   4 – 5 – 6   7 – 8 – 9

Fiction
Novels / Short Stories

Like Water for Chocolate
by Laura Esquivel (1993) 224p, ISBN-13: 978-0552995870

Standard book equivalent: 0.9
First published: 1989

Esquivel (b. 1950) is a Mexican author whose works often are described as examples of magical realism. This novel is set in Mexico during the Mexican Revolution of the early twentieth century. It is about Tita who longs to marry her lover. However, she is the youngest daughter and her mother insists that she follow custom by staying at home and remaining unmarried. Tita responds by pouring her passion into her cooking with the result that anyone who eats her food can feel what she feels. Eventually the lovers unite but to fateful consequences.

Keywords: Mexican author, woman author, family, food, feminism, magical realism, Mexico

Websites:
http://www.sparknotes.com/lit/likewater/index.html
http://www.greenmanreview.com/book/book_esquivel_wat
    erchocolate.html
http://en.wikipedia.org/wiki/Laura_Esquivel

Rate this book: 1 – 2 – 3   4 – 5 – 6   7 – 8 – 9

Fiction
Novels / Short Stories

Lord of the Flies
by William Golding (1997) 272p, ISBN-13: 978-1573226127

Standard book equivalent: 1.0
First published: 1954

British author Golding (1911 – 1993) won the 1983 Nobel Prize in Literature. *Lord of the Flies* is his classic tale about a group of English schoolboys who are stranded on a deserted island during a nuclear war. A major theme of the novel is that the defects of society trace back to the defects of human nature. It examines the savage side of human nature as the group becomes ever less civilized. The plot revolves around the power struggle between two of the boys, Ralph and Jack, symbolizing civilization and savagery, respectively.

Keywords: British author, adventure, children, dictatorship, Nobel Prize (Literature), violence

Websites:
http://www.sparknotes.com/lit/flies/
http://www.cliffsnotes.com/WileyCDA/LitNote/id-64.html
http://www.william-golding.co.uk/

Rate this book: 1 – 2 – 3   4 – 5 – 6   7 – 8 – 9

Fiction
Novels / Short Stories

Lost Horizon *
by James Hilton (1988) 240p, ISBN-13: 978-0671664275

Standard book equivalent: 0.9
First published: 1933

Hilton (1900 – 1954) was a British author. *Lost Horizon* is the novel that popularized the term "Shangri-La". It is about Hugh Conway, a British diplomat who finds inner peace in Shangri-La. Shangri-La is a utopian lamasery hidden in the Himalayas whose inhabitants enjoy incredible longevity. Conway and three others find their way there after a plane crash. *Lost Horizons*' main theme is the contrast between Eastern and Western cultures. An interesting side theme is the suggestion that another cataclysmic world war is imminent, just six years before World War II actually began.

Keywords: British author, adventure, cross-cultural, Himalayas, religion, Tibet

Websites:
http://www.sfsite.com/~silverag/hilton.html
http://www.harperacademic.com/catalog/excerpt_xml.asp?isbn=0060594527
http://en.wikipedia.org/wiki/James_Hilton

Rate this book: 1 – 2 – 3   4 – 5 – 6   7 – 8 – 9

Fiction
Novels / Short Stories

Lost in the City *
by Edward P. Jones (2004) 288p, ISBN-13: 978-0060795283

Standard book equivalent: 1.1
First published: 1991

Jones (b. 1951) is an American author who won the 1992 PEN/Hemingway Award for *Lost in the City*. It is a collection of fourteen short-stories, all set in the African American neighborhoods of Washington D.C. during the 1960s and 1970s. The imagery depicts poverty and tragedy but the characters are survivors and full of hope. Jones' characters are real and free of stereotypes and clichés. He depicts them, and their situations, with honesty and frankness. Compare with *Elbow Room*.

Keywords: American author, African-American author, African American experience, PEN/Hemingway Award, short-stories, Washington D.C.

Websites:
http://www.hackwriters.com/lostcity.htm
http://www.allaunthagarschildren.com/
http://www.bookbrowse.com/author_interviews/full/index.cfm?author_number=930

Rate this book:　　1 – 2 – 3　　4 – 5 – 6　　7 – 8 – 9

Fiction
Novels / Short Stories

Medicine River
by Thomas King (2006) 264p. ISBN-13: 978-0143054351

Standard book equivalent: 1.0
First published: 1990

King (b. 1943) is an American author of Native American descent. The title takes its name from a small town near an Indian reserve in Western Canada. It is narrated by Will, a Native American photographer, returning to his hometown to attend his mother's funeral. The loosely woven episodes revolve around Harlen Bigbear, who constantly meddles in the affairs of the locals. Interwoven into the story are the narrator's bittersweet experiences of growing up with his brother James, the eccentricities of his Native American mother, and his questions about the white father he doesn't remember.

Keywords: Native American author, Canada, cross-cultural, Native American experience

Websites:
http://www.nwpassages.com/bios/king.asp
http://www.suite101.com/article.cfm/5705/115705
http://www.litencyc.com/php/speople.php?rec=true&UID=
   5303

Rate this book: 1 – 2 – 3   4 – 5 – 6   7 – 8 – 9

Fiction
Novels / Short Stories

The Mistress of Spices
by Chitra Banerjee Divakaruni (1998) 352p, ISBN-13: 978-0385482387

Standard book equivalent: 1.4
First published: 1997

Divakaruni (b. 1956) is an Indian American author. Her novel mixes prose with poetry. She describes her novel as, "… collapsing the divisions between the realistic world of twentieth century America and the timeless one of myth and magic." It is about a spice seller, Tilo, and those customers who visit her Indian spice shop in Oakland, California. She dispenses wisdom with the appropriate spice: coriander for sight, turmeric for wrinkles, and fenugreek to make a rejected wife desirable. Unfortunately, Tilo's powers are not everlasting. Her powers vanish the instant she falls in love.

Keywords: American author, Indian author, woman author, California, food, India

Websites:
http://www.chitradivakaruni.com/
http://www.time.com/time/daily/special/india/chitra.html
http://www.indiastar.com/mitra.html

Rate this book: 1 – 2 – 3   4 – 5 – 6   7 – 8 – 9

Fiction
Novels / Short Stories

Native Speaker
by Chang-Rae Lee (1998) 324p, ISBN-13: 978-1862071148

Standard book equivalent: 1.4
First published: 1994

Lee (b. 1965) is a Korean American author. His novel, *Native Speaker* won the 1995 PEN/Hemingway Award. In this novel, espionage is a metaphor for the relationship Amerasians experience with American society. It is about Henry Park, a young Korean American man struggling to piece together the fragments of his personality as he strives to find a place in culturally diverse New York City. The dichotomy of Korean culture's penchant for careful control of emotions versus the "in-your-face" style of New York wears heavily on Henry, the son of a successful Korean-American grocer.

Keywords: American author, Korean author, Asia, cross-cultural, immigrants, Korea, New York City, PEN/Hemingway Award

Websites:
http://us.penguingroup.com/static/rguides/us/native_speaker.html
http://www.mysteryguide.com/bkLeeSpeaker.html
http://www.yale.edu/opa/v28.n28/story10.html

Rate this book: 1 – 2 – 3   4 – 5 – 6   7 – 8 – 9

Fiction
Novels / Short Stories

Night
by Elie Wiesel (2006) 144p, ISBN-13: 978-0374500016

Standard book equivalent: 0.6
First published: 1956

Wiesel (b. 1928) is a Jewish American author, philosopher and humanitarian. He was born in Transylvania, Romania. *Night* is his autobiographical novel about a boy's experience of the holocaust. It is a reflection of the time leading up to and including his experiences in the Auschwitz and Buchenwald concentration camps. The time frame covered is 1941 to 1945 and central themes include belief in God in the face of tragedy and the inhumanity of man toward his fellow humans. He wrote it as the first part of a trilogy that is completed with the books *Dawn* and *Day*.

Keywords: American author, Auschwitz, Romanian author, Germany, holocaust, war, WWII

Websites:
http://www.sparknotes.com/lit/night/
http://www.bookrags.com/Night_%28book%29
http://www.eliewieselfoundation.org/ElieWiesel/index.html

Rate this book: 1 – 2 – 3   4 – 5 – 6   7 – 8 – 9

Fiction
Novels / Short Stories

Now in November
by Josephine W. Johnson (1991) 288p, ISBN-13: 978-1558610354

Standard book equivalent: 1.1
First published: 1934

Johnson (1910 – 1990) was an American author born in Kirkwood, Missouri. She won a 1935 Pulitzer Prize for *Now in November*. It describes the austere and often dreary world of Midwestern farmers desperate to make a living during the Great Depression. *Now in November* is often favorably compared to Steinbeck's *Grapes of Wrath*. It is narrated by Margaret Haldmarne, the middle-born of three daughters and traces her family's struggle to pay off the mortgage on their farm. The family faces many hardships including fire, drought and loneliness.

Keywords: American author, woman author, agriculture, family, farming, Great Depression, Midwest, Pulitzer Prize

Websites:
http://www.citypaper.com/special/story.asp?id=6684
http://www.womenwriters.net/domesticgoddess/Weiser.html
http://library.wustl.edu/units/spec/manuscripts/mlc/johnsonj/johnsonj.html

Rate this book: 1 – 2 – 3   4 – 5 – 6   7 – 8 – 9

Fiction
Novels / Short Stories

The Odyssey *
by Homer, George Herbert Palmer (translator) (1999) 256p, ISBN-13: 978-0486406541

Standard book equivalent: 1.0
Translation first published in 1921

Homer's poem was likely written between 800 and 600 BC. Palmer provides a prose translation of the ancient epic poem. It recounts the adventures of the heroic Odysseus on his homeward voyage from the Trojan War to his wife and family. The war took ten years to fight and the voyage another ten years to complete because of the many adventures he encounters. When Odysseus finally returns home he finds his faithful wife surrounded by suitors eager to assume his place.

Keywords: Greek author, ancient, mythology, war

Websites:
http://www.encyclopedia.com/doc/1E1-Palmer-G.html
http://www.mythweb.com/odyssey/index.html
http://www.sparknotes.com/lit/odyssey/

Rate this book: 1 – 2 – 3   4 – 5 – 6   7 – 8 – 9

Fiction
Novels / Short Stories

Of Mice and Men *
by John Steinbeck (1993) 112p, ISBN-13: 978-0140177398

Standard book equivalent: 0.4
First published: 1937

Steinbeck (1902 – 1968) was an American author and 1962 Nobel Prize in Literature winner. This is a novel about the friendship between two men and a murder. The main characters are two friends: Lenny, a large man with a mental disability, and George, a smaller quick-witted man. They are migrant workers in California during the 1930s. George's friendship with Lenny puts him in the situation of having to deal severely with him. The novel's themes are the predatory nature of human existence and the importance of friendships.

Keywords: American author, California, friendship, Great Depression, Nobel Prize (Literature)

Websites:
http://www.sparknotes.com/lit/micemen/
http://www.gradesaver.com/classicnotes/titles/miceandmen/
http://www.kirjasto.sci.fi/johnstei.htm

Rate this book: 1 – 2 – 3   4 – 5 – 6   7 – 8 – 9

Fiction
Novels / Short Stories

Old Man and the Sea *
by Ernest Hemingway (1995) 128p, ISBN-13: 978-0684801223

Standard book equivalent: 0.5
First published: 1952

Hemingway (1899 – 1961) was an American author. He won a 1953 Pulitzer Prize, and the 1954 Nobel Prize in Literature. *The Old Man and the Sea* is a fable about an epic struggle between an old fisherman, Santiago, and the greatest catch of his life a gigantic blue marlin. Santiago had gone 84 days without a catch before meeting the blue marlin, and people had begun to believe he should be avoided for fear that they might catch his bad luck. The book's central theme is the honor in struggling against adversity.

Keywords: American author, fable, inspirational, Nobel Prize (Literature), Pulitzer Prize, sea

Websites:
http://www.sparknotes.com/lit/oldman/
http://www.gradesaver.com/classicnotes/titles/oldman/
http://www.kirjasto.sci.fi/hemingwa.htm

Rate this book: 1 – 2 – 3   4 – 5 – 6   7 – 8 – 9

Fiction
Novels / Short Stories

One Flew Over the Cuckoo's Nest
by Ken Kesey (1963) 272p, ISBN-13: 978-0451163967

Standard book equivalent: 1.0
First published: 1962

Kesey (1935 – 2001) was an American author. *One Flew Over the Cuckoo's Nest* is set in an Oregon asylum and is an examination of the institutionalization process. The narrator, Chief Bromden, is a Native American who suffers from paranoia. He believes an organization, which he calls the Combine, is forcing people into conformity. A major theme of the book is that society restricts the natural tendencies of people and that many diagnoses of insanity are in fact misdiagnoses. Most of the book concerns the power struggle between the female nursing staff—particularly, Head Nurse Ratchet—and the male patients.

Keywords: American author, mental illness, power

Websites:
http://www.sparknotes.com/lit/cuckoo/index.html
http://www.gradesaver.com/classicnotes/titles/cuckoosnest/
http://www.lib.virginia.edu/small/exhibits/sixties/kesey.html

Rate this book: 1 – 2 – 3   4 – 5 – 6   7 – 8 – 9

Fiction
Novels / Short Stories

The Optimist's Daughter
by Eudora Welty (1990) 192p, ISBN-13: 978-0679728832

Standard book equivalent: 0.7
First published: 1972

Welty (1909 – 2001) was an American author from Jackson Mississippi. *The Optimist's Daughter* won a Pulitzer Prize in 1973. The story concerns a daughter, Laurel McKelva Hand, who returns to her rural Mississippi home town after her father's death. Laurel explores her roots in the town and her family relationships. Welty's themes include the love between parents and children, the grief they endure at the loss of these relationships, and how the passage of time affects lives.

Keywords: American author, woman author, family, love, Pulitzer Prize, the South

Websites:
http://www.bookrags.com/The_Optimist's_Daughter
http://www.bookreporter.com/reviews/067972883X.asp
http://clem.mscd.edu/~english/413h/todnotes.html

Rate this book: 1 – 2 – 3   4 – 5 – 6   7 – 8 – 9

Fiction
Novels / Short Stories

The Orchid House
by Phyllis S. Allfrey, Lizabeth Paravisini-Gebert (Introduction) (1996) 185p, ISBN-13: 978-0813523323

Standard book equivalent: 0.7
First published: 1953

Allfrey (1908 – 1986) is a Dominican (Commonwealth of Dominica) author. Her novel, *The Orchid House*, is a classic of Caribbean literature. It is an autobiographical novel of the three daughters of a once-powerful but now impoverished white family. Allfrey's novel gives a rich picture of the island of Dominica's history during the twentieth century. The story is told through the eyes of Lally, the Black nurse to the three sisters. The novel is set during the period when Dominica was gaining its independence.

Keywords: Caribbean author, woman author, Caribbean, colonialism, Dominica

Websites:
http://www.ocpl.lib.ny.us/website/reading/fearless_reader/orchid_house.htm
http://books.bankhacker.com/The+Orchid+House/

Rate this book: 1 – 2 – 3   4 – 5 – 6   7 – 8 – 9

Fiction
Novels / Short Stories

The Outsiders *
by S. E. Hinton (1997) 192p, ISBN-13: 978-0140385724

Standard book equivalent: 0.7
First published: 1967

Hinton (b. 1948) is an American author, primarily of young adult fiction. *The Outsiders* is set in Oklahoma and is a tale about two gangs, the Greasers and the Socs. The Greasers are lower class youths while the Socs, or Socials, represent upper class privileged youth. Ponyboy Curtis, a Greaser, is the narrator. The plot races toward conflict between these two groups with the theme of incompatibility between socioeconomic groups ever present. A secondary theme is the danger lurking behind male-female relationships.

Keywords: American author, woman author, coming-of-age, gangs, Oklahoma, prejudice

Websites:
http://www.sparknotes.com/lit/outsiders/
http://www.bookrags.com/notes/outs/
http://www.sehinton.com/

Rate this book: 1 – 2 – 3   4 – 5 – 6   7 – 8 – 9

Fiction
Novels / Short Stories

The Palm-Wine Drinkard and My Life in the Bush of Ghosts
by Amos Tutuola, (1993) 256p, ISBN-13: 978-0802133632

Standard book equivalent: 1.2
First published: 1952 and 1954, respectively

Tutuola (1920 – 1997) was a Nigerian author. The writing is in pidgin-English, which sets the mood for colonial West Africa. It is a culturally authentic example of magical realism. The plot of *The Palm-wine Drinkard*, based on Yoruba folktales, is about a man who journeys to the land of the dead to bring back his favorite palm-wine tapper (A palm-wine tapper is a person who produces palm-wine from palm trees). The second story is the story of a boy who is lost in the spiritual world, and struggles to return to his family.

Keywords: Nigerian author, Africa, magical realism, Nigeria

Websites:
http://www.qub.ac.uk/schools/SchoolofEnglish/imperial/nigeria/amos.htm
http://www.kirjasto.sci.fi/tutuola.htm
http://www.hrc.utexas.edu/research/fa/tutuola.html

Rate this book: 1 – 2 – 3   4 – 5 – 6   7 – 8 – 9

Fiction
Novels / Short Stories

The Painted Bird **
by Jerzy Kosinski (1995) 234p, ISBN-13: 978-0802134226

Standard book equivalent: 0.9
First published: 1965

Kosinski (1933 – 1991) was a Polish born Jewish author. This novel is a controversial story that follows the wanderings of a boy in Europe during World War II. One of the characters he meets is a bird catcher who, for sport, paints one of his captured birds in bright colors. When the painted bird is released and attempts to rejoin its flock, it is not recognized and attacked as an intruder. A central theme is the often close proximity of terror and savagery to innocence. The book has been criticized for depicting peasants in a poor light.

Keywords: Polish author, Europe, war, WWII

Websites:
http://www.wtamu.edu/academic/fah/eng/wc/jk.htm
http://www.bookrags.com/The_Painted_Bird_(novel)
http://query.nytimes.com/gst/fullpage.html?res=950DE7D
    A1039F931A15757C0A96F948260

Rate this book: 1 – 2 – 3   4 – 5 – 6   7 – 8 – 9

Fiction
Novels / Short Stories

Pedro Paramo
by Juan Rulfo, Margaret Sayers Peden (translator) (1994)
124p, ISBN-13: 978-0802133908

Standard book equivalent: 0.5
First published: 1955

Rulfo (1917 – 1986) was a Mexican author. This novel is noted for its realism in capturing life in rural Mexico at the beginning of the twentieth century. It is also an early example of magical realism. The main character is Pedro Paramo who is the son of failing landowners. His father dies and he assumes control of the estate. His success is based on becoming increasingly manipulative, greedy and exploitive. However, he ultimately pays a great price for his transgressions.

Keywords: Mexican author, family, greed, love, magical realism, Mexico

Websites:
http://www.utexas.edu/utpress/excerpts/rulped-intro.html
http://www.kirjasto.sci.fi/rulfo.htm
http://www.lclark.edu/~woodrich/seligmanparamo.html

Rate this book: 1 – 2 – 3   4 – 5 – 6   7 – 8 – 9

Fiction
Novels / Short Stories

Persepolis: The Story of a Childhood *
by Marjane Satrapi. (2004) 160 p, ISBN-13: 978-0375714573

Standard book equivalent: 0.6
First published: 2001

Satrapi (b. 1969) is an Iranian graphic novelist (graphic novels are written in the style of comic books). This is an autobiographical novel depicting how the author lived in Tehran, Iran until the country came under the control of the Islamic regime. It covers the period of her life from the ages of six to fourteen and provides a glimpse at everyday life during a time of political upheaval. In addition to presenting a child's view of the politics around her, Satrapi's book is an introduction to some of the differences between Western and Islamic culture.

Keywords: Iranian author, woman author, graphic book, Iran, Muslim experience, religion

Websites:
http://www.complete-review.com/reviews/iran/satrapim.htm
http://seattlepi.nwsource.com/books/123973_momentwith29.html
http://www.randomhouse.com/pantheon/graphicnovels/satrapi2.html

Rate this book: 1 – 2 – 3   4 – 5 – 6   7 – 8 – 9

Fiction
Novels / Short Stories

A Personal Matter
by Kenzaburo Oë, John Nathan (translator) (1982) 165p, ISBN-13: 978-0802150615

Standard book equivalent: 0.6
First published: 1964

Oë (b. 1935) is a Japanese novelist and 1994 Nobel Prize in Literature winner. *A Personal Matter* weaves together issues of ethics, fatherhood, and responsibility. Bird is the protagonist. He dreams of going to Africa, of undemanding love, and of a perfect son. These are all things that elude him. His child is born with a herniated brain, and his wife's physician speaks of an autopsy for the baby even though it stubbornly continues to live. Bird's responsibility to decide his son's fate pushes him into denial of his reality as he attempts to flee.

Keywords: Japanese author, family, Japan, Nobel Prize (Literature)

Websites:
http://www.ucalgary.ca/~xyang/j341_01f/oef20.htm
http://mchip00.nyu.edu/lit-med/lit-med-db/webdocs/webdescrips/oe836-des-.html
http://www.kirjasto.sci.fi/oe.htm

Rate this book: 1 – 2 – 3   4 – 5 – 6   7 – 8 – 9

Fiction
Novels / Short Stories

The Plague
by Albert Camus (1965) 278p, ISBN-13: 978-0075536499

Standard book equivalent: 1.2
First published: 1947

Camus (1913 – 1960) was a French author and philosopher who received the 1957 Nobel Prize in Literature. Camus' work often dealt with the absurd, or our attempt to find meaning where none exists. In this novel the bubonic plague strikes a North African city, which is then quarantined. The setting is the Algerian city, Oran. The novel deals with the reactions of the inhabitants to the disease and the quarantine. Dr. Rieux is the main character and the novel describes, mostly by relating his journal entries, his attempts to stop the plague.

Keywords: French author, absurdism, Africa, disease, Nobel Prize (Literature), bubonic plague

Websites:
http://www.sparknotes.com/lit/plague/index.html
http://www.camus-society.com/camus-thought.htm
http://www.bookrags.com/The_Plague

Rate this book: 1 – 2 – 3   4 – 5 – 6   7 – 8 – 9

Fiction
Novels / Short Stories

The Power and the Glory
by Graham Greene (2003) 240p, ISBN-13: 978-0142437308

Standard book equivalent: 0.9
First published: 1940

Greene (1904 – 1991) was a British author whose work was influenced by his Catholic faith. Greene's novel is set in 1930s Mexico and follows "the whiskey Priest" in his flight from authorities who are trying to eradicate the Catholic Church in the Mexican state. The antagonist is a lieutenant of the police whose task it is to pursue and capture the priest. The story is rich in symbolism as the role of sacraments and clergy are examined. The Mexican government's antagonism to the Catholic Church during this period has a basis in history.

Keywords: American author, Mexico, religion

Websites:
http://www.sparknotes.com/lit/powerglory/index.html
http://www.kirjasto.sci.fi/greene.htm
http://www.americamagazine.org/gettext.cfm?articleTypeID=1&textID=2311&issueID=388

Rate this book: 1 – 2 – 3   4 – 5 – 6   7 – 8 – 9

Fiction
Novels / Short Stories

The Prisoner of Zenda *
by Anthony Hope (2001) 184p, ISBN-13: 978-0755107094

Standard book equivalent: 0.7
First published: 1894

Hope (1863 – 1933) was a British author. Hope's novel is an adventure story set in the fictional Ruritania—a German-speaking, Roman Catholic monarchy in central Europe—during the nineteenth century. The protagonist is Rudolf Rassendyll, an Englishman on vacation to Ruritania. He discovers that he bears a striking resemblance to the King and through a series of adventures is required to impersonate the king to protect him. Unfortunately, along the way he falls in love with Princess Flavia, the King's love interest.

Keywords: British author, adventure, love, Ruritania

Websites:
http://www.bibliomania.com/0/0/25/53/frameset.html
http://www.1911encyclopedia.org/Anthony_Hope
http://en.wikipedia.org/wiki/Ruritania

Rate this book: 1 – 2 – 3   4 – 5 – 6   7 – 8 – 9

Fiction
Novels / Short Stories

The Professor's House
by Willa Cather (1990) 272p, ISBN-13: 978-0679731801

Standard book equivalent: 1.1
First published: 1922

Cather (1873 – 1947) was an American author. *The Professor's House* is about Professor Godfrey St. Peter who is in his fifties and seems to be happy. The novel traces the year following his move into a new house. However, the hollowness of his happiness is soon exposed. He almost dies in an accident in his old house that he has refused to leave behind. The emptiness of his professional success and of his relationships with his wife and daughters depicts an unhappy entry into old age. Major themes of loneliness and old age are explored in the novel.

Keywords: American author, woman author, family, Midwest

Websites:
http://www.newcriterion.com/archive/18/jan00/lyons.htm
http://gutenberg.net.au/ebooks02/0200831h.html
http://www.gradesaver.com/classicnotes/titles/professor/essay1.html

Rate this book: 1 – 2 – 3   4 – 5 – 6   7 – 8 – 9

Fiction
Novels / Short Stories

Purple Hibiscus
by Chimamanda Ngozi Adichie (2003) 307p, ISBN-13: 978-1565123878

Standard book equivalent: 1.2
First published: 2003

Purple Hibiscus is the debut novel of Nigerian author Adichie (b. 1977). It is set against the political turmoil of late 1990s Nigeria. The story centers on Kambili Achike, a fifteen-year-old schoolgirl, and her family. Kambili's father, Eugene, is a complex character—a devout Catholic and political rights activist who rules his household with a heavy hand. The narrative is told from the perspective of Kambili. It explores her and her brother Jaja's response to their father's authority. Other main characters include their more liberal aunt Ifeoma and their Igbo traditionalist grandfather, whom Eugene dismisses as a "heathen".

Keywords: Nigerian author, woman author, Africa, family, Nigeria, religion, tolerance

Websites:
http://www.nigeriavillagesquare1.com/purplehibiscus.html
http://www.curledup.com/hibiscus.htm
http://www.ulg.ac.be/facphl/uer/d-german/L3/cnaindex.html

Rate this book: 1 – 2 – 3   4 – 5 – 6   7 – 8 – 9

Fiction
Novels / Short Stories

Rabbit, Run
by John Updike (1996) 272p, ISBN-13: 978-0449911655

Standard book equivalent: 1.0
First published: 1960

Updike (b. 1932) is an American author. *Rabbit, Run* is about Harry "Rabbit" Angstrom. He is a young married man feeling tied down and overwhelmed by family-life. He has one child and another on the way. He has little affection for his alcoholic wife, and the feeling is mutual. He is constantly reminiscing about his days as the star basketball player for his high school team. He desperately wants to retrieve that status, but does not see how his current life can progress to that end. So, Rabbit runs from his domestic quagmire.

Keywords: American author, alcoholism, basketball, family, marriage, midlife crisis

Websites:
http://www.bookrags.com/studyguide-rabbitrun/
http://www.gradesaver.com/classicnotes/titles/rabbit/essay1.html
http://www.kirjasto.sci.fi/updike.htm

Rate this book: 1 – 2 – 3   4 – 5 – 6   7 – 8 – 9

Fiction
Novels / Short Stories

The Red Badge of Courage *
by Stephen Crane (1990) 112p. ISBN-13: 978-0486264653

Standard book equivalent: 0.7
First published: 1894

Crane (1871 – 1900) was an American author of novels and poetry who died of tuberculosis in Germany. This novel is about the Civil War, and a Union soldier's effort to control his fears and inner demons as he prepares to fight in his first battle. It is less condemning of war than *All Quiet on the Western Front*, but still reveals the horror of war, and the unpredictability of one's response to battle. A major theme of the novel is the meaning of courage. Compare to *Going After Cacciato*.

Keywords: American author, coming-of-age, Civil War, war

Websites:
http://www.sparknotes.com/lit/redbadge/
http://www.gradesaver.com/classicnotes/titles/redbadge/
http://www.online-literature.com/crane/redbadge/

Rate this book: 1 – 2 – 3   4 – 5 – 6   7 – 8 – 9

Fiction
Novels / Short Stories

The Red Tent
by Anita Diamant (1998) 336p, ISBN-13: 978-0312195519

Standard book equivalent: 1.3
First published: 1997

Diamant (b. 1951) is an American author. *The Red Tent* interweaves biblical tales with fictional events and characters. It is a fictionalized recounting of the life of Dinah—daughter of Leah and Jacob, and sister to Joseph—from her birth in Mesopotamia through her years in Canaan and death in Egypt. The title refers to the place women visit when they are in their menses or giving birth. When Dinah reaches puberty and enters the red tent, her mother and Jacob's three other wives initiate her into the mores of the tribe's women.

Keywords: American author, woman author, ancient, Jewish experience, women

Websites:
http://www.anitadiamant.com/
http://www.citybeat.com/2001-05-17/books2.shtml
http://www.curledup.com/redtent.htm

Rate this book: 1 – 2 – 3   4 – 5 – 6   7 – 8 – 9

Fiction
Novels / Short Stories

Rip Van Winkle and Other Stories *
by Washington Irving (1996) 208p, ISBN-13: 978-0140367713

Standard book equivalent: 0.8
First published in the early nineteenth century

Washington Irving (1783 – 1859) was a pioneer of American fiction who was born in Manhattan and once served as the U.S. Ambassador to Spain. He was the first American to make a living solely as a writer. This collection includes: 'Rip Van Winkle', 'The Legend of Sleepy Hollow', 'The Spectre Bridegroom', 'The Pride of the Village', and 'Mountjoy'. 'Rip van Winkle' and 'The Legend of Sleepy Hollow' first appeared in Irving's *Sketchbook of Geoffrey Crayon* in 1820.

Keywords: American author, fable, horror, short-stories

Websites:
http://www.bartleby.com/195/4.html
http://www.bartleby.com/310/2/2.html
http://www.kirjasto.sci.fi/wirving.htm

Rate this book: 1 – 2 – 3   4 – 5 – 6   7 – 8 – 9

Fiction
Novels / Short Stories

Roofwalker
by Susan Power (2004) 224p, ISBN-13: 978-1571310415

Standard book equivalent: 0.9
First published: 2001

Power (b. 1961) is a Native American author (a member of the Standing Rock Sioux tribe) from Chicago who won the Milkweed National Fiction Prize in 2002 for *Roofwalker*. She won the 1995 PEN/Hemingway Award for *Grass Dancer*. *Roofwalker* is an anthology about the lives of Native Americans and mixed bloods living away from the reservation. It is a realistic portrayal of Sioux culture in modern American society. Part fiction, part autobiography, these stories emphasize the cross-cultural issues faced by Native Americans.

Keywords: Native American author, Chicago, cross-cultural, Native American experience, PEN/Hemingway Award, short-stories

Websites:
http://newpages.com/bookreviews/archive/reviews/roofwalker.htm
http://voices.cla.umn.edu/vg/Bios/entries/power_susan.html
http://www.ipl.org/div/natam/bin/browse.pl/A259

Rate this book: 1 – 2 – 3   4 – 5 – 6   7 – 8 – 9

Fiction
Novels / Short Stories

The Screwtape Letters
by C. S. Lewis (2001) 224p, ISBN-13: 978-0060652937

Standard book equivalent: 0.9
First published: 1942

Lewis (1898 – 1963) was an Irish author now best known for his *Chronicles of Narnia*. *The Screwtape Letters*, a work of Christian fiction, is written as a series of letters from a senior demon to his inexperienced nephew, Wormwood. Screwtape mentors Wormwood on the "tricks of the trade" in tempting people away from God. Lewis provides readers with an understanding of temptation using an inside look at the workings of evil, which he depicts as a heartless bureaucracy.

Keywords: Irish author, bureaucracy, devil, epistolary novel, magical realism, religion

Websites:
http://www.harpercollins.com/author/authorExtra.aspx?authorID=5865&isbn13=9780060652937&displayType=readingGuide
http://ic.net/~erasmus/RAZ26.HTM
http://www.kirjasto.sci.fi/cslewis.htm

Rate this book: 1 – 2 – 3   4 – 5 – 6   7 – 8 – 9

Fiction
Novels / Short Stories

The Sea
by John Banville (2006) 208p, ISBN-13: 978-1400097029

Standard book equivalent: 0.8
First published: 2005

Banville (b. 1945) is an Irish author whose book, *The Sea*, won the 2005 Man Booker Award. It is about Max Morden, a middle-aged Irishman who retreats to the seaside town of his childhood to reflect on the deaths of his loved ones—both recent and long ago. Max contemplates the effects his past has on him. His wife has recently died, and the town revives memories of a childhood love that drowned as a child. Banville explores the issues of love, loss and memory as they shape our lives.

Keywords: Irish author, Ireland, loss, love, Man Booker Award, memory, midlife crisis

Websites:
http://www.themodernword.com/scriptorium/banville.html
http://www.complete-review.com/reviews/banvillej/sea.htm
http://www.threemonkeysonline.com/threemon_article_John_Banville_interview.htm

Rate this book: 1 – 2 – 3   4 – 5 – 6   7 – 8 – 9

Fiction
Novels / Short Stories

The Secret Life of Bees
by Sue Monk Kidd (2005) 320p, ISBN-13: 978-0143036401

Standard book equivalent: 1.2
First published: 2002

Kidd (b. 1948) is an American author. *The Secret Life of Bees* is set in 1964 South Carolina and the protagonist is 14-year-old Lily. She is growing up with an abusive father; her mother had died under puzzling circumstances. Lily and her nanny finally take an opportunity to flee their stifling and harmful environment. Eventually, Lily ends up becoming an apprentice beekeeper. The novel carries themes of social unrest, racism, love, and maternal bonds that extend beyond death.

Keywords: American author, woman author, abuse, family, inspirational, love, motherhood, racism, the South

Websites:
http://www.suemonkkidd.com/
http://www.trashionista.com/2006/08/book_review_the_4.html
http://www.readinggroupguides.com/guides3/secret_life_of_bees1.asp

Rate this book: 1 – 2 – 3   4 – 5 – 6   7 – 8 – 9

Fiction
Novels / Short Stories

Seize the Day
by Saul Bellow (2003) 144p, ISBN-13: 978-0142437612

Standard book equivalent: 0.6
First published: 1956

Bellow (1915 – 2005) was an American author and 1976 Nobel Prize in Literature winner. *Seize the Day* describes one day in the life of Wilhelm Adler. Wilhelm is undergoing a midlife crisis. He is an unemployed broke actor estranged from his wife, children and father. He has always found a way to evade taking personal responsibility for his life. However, today he comes to see himself as he is—isolated, lacking maturity and a failure.

Keywords: American author, family, Jewish experience, midlife crisis, New York City, Nobel Prize (Literature)

Websites:
http://www.sparknotes.com/lit/seize/
http://us.penguingroup.com/static/rguides/us/seize_the_day.html
http://www.litencyc.com/php/sworks.php?rec=true&UID=2189

Rate this book: 1 – 2 – 3   4 – 5 – 6   7 – 8 – 9

Fiction
Novels / Short Stories

A Separate Peace
by John Knowles (2003) 208p, ISBN-13: 978-0743253970

Standard book equivalent: 0.8
First published: 1959

Knowles (1926 – 2001) was an American novelist most famous for *A Separate Peace*. It is about the rivalries and friendships at Devon School, a fictional prep school for boys, during WWII. Gene is the narrator, a man looking back on his last year at Devon. The plot centers on the relationship between Gene and Phineas. Their school days were a complicated blend of friendship and jealousy that sees the best and worst of each boy and leads to violence, a confession, and the betrayal of trust.

Keywords: American author, betrayal, coming-of-age, friendship, violence, war, WWII

Websites:
http://www.sparknotes.com/lit/separate/
http://www.gradesaver.com/classicnotes/titles/separate/
http://www.cliffsnotes.com/WileyCDA/LitNote/id-168.html

Rate this book: 1 – 2 – 3   4 – 5 – 6   7 – 8 – 9

Fiction
Novels / Short Stories

Shame **
by Salman Rushdie (2000) 307p, ISBN-13: 978-0312270933

Standard book equivalent: 1.2
First published: 1983

Rushdie (b. 1947) is a British-Indian author. *Shame* explores the theme of shame in the context of an Islamic society. It is set in the fictional city of Q and is an allegory about the first forty years of Pakistan and the people who have governed it. The storyline is that of a fable about the conflict between two men and their families, who represent Pakistan's Zulfiquar Ali Bhutto and General Mohammed Zia ul-Haq. Rushdie fills the story with myth, and magical characters.

Keywords: Indian author, British author, Muslim experience, Pakistan, politics, religion, shame

Websites:
http://www.postcolonialweb.org/pakistan/literature/rushdie/shameov.html
http://www.ipl.org/div/litcrit/bin/litcrit.out.pl?ti=sha-271
http://www.kirjasto.sci.fi/rushdie.htm

Rate this book: 1 – 2 – 3   4 – 5 – 6   7 – 8 – 9

Fiction
Novels / Short Stories

The Sheltering Sky
by Paul Bowles (1998) 368p, ISBN-13: 978-0880015820

Standard book equivalent: 1.4
First published: 1949

Bowles (1910 - 1999) was an American author. The setting of *The Sheltering Sky* is the North African desert shortly after World War II. The story centers on Port and Kit Moresby, a married couple originally from New York who travel to the North African desert accompanied by their friend Tunner. Port and Kit hope to resolve their marital difficulties through this journey, but the trip is soon made treacherous by their ignorance of local culture and the dangers that surround them.

Keywords: American author, Africa, cross-cultural, desert, love, marriage, nature, slavery

Websites:
http://www.paulbowles.org/
http://www.readinggroupguides.com/guides3/sheltering_sky1.asp
http://www.harpercollins.com/author/authorExtra.aspx?isbn13=9780060834821&displayType=readingGuide

Rate this book: 1 – 2 – 3   4 – 5 – 6   7 – 8 – 9

Fiction
Novels / Short Stories

Shizuko's Daughter *
by Kyoko Mori (1994) 224p, ISBN-13: 978-0449704332

Standard book equivalent: 0.9
First published: 1993

Mori (b. 1957) is a Japanese-American author. *Shizuko's Daughter* is about twelve year-old Yuki Okudo. The central theme is death and how it affects those left behind. After her mother's suicide, Yuki lives with her aloof father and his resentful new wife. She is cut off from her mother's family, and has no one to help her grieve the loss of her mother. However, Yuki becomes strong and learns to appreciate both the good and difficult times life has to offer.

Keywords: Japanese author, American author, woman author, coming-of-age, death, family, love, Japan, suicide

Websites:
http://www.randomhouse.com/highschool/catalog/display.pperl?isbn=9780449704332&view=tg
http://www.bookrags.com/studyguide-shizukosdaughter/
http://goldsea.com/Bookview/Kids/Shizuko/shizuko.html

Rate this book: 1 – 2 – 3   4 – 5 – 6   7 – 8 – 9

Fiction
Novels / Short Stories

Siddhartha **
by Hermann Hesse (1998) 112p, ISBN-13: 978-0486406534

Standard book equivalent: 0.4
First published: 1922

Hesse (1877 – 1962) is a German author who became a Swiss citizen. He won the 1946 Nobel Prize in Literature. *Siddhartha* is an allegorical novel about enlightenment. Siddhartha means "one who has attained his goals." It is set in India, about the time of Buddha. Siddhartha is the main character (he is not the Buddha). The novel is written in the third person and follows Siddhartha in his search for enlightenment and the experiences he has along the way. One theme of the novel is that enlightenment must come from experience; it cannot come from listening or reading.

Keywords: German author, Buddhism, India, Nobel Prize (Literature), religion

Websites:
http://www.online-literature.com/hesse/siddhartha/
http://www.sparknotes.com/lit/siddhartha/
http://www.gradesaver.com/classicnotes/titles/siddhartha/

Rate this book: 1 – 2 – 3   4 – 5 – 6   7 – 8 – 9

Fiction
Novels / Short Stories

Silas Marner
by George Eliot (1996) 160p, ISBN-13: 978-0486292465

Standard book equivalent: 0.6
First published: 1861

Eliot (1819 – 1880) was the penname of British author Mary Anne Evans. The setting of *Silas Marner* is early 18th century England. Silas Marner is a poor linen-weaver who leaves his village after being framed for a robbery by his friend William Dane. William then goes on to marry Silas' lover. Silas, embittered, ends up in the village of Raveloe and is again wronged when his money is stolen by the son of the village's wealthiest landowner. However, through an orphaned girl that he adopts, he learns to love again.

Keywords: British author, woman author, betrayal, England, family, love

Websites:
http://www.sparknotes.com/lit/silas/
http://www.bookrags.com/notes/sm/
http://www.online-literature.com/george_eliot/silas_marner/

Rate this book: 1 – 2 – 3 4 – 5 – 6 7 – 8 – 9

Fiction
Novels / Short Stories

Snow Flower and the Secret Fan *
by Lisa See (2006) 288p, ISBN-13: 978-0812968064

Standard book equivalent: 1.1
First published: 2005

See (b. 1955) is an American author. *Snow Flower and the Secret Fan* is set in remote 19th-century China. The novel is noted for its historical accuracy regarding women's ceremonies and duties, and other aspects of culture in China during this period. It traces the lifelong friendship of Lily and Snow Flower, their imprisonment by the rigid codes of conduct for women and their betrayal by pride and love. The two women find comfort in their decades' old friendship. However, when a misunderstanding arises, their lifelong friendship is suddenly threatened.

Keywords: American author, woman author, betrayal, China, feminism, friendship

Websites:
http://www.lisasee.com/
http://www.randomhouse.com/catalog/display.pperl?isbn=9781588364746
http://www.waterbridgereview.org/092005/cnv_see.php

Rate this book: 1 – 2 – 3   4 – 5 – 6   7 – 8 – 9

Fiction
Novels / Short Stories

So Long, See You Tomorrow
by William Maxwell (1996) 144p, ISBN-13: 978-0679767206

Standard book equivalent: 0.6
First published 1980

Maxwell (1908 – 2000) was an American author. *So Long, See You Tomorrow* won the National Book Award in 1982. The novel's setting is rural Lincoln, Illinois during the 1920s. It is about a murder on a farm and the effect it has on the friendship between two boys. It is narrated by an elderly man as a remembrance of events long past. The novel explores the role that unresolved guilt plays in shaping our lives. Coming to terms with one's memory is a theme of the novel.

Keywords: American author, friendship, memory, Midwest, National Book Award

Websites:
http://www.washingtonpost.com/wp-dyn/articles/A14217-2004Jun3.html
http://www.writingsite.com/index.htm?pages/reviews/maxwell_solong.htm~mainFrame
http://www.snreview.org/0405Burkhardt.html

Rate this book: 1 – 2 – 3   4 – 5 – 6   7 – 8 – 9

Fiction
Novels / Short Stories

Something Wicked This Way Comes *
by Ray Bradbury (1998) 304p, ISBN-13: 978-0380729401

Standard book equivalent: 1.2
First published: 1962

Bradbury (b. 1920) is an American author noted for his science fiction novels, short-stories and screenplays. *Something Wicked This Way Comes* is the story of two boys, James Nightshade and William Halloway, and the evil that enters their small Midwestern town when a "dark carnival" arrives one autumn midnight. It is up to these two thirteen year-old boys to save their own souls and those of the town as well. Themes developed in this novel include accepting oneself and the importance of common cause in getting people to live and struggle together.

Keywords: American author, carnival, horror, Midwest

Websites:
http://www.sparknotes.com/lit/wicked/index.html
http://www.harperacademic.com/catalog/instructors_guide_
    xml.asp?isbn=0380729407
http://www.sfsite.com/05a/some32.htm

Rate this book: 1 – 2 – 3   4 – 5 – 6   7 – 8 – 9

Fiction
Novels / Short Stories

The Spy Who Came in from the Cold
by John le Carre (2001) 224p, ISBN-13: 978-0743442534

Standard book equivalent: 0.9
First published: 1963

Le Carre (b. 1931) is a British author. Graham Greene called *The Spy Who Came in from the Cold* the best spy story he had ever read. It takes place during the cold war, when Germany was still divided into two countries. The novel tells the story of Alec Leamas, a British spy, who defects to East Germany. Leamas is actually being manipulated by the director of the Circus (i.e., British Intelligence). His defection is part of a scheme to protect a British agent in the East German Secret Service from discovery and discredit an East German spymaster.

Keywords: British author, cold war, Germany, mystery, spy

Websites:
http://www.mysteryguide.com/bkLecarrCold.html
http://www.brothersjudd.com/index.cfm/fuseaction/reviews.detail/book_id/727
http://www.johnlecarre.com/

Rate this book: 1 – 2 – 3   4 – 5 – 6   7 – 8 – 9

Fiction
Novels / Short Stories

Sula
by Toni Morrison (2004) 192p, ISBN-13: 978-1400033430

Standard book equivalent: 0.7
First published: 1973

Morrison (b. 1931) is an American author and winner of the 1993 Nobel Prize in Literature. *Sula*—set in Medallion, Ohio during the first half of the twentieth century—is her second novel. It is about Nel Wright and Sula Peace, two girls who grow up as friends but then become bitter enemies. Their friendship endures even after Nel becomes a mainstay of the African American community and Sula an outcast. However, an act of betrayal changes everything.

Keywords: American author, African American author, woman author, African American experience, betrayal, friendship, Midwest, Nobel Prize (Literature)

Websites:
http://www.sparknotes.com/lit/sula/
http://www.luminarium.org/contemporary/tonimorrison/sula.htm
http://www.oprah.com/obc/pastbooks/toni_morrison/obc_20020405_about.jhtml

Rate this book: 1 – 2 – 3   4 – 5 – 6   7 – 8 – 9

Fiction
Novels / Short Stories

The Swallows of Kabul
by Yasmina Khadra, John Cullen (translator) (2005) 208p,
ISBN-13: 978-1400033768

Standard book equivalent: 0.8
First published: 2004

Khadra (b. 1955) is a pseudonym of the Algerian author Mohammed Moulessehoul. *The Swallows of Kabul* takes place in Afghanistan during the reign of the Taliban. The story is about two couples, one is persecuted by the Taliban, and the husband of the other is a jailer sympathetic to the Taliban's rule. The main characters are brought together under tragic circumstances driven by the coldhearted fundamentalism of the regime. The novel describes the humiliation endured by women who at one time were free to become educated and assume important roles in society.

Keywords: Algerian author, Afghanistan, feminism, Muslim experience, religion, violence

Websites:
http://www.asianreviewofbooks.com/arb/article.php?article=366
http://www.curledup.com/swallows.htm
http://www.csmonitor.com/2004/0210/p14s03-bogn.html

Rate this book: 1 – 2 – 3   4 – 5 – 6   7 – 8 – 9

Fiction
Novels / Short Stories

Their Eyes Were Watching God
by Zora Neale Hurston (1998) 240p, ISBN-13: 978-0060931414

Standard book equivalent: 0.9
First published: 1937

Hurston (1891 – 1960) was an American author. Her novel *Their Eyes Were Watching God* is about male-female and female-female relationships. It tells the life story of Janie, an African American woman, as she experiences the different men in her life. Hurston captures the conflicts, joys, and tender moments of Janie's male relationships with realistic dialog. Janie's relationships with other African American women are important in her life and Hurston emphasizes themes of empowerment and female bonding throughout the book.

Keywords: American author, African American author, woman author, African American experience, feminism, friendship

Websites:
http://www.sparknotes.com/lit/eyes/
http://www.bookrags.com/notes/tewg/
http://lkwdpl.org/wihohio/hurs-zorx.htm

Rate this book: 1 – 2 – 3   4 – 5 – 6   7 – 8 – 9

Fiction
Novels / Short Stories

Things Fall Apart
by Chinua Achebe (1994) 224p, ISBN-13: 978-0385474542

Standard book equivalent: 0.9
First published: 1958

Achebe (b. 1930) is a Nigerian author most famous for *Things Fall Apart*. The novel's setting is during the 1890s in Ibo villages of what is now Nigeria. The main character is Okonkwo, a proud village leader in conflict with the changes being brought to Ibo culture by colonialism and Christianity. The climax is precipitated by a murder Okonkwo commits. Major themes of the novel include the struggle between tradition and change, and the clash of cultures. Compare with *Kokoro*.

Keywords: Nigerian author, Africa, colonialism, cross-cultural, Nigeria

Websites:
http://www.kirjasto.sci.fi/achebe.htm
http://www.sparknotes.com/lit/things/index.html
http://www.gradesaver.com/classicnotes/titles/things/

Rate this book: 1 – 2 – 3   4 – 5 – 6   7 – 8 – 9

Fiction
Novels / Short Stories

To Kill a Mockingbird *
by Harper Lee (1988) 288p, ISBN-13: 978-0446310789

Standard book equivalent: 1.1
First published: 1960

Lee (b. 1926) is an American author who won a 1961 Pulitzer Prize for *To Kill a Mockingbird*. The novel is narrated by a child, Scout Finch, and the setting is 1930s rural Alabama. It is a story about her father, Atticus Finch, who is a lawyer in the Depression-era South. He defends an African American man against an unwarranted rape charge and his own children against prejudice. Lee explores themes of the importance of a moral education, and the coexistence of good and evil.

Keywords: American author, woman author, African American experience, Great Depression, prejudice, Pulitzer Prize, racism, the South

Websites:
http://www.sparknotes.com/lit/mocking/index.html
http://www.gradesaver.com/classicnotes/titles/killmockingbird/
http://www.bookrags.com/notes/tkm/

Rate this book: 1 – 2 – 3   4 – 5 – 6   7 – 8 – 9

Fiction
Novels / Short Stories

To the Lighthouse **
by Virginia Woolf, Eudora Welty (Introduction) (1989)
228p, ISBN-13: 978-0156907392

Standard book equivalent: 0.9
First published: 1927

Woolf (1882 – 1941) was a British author. *To the Lighthouse* is set between 1910 and 1920. It is a philosophical narrative about the Ramsey family and their summer home on the Isle of Skye. Part I describes the family and their summer home. Part II describes the deaths of one of the sons in war, a daughter in pregnancy, and Mrs. Ramsey, the matriarch. Part III returns to their summer home; it is a reflection on the events that have occurred. The novel ends as it began, with a proposed trip to the lighthouse.

Keywords: British author, woman author, family, Scotland

Websites:
http://www.sparknotes.com/lit/lighthouse/
http://etext.library.adelaide.edu.au/w/woolf/virginia/w91t/
http://www.kirjasto.sci.fi/vwoolf.htm

Rate this book: 1 – 2 – 3   4 – 5 – 6   7 – 8 – 9

Fiction
Novels / Short Stories

Too Loud a Solitude **
by Bohumil Hrabal, Michael Henry Heim (translator) 1992
98p, ISBN-13: 978-0156904582

Standard book equivalent: 0.4
First published: 1976

Hrabel (1914 – 1997) was a Czech author. *Too Loud a Solitude* is about Hanta, a man who has worked 35 years as a hydraulic press operator in a dark cellar, compacting waste paper and books outlawed by successive regimes. The books that he must destroy become his whole life and only companions. When he is to be replaced by younger workers and a more productive machine, Hanta dreams of a gigantic press that destroys not only him but the entire city with its traditions and culture.

Keywords: Czech author, absurdism, bureaucracy, change, Czechoslovakia, Prague, technology

Websites:
http://www.kirjasto.sci.fi/hrabal.htm
http://www.webster.edu/~corbetre/personal/reading/hrabal-silence.html
http://www.lrb.co.uk/v23/n01/wood02_.html

Rate this book: 1 – 2 – 3   4 – 5 – 6   7 – 8 – 9

Fiction
Novels / Short Stories

The Trial
by Franz Kafka (1999) 304p, ISBN-13: 978-0805209990

Standard book equivalent: 1.2
First published: 1925

Kafka (1883 – 1924) was a Jewish-Bohemian author, born in Prague, who wrote in German. *The Trial* is a novel about a character named Joseph K and is set in an unnamed European city. Joseph awakens one morning, is arrested and subjected to the judicial process for an unspecified crime. The reasons for his predicament are never specified. The novel's theme is the inhumanity of bureaucracy and foreshadows the coming of totalitarian regimes that would use such tactics. It was left unfinished at Kafka's death, and was never intended to be published.

Keywords: Jewish-Bohemian author, Czech author, absurdism, bureaucracy, totalitarianism

Websites:
http://www.sparknotes.com/lit/trial/
http://www.gutenberg.org/etext/7849
http://www.britishcouncil.org/learnenglish-central-stories-the-trial.htm

Rate this book: 1 – 2 – 3   4 – 5 – 6   7 – 8 – 9

Uncle Tom's Cabin
by Harriet Beecher Stowe (2005) 384p, ISBN: 0486440281

Standard book equivalent: 1.5
First published: 1852

Stowe (1811 - 1896) was an American author. She wrote *Uncle Tom's Cabin* in response to passage of the Fugitive Slave Act of 1850, which made it illegal to aid runaway slaves. The main character is Uncle Tom, a long-suffering slave who is separated from his family and repeatedly sold. On meeting Stowe, Lincoln is reputed to have said, "So you are the little woman who started this big war." Ironically, the anti-slavery *Uncle Tom's* Cabin—as the best selling novel of the 19th century—cemented negative stereotypes of African Americans. Also, it depicted slavery less harshly than the reality.

Keywords: American author, woman author, racism, slavery

Websites:
http://www.sparknotes.com/lit/uncletom/
http://www.iath.virginia.edu/utc/
http://www.online-literature.com/stowe/uncletom/

Rate this book: 1 – 2 – 3   4 – 5 – 6   7 – 8 – 9

Fiction
Novels / Short Stories

Waiting for the Vote of the Wild Animals
by Ahmadou Kourouma, Carrol F. Coates (translator)
(2001) 277p, ISBN-13: 978-0813920221

Standard book equivalent: 1.1
First published in: 1998

Kourouma (1927 – 2003) was an Ivorian novelist whose writing often attacked political corruption in Africa. *Waiting for the Vote of the Wild Animals* is an English translation of his French text. Its main character is Koyaga, the leader of a fictional African country. The novel traces his rise to power and the events that shape his rule. Koyaga is actually a thinly veiled caricature of Eyadema, Togo's leader of many years and the novel is more factual than fiction. Another English translation of this text has been done by Frank Wynne.

Keywords: Ivorian author, Africa, dictatorship, politics, Togo

Websites:
http://www.complete-review.com/reviews/cdivoire/kourma4.htm
http://www.nathanielturner.com/waitingforvoteofwildanimals.htm
http://books.guardian.co.uk/review/story/0,12084,913652,00.html

Rate this book: 1 – 2 – 3   4 – 5 – 6   7 – 8 – 9

Fiction
Novels / Short Stories

Waiting for the Barbarians
by J.M. Coetzee (1999) 160p. ISBN-13: 978-0140283358

Standard book equivalent: 0.9
First published: 1980

Coetzee (b. 1940) is a South African author and winner of the 2003 Nobel Prize in Literature. This novel is about a magistrate of an empire who has run the affairs of a tiny frontier settlement for years. He has ignored the trouble brewing with the "barbarians" and war is imminent. However, when the interrogation experts arrive, he becomes sympathetic toward the victims. His actions to aid the barbarians land him in jail as an enemy of the state. The magistrate represents all men living in complicity with regimes that ignore justice and decency.

Keywords: South African author, Africa, colonialism, dictatorship, Nobel Prize (Literature), politics, racism

Websites:
http://www.wmich.edu/dialogues/texts/waitingforthebarbarians.html
http://turtleneck.net/summer01/tweedjacket/coetzee.htm
http://www-news.uchicago.edu/releases/03/031002.coetzee.shtml

Rate this book: 1 – 2 – 3   4 – 5 – 6   7 – 8 – 9

Fiction
Novels / Short Stories

Walk in the Light & Twenty-Three Tales
by Leo Tolstoy (2003) 360p, ISBN-13: 978-1570754609

Standard book equivalent: 1.4
First published: 1928

Tolstoy (1828 – 1910) was a famous Russian author whose works are noted for their themes about morality. This anthology of 24 short stories includes "Two Old Men" (1885), "Prisoner of the Caucasus" (1886), "Ivan the Fool" (1886), "The Empty Drum" (1887), "Walk in the Light While the Light is With You" (1893), and "Three Questions" (1903). The title story, "Walk in the Light" takes place during the early Christian era. It follows the lives of ordinary men who convert from paganism to Christianity. "Three Questions" is a short parable about an emperor who learns the importance of time and people.

Keywords: Russian author, Christianity, morality, parable, short-stories

Websites:
http://www.ccel.org/ccel/tolstoy/23_tales.titlepage.html
http://www.ltolstoy.com/
http://www.kirjasto.sci.fi/ltolstoi.htm

Rate this book: 1 – 2 – 3   4 – 5 – 6   7 – 8 – 9

Fiction
Novels / Short Stories

The War of the Worlds *
by H. G. Wells (1997) 160p, ISBN-13: 978-0486295060

Standard book equivalent: 0.6
First published: 1898

Wells (1866 – 1946) was a British author of science fiction. *The War of the Worlds* depicts an invasion of earth by Martians. The setting is England during the early twentieth century. Ten landings of Martians occur followed by a three week-long war. Wells wrote the book at a time when the possibility of life on Mars was popularized by observations of its canal-like features by Italian astronomers. The book has been interpreted as a condemnation of colonialism practiced by many European countries of the day.

Keywords: British author, colonialism, Martians, science fiction, war

Websites:
http://www.sfreviews.net/wotw.html
http://www.online-literature.com/wellshg/
http://www.kirjasto.sci.fi/hgwells.htm

Rate this book: 1 – 2 – 3   4 – 5 – 6   7 – 8 – 9

Fiction
Novels / Short Stories

Weep Not, Child
by Ngugi wa Thiong'o (1988) 144p, ISBN-13: 978-0435908300

Standard book equivalent: 0.6
First published: 1964

Thiong'o (b. 1938) is a Kenyan author. *Weep Not, Child* follows a young boy, Njoroge, as he grows up during the Mau Mau war of 1950s Kenya. It is about the hopes and dreams of Njoroge, his coming-of-age, and the affects the changes in the outside world have on him. The author describes the power of the white rulers, the bitterness of the Africans at being enslaved on their own land, and their attempt to rise up against tyranny. It also deals with the poor relations between Africans and the Indian merchants.

Keywords: Kenyan author, Africa, colonialism, coming-of-age, Kenya, Mau Mau, racism

Websites:
http://www.kirjasto.sci.fi/ngugiw.htm
http://exploringafrica.matrix.msu.edu/students/curriculum/m11/activity3.php
http://www.washingtonpost.com/wp-dyn/content/article/2006/09/16/AR2006091600943.html?referrer=delicious

Rate this book: 1 – 2 – 3   4 – 5 – 6   7 – 8 – 9

Fiction
Novels / Short Stories

Where We Once Belonged
by Sia Figiel (2000) 247p, ISBN-13: 978-1885030276

Standard book equivalent: 1.0
First published: 1996

Figiel (b. 1967) is often considered to be Samoa's first woman novelist. *Where We Once Belonged* describes Alofa, a Samoan girl coming-of-age through a series of linked stories. It was awarded the Commonwealth Prize for Best Novel (Southeast Asia/South Pacific region). Many of the episodes emphasize the tensions between guilt and cruelty felt by girls of Alofa's age, while others show the naiveté of children who are still utterly dependent on their families. A central theme of the novel is the dominance of the community over the individual in Samoan culture.

Keywords: Pacific Island author, woman author, coming-of-age, Samoa

Websites:
http://www.trout.auckland.ac.nz/journal/2/sullivan/sia.htm
http://www.thei.aust.com/sydney/biographies/figiel.html
http://www.southproject.org/profiles/figiel1.htm

Rate this book: 1 – 2 – 3   4 – 5 – 6   7 – 8 – 9

Fiction
Novels / Short Stories

Wide Sargasso Sea
by Jean Rhys (2001) 192p, ISBN-13: 978-0140818031

Standard book equivalent: 0.7
First published: 1966

Rhys (1890 – 1979) was a Caribbean author born in Dominica. *Wide Sargasso Sea* is a "prequel" to Bronte's 1847 novel, *Jane Eyre*, with the focus on Bertha Mason—the first Mrs. Rochester as depicted in *Jane Eyre*. When Bertha comes-of-age she is married off to Mr. Rochester. He takes her to England, away from Jamaica the only place she has known. Bertha descends into madness when she realizes he does not love her. A theme of the novel is women transplanted from their roots and left to fend for themselves in alien societies.

Keywords: Caribbean author, woman author, England, Jamaica, marriage, social class, West Indies

Websites:
http://www.sparknotes.com/lit/sargasso/
http://www.eng.fju.edu.tw/worldlit/caribbean/rhys.htm
http://www.postcolonialweb.org/caribbean/dominica/rhys/ripple18.html

Rate this book: 1 – 2 – 3   4 – 5 – 6   7 – 8 – 9

Fiction
Novels / Short Stories

Winesburg, Ohio *
by Sherwood Anderson (1999) 240p, ISBN-13: 978-0192839770

Standard book equivalent: 1.0
First published: 1919

Anderson (1876 – 1941) was an American author. *Winesburg, Ohio* is part novel and part collection of short stories. The stories are all centered on the main character, a young reporter for the local paper named George Willard and the fictional town of Winesburg. He views the inhabitants as "grotesques"—simple-minded and handicapped in some way, e.g., emotionally, morally, or intellectually. A central theme of the stories is the loneliness and frustration of small-town life in the Midwest.

Keywords: American author, Midwest, Ohio, short-stories

Websites:
http://www.sparknotes.com/lit/winesburgohio/
http://www.gradesaver.com/classicnotes/titles/winesburg/
http://www.bartleby.com/156/

Rate this book: 1 – 2 – 3   4 – 5 – 6   7 – 8 – 9

Fiction
Novels / Short Stories

A Yellow Raft in Blue Water
by Michael Dorris (2003) 383p, ISBN-13: 978-0312421854

Standard book equivalent: 1.5
First published: 1987

Dorris (1945 – 1997) was a Native American author. Three generations of Native American women recount their searches for identity and love: Ida, the grandmother, Christine, the mother and Raymona, the daughter. Ida is a traditionalist and lives on a reservation. Christine lives in a city as a single mother formerly with an African American husband. Raymona is a mixed-blood offspring and faces prejudice because of her African American features and "city ways". The story moves back and forth in time between the 1930s and the present, providing a history of reservation life.

Keywords: Native American author, cross-cultural, love, motherhood, Native American experience, women

Websites:
http://www.sparknotes.com/lit/yellowraft/
http://www.mnsu.edu/emuseum/information/biography/abcde/dorris_michael.html
http://www.kstrom.net/isk/books/ya/ya334.html

Rate this book: 1 – 2 – 3   4 – 5 – 6   7 – 8 – 9

Fiction
Novels / Short Stories

You Know Me Al
by Ring Lardner (2004) 119p, ISBN-13: 978-1419195273

Standard book equivalent: 0.5
First published: 1914

Ring Lardner (1885 - 1933) was an American sports columnist and author. *You Know Me Al* shows him to be a great humorist as well. It is a collection of short stories in the form of letters by Jack Keefe, a fictional bush-league pitcher who finally gets his chance in the majors. He is talented but also extraordinarily naïve, which Lardner uses to hilarious effect. The stories were originally published as six installments in the *Saturday Evening Post*.

Keywords: American author, baseball, short-stories, sports

Websites:
http://www.tridget.com/lardnermania/index.htm
http://www.ibiblio.org/eldritch/rl/unomeal.htm
http://www.bookrags.com/shortguide-you-know-me-al/

Rate this book: 1 – 2 – 3   4 – 5 – 6   7 – 8 – 9

Fiction
Novels / Short Stories

Zorba the Greek
by Nikos Kazantzakis (1996) 320p, ISBN-13: 978-0684825540

Standard book equivalent: 1.2
First published: 1946

Kazantzakis (1883 – 1957) was a Greek author from Crete. The unnamed narrator is an intellectual Greek writer who opens a coal mine on the island of Crete. He develops a friendship with an elderly employee named Zorba, who delights in sensual pleasures and lives his life with great passion. The two become curious about each other's lifestyles, with the narrator learning to become more experiential. He takes a lover, the village widow, and experiences both great pleasure and great sorrow.

Keywords: Greek author, Crete, cross-cultural, friendship, Greece, violence

Websites:
http://www.bookrags.com/Zorba_the_Greek_(novel)
http://www.webster.edu/~corbetre/personal/reading/kazantzakis-zorba.html
http://www.kirjasto.sci.fi/kazantza.htm

Rate this book: 1 – 2 – 3   4 – 5 – 6   7 – 8 – 9

Fiction
Novels / Short Stories

FICTION

Drama

Fiction
Drama

3 by Shakespeare: A Midsummer Night's Dream, Romeo and Juliet and Richard III
by William Shakespeare (2006) 288p, ISBN-13: 978-0486447216

Standard book equivalent: 1.1
First published: early seventeenth century

Shakespeare (1564 – 1616) was a British author. This anthology of unabridged plays (with informative footnotes) contains a comedy, a tragedy, and a history. *A Midsummer Night's Dream* is about the imaginative powers of love. It is set in a forest with four young lovers, a group of actors and fairies. *Romeo and Juliet* is a passionate romantic drama about two young lovers who would do anything to be together. *Richard III* is a portrait of a villain who murders and betrays his way to the throne.

Keywords: British author, betrayal, comedy, tragedy

Websites:
http://www.sparknotes.com/shakespeare/msnd/
http://www.sparknotes.com/shakespeare/romeojuliet/
http://www.sparknotes.com/shakespeare/richardiii/
http://www-tech.mit.edu/Shakespeare/

Rate this book: 1 – 2 – 3   4 – 5 – 6   7 – 8 – 9

Fiction
Drama

The Cherry Orchard
by Anton Chekhov (1991) 64p, ISBN-13: 978-0486266824

Standard book equivalent: 0.2
First published: 1904

Chekhov (1860 – 1904) was a Russian author and physician. *The Cherry Orchard* is about an aristocratic Russian woman who returns to her estate just before it is auctioned to pay the mortgage. Presented with options to save the estate, she does nothing. The play ends with the estate being sold and the family leaving to the sound of its well-known and productive cherry orchard being cut down. Central themes include the futility of both the aristocracy to maintain its status and the bourgeoisie to find meaning in its newfound materialism.

Keywords: Russian author, Russia, tragedy

Websites:
http://www.sparknotes.com/drama/cherryorchard/index.html
http://www.gradesaver.com/classicnotes/titles/cherry/
http://www.ibiblio.org/eldritch/ac/chorch.htm

Rate this book: 1 – 2 – 3   4 – 5 – 6   7 – 8 – 9

Fiction
Drama

The Complete Greek Tragedies: Aeschylus II
by David Grene (translator), (1992) 188p, ISBN-13: 978-0226307947

Standard book equivalent: 0.7
First published: circa 4th century BC

Aeschylus (525 BC – 456 BC) was a Greek playwright. Four plays. *The Suppliant Maidens* is about fifty Egyptian sisters who flee to Argos when forced to marry their cousins; they are protected there from the Egyptians. *The Persians* is about the Battle of Salamis in which King Xerxes was defeated by Athens. *Seven against Thebes* is the same story as told in the *Poenecian Women* by Euripides; it is about the conflict between Oedipus' sons. *Prometheus Bound* is about the titan punished by Zeus for giving man fire; Zeus is enraged because Prometheus won't reveal who will overthrow Zeus.

Keywords: Greek author, ancient, tragedy

Websites:
http://classics.mit.edu/Browse/browse-Aeschylus.html
http://www.gradesaver.com/classicnotes/authors/about_aeschylus.html
http://www.sparknotes.com/drama/prometheus/
http://www.pathguy.com/7thebes.htm

Rate this book: 1 – 2 – 3   4 – 5 – 6   7 – 8 – 9

Fiction
Drama

The Complete Greek Tragedies: Euripides V
by Euripides, David Grene (translator) (2002) 234p,
ISBN-13: 978-0226307848

Standard book equivalent: 0.9
First published: circa 4th century BC

Euripedes (480BC – 406BC) was a Greek playwright. This collection contains three of his plays. The title character of *Electra* is the daughter of Agamemnon who is murdered by his wife and her lover when he returns from the Trojan War; the play is about Electra's desire for revenge. *The Poenician Women* follows the story of Oedipus; after Oedipus blinds himself his sons fight each other for control of Thebes. *The Bacchae* is about a young king who attempts to rid his kingdom of the new cult of Dionysus; Dionysus has him murdered.

Keywords: Greek author, ancient, tragedy

Websites:
http://www.sparknotes.com/drama/electra/
http://www.theatredatabase.com/ancient/euripides_013.html
http://www.gradesaver.com/classicnotes/titles/bacchae/about.html
http://classics.mit.edu/Browse/browse-Euripides.html

Rate this book: 1 – 2 – 3   4 – 5 – 6   7 – 8 – 9

Fiction
Drama

The Complete Greek Tragedies: Sophocles I
by Sophocles, David Grene (translator) (1991) 218p, ISBN-13: 978-0226307923

Standard book equivalent: 0.8
First published: circa 4th century BC

Sophocles (496 BC – 406 BC) was a Greek playwright. This collection contains three plays: *Oedipus the King* is the story of Oedipus, a man fated to kill his father and marry his mother; horrified, he blinds himself and is exiled. *Oedipus at Colonus* continues with the wanderings of Oedipus, the fighting among his sons, and his death. *Antigone*, is about the daughter of Oedipus who morns her brother's death by attempting to bury him against the new King's orders; the King punishes her with death and is in turn punished by the gods.

Keywords: Greek author, ancient, tragedy

Websites:
http://www.online-literature.com/sophocles/oedipus/
http://www.bookrags.com/notes/oed/
http://www.bookrags.com/Oedipus_at_Colonus
http://www.bookrags.com/notes/ant/

Rate this book: 1 – 2 – 3   4 – 5 – 6   7 – 8 – 9

Fiction
Drama

The Crucible *
by Arthur Miller (2003) 176p, ISBN-13: 978-0142437339

Standard book equivalent: 0.7
First published: 1952

Miller (1915 – 2005) was an American playwright. *The Crucible* is a play about the Salem witch trials and McCarthyism. The witch trials are a historical event that occurred in the Puritan town of Salem, Massachusetts in 1692. The play concerns a group of girls falsely accused of witchcraft. The hysteria that follows the trial results in much tragedy for the people of Salem. The play is an allegory about McCarthyism, the anticommunism fear fueled by Senator Joe McCarthy of Minnesota, which swept through the United States during the 1950s.

Keywords: American author, McCarthyism, power, Salem, tragedy, witchcraft

Websites:
http://www.newyorker.com/archive/content/?020422fr_archive02
http://www.sparknotes.com/lit/crucible/
http://www.gradesaver.com/classicnotes/titles/crucible/

Rate this book: 1 – 2 – 3   4 – 5 – 6   7 – 8 – 9

Fiction
Drama

The Death of a Salesman *
by Arthur Miller (1998) 144p, ISBN-13: 978-0140481341

Standard book equivalent: 0.4
First published: 1949

Miller (1915 – 2005) was an American playwright. The *Death of a Salesman* is a play about broken-hearted salesman Willy Loman. Loman, no longer living in the real world, is trapped in his own delusional world. He cannot let go of the past and it's eating him up inside. He wants to believe that his family is destined for greatness, no matter how much reality points to otherwise. *The Death of a Salesman* is a powerful glimpse into an American tragedy that is as heartbreaking today as when it was when first produced.

Keywords: American author, family, midlife crisis, New York City, tragedy

Websites:
http://www.sparknotes.com/lit/salesman/
http://www.gradesaver.com/classicnotes/titles/salesman/
http://www.kirjasto.sci.fi/amiller.htm

Rate this book: 1 – 2 – 3   4 – 5 – 6   7 – 8 – 9

Fiction
Drama

A Doll's House
by Henrik Ibsen (1992) 72p, ISBN-13: 978-0486270623

Standard book equivalent: 0.3
First published: 1879

Ibsen (1828 – 1906) was a Norwegian playwright. Nora Helmer is the main character of *A Doll's House*. She saves her husband's life by forging her father's signature on a note. Her husband is disgusted by her action, the more so because she is blackmailed for doing it. Norma then leaves her husband—a man who has always treated her like a doll rather than a human being—in order to establish a life of her own. The play was highly controversial when first published, as it is sharply critical of Victorian marriage norms.

Keywords: Norwegian author, family, feminism, marriage

Websites:
http://www.sparknotes.com/lit/dollhouse/
http://www.cummingsstudyguides.net/DollHouse.html#Doll's%20House
http://www.mala.bc.ca/~johnstoi/introser/ibsen.htm

Rate this book: 1 – 2 – 3   4 – 5 – 6   7 – 8 – 9

Fiction
Drama

Faust Part One
by Johann Wolfgang von Goethe (1994) 192p, ISBN-13: 978-0486280462

Standard book equivalent: 0.7
First published: 1806

Goethe (1749 – 1832) was a German author. This is the Anna Swanwick translation, published in 1858. The story is based on a German folk legend from the 16th century. In that legend, the devil makes a bet with God that he can seduce Faust, God's favorite human. The devil appears to Faust and convinces him to sign his name in blood to an agreement. The agreement states that the devil will aid Faust in all things while he is on earth. However, when he dies he must do the devil's bidding in hell.

Keywords: German author, devil, fable, religion

Websites:
http://www.cummingsstudyguides.net/Faust.html#Faust
http://www.levity.com/alchemy/faustidx.html
http://www.kirjasto.sci.fi/goethe.htm

Rate this book: 1 – 2 – 3   4 – 5 – 6   7 – 8 – 9

Fiction
Drama

Glengarry Glen Ross
by David Mamet (1992) 122p, ISBN-13: 978-0802130914

Standard book equivalent: 0.5
First published: 1992

Mamet (b. 1947) is an American author who won a Pulitzer Prize in 1984 for *Glengarry Glen Ross*. It is a play about four Chicago salesmen who work together selling undesirable real estate at inflated prices. The play is an attack on American business practices. It takes place at the end of a month in which the company bosses have declared a "sales contest". The rules are that the salesman who clears a certain high-dollar amount will win a Cadillac, and the two salesmen who perform worst will be fired.

Keywords: American author, business, Chicago, Pulitzer Prize, tragedy

Websites:
http://www.sparknotes.com/drama/glengarry/
http://www.stageagent.com/shows.php?id=1282
http://mamet.eserver.org/review/2002/brucherglen.html

Rate this book: 1 – 2 – 3   4 – 5 – 6   7 – 8 – 9

Fiction
Drama

The Importance of Being Earnest
by Oscar Wilde (1990) 64p, ISBN-13: 978-0486264783

Standard book equivalent: 0.2
First published: 1895

Oscar Wilde's (1854 – 1900) was an Irish author. *The Importance of Being Earnest* is a farce about mistaken identities, secret engagements, and lovers' entanglements. It is set in 1890s England and makes fun of the English upper class with light-hearted satire. The main characters are Jack Worthington and Algernon Mongrieff, two young men in love with girls who are both determined to marry someone named Earnest. This play is noted for its rapid-fire wit and eccentric characters.

Keywords: Irish author, comedy, social class

Websites:
http://www.sparknotes.com/lit/earnest/
http://www.cliffsnotes.com/WileyCDA/LitNote/id-29.html
http://www.online-literature.com/wilde/being_earnest/

Rate this book: 1 – 2 – 3   4 – 5 – 6   7 – 8 – 9

Fiction
Drama

Life Is a Dream
by Pedro Calderón de la Barca (2002) 96p, ISBN-13: 978-0486421247

Standard book equivalent: 0.4
First published: the 17th century

Calderón (1600 – 1681) was a Spanish playwright. *Life Is a Dream* is one of the great dramas of Spanish literature. It tells the story of the King of Poland. Astrologers have predicted his son will take his throne, so he has his son imprisoned in a tower from birth. The King has a change of heart and orders his son drugged and brought to his palace. The young man behaves badly, and the King banishes him back to his prison. Waking up in the tower, the son is convinced that it was all just a dream.

Keywords: Spanish author, Poland, predestination, religion

Websites:
http://www.gutenberg.org/etext/6363
http://www.newadvent.org/cathen/03156a.htm
http://www.theatrehistory.com/spanish/calderon001.html

Rate this book:	1 – 2 – 3	4 – 5 – 6	7 – 8 – 9

Fiction
Drama

The Lion and the Jewel *
by Wole Soyinka (1966) 72p, ISBN-13: 978-0199110834

Standard book equivalent: 0.3
First published: 1963

Soyinka (b. 1934) is a Nigerian playwright and winner of the 1986 Nobel Prize in Literature. *The Lion and the Jewel* is a play about the issues of colonization, cross-cultural interaction, and gender roles. It is set in a Yoruba village and the plot concerns the competition between a teacher and the village chief (the lion) for the affection of a village girl who is the jewel of the title. The girl's choice is between modern and traditional values. A complication arises when her photograph appears on a magazine cover, which in her eyes raises her worth.

Keywords: Nigerian author, Africa, colonialism, marriage, Nigeria, Nobel Prize (Literature)

Websites:
http://www.dailyinfo.co.uk/reviews/theatre/The%20Lion%20and%20The%20Jewel.htm
http://www.kirjasto.sci.fi/soyinka.htm
http://www.albany.edu/writers.inst/soyinka.html

Rate this book: 1 – 2 – 3   4 – 5 – 6   7 – 8 – 9

Fiction
Drama

Long Day's Journey into Night *
by Eugene O'Neil (2002) 192p, ISBN-13: 978-0300093056

Standard book equivalent: 0.7
First published: 1956 (written in 1941)

O'Neil (1888 – 1953) was an American playwright who won the 1936 Nobel Prize in Literature. The play is the story of the Tyrone family. James Tyrone is a now aging, once-famous stage actor. His wife, Mary, is a delicate and fragile woman. Their two sons, Jamie and Edmund, are opposites. Jamie is in his late 30s, and fond of wine, women and song. Edmund is physically frail but intellectually sharp. The setting takes place in New London, Connecticut and the plot covers one heart-wrenching day in their lives filled with alcohol and brutal conversation.

Keywords: American author, alcoholism, family, Nobel Prize (Literature), tragedy

Websites:
http://www.sparknotes.com/lit/longdays/
http://www.gradesaver.com/classicnotes/titles/journey/
http://www.cummingsstudyguides.net/Guides2/LongDay.html#Top

Rate this book: 1 – 2 – 3   4 – 5 – 6   7 – 8 – 9

Fiction
Drama

Lost in Yonkers *
by Neil Simon (1993) 128p, ISBN-13: 978-0452268838

Standard book equivalent: 0.5
First published: 1991

Simon (b. 1927) is an American playwright and screenwriter who won a 1991 Pulitzer Prize for *Lost in Yonkers*. The play is a comedy set in Yonkers, New York in 1942. Brothers Jay and Artie must stay for one year with their domineering grandmother while their father takes a job in another state to clear a debt. Seen through their eyes, she is cold-hearted, inflexible, emasculating and miserly. Other characters include the likeable thug Uncle Louie, and sweet but childlike Aunt Bella.

Keywords: American author, family, New York City, Pulitzer Prize

Websites:
http://en.wikipedia.org/wiki/Lost_in_Yonkers
http://www.pbs.org/wnet/americanmasters/database/simon_n.html
http://www.kennedy-center.org/calendar/index.cfm?fuseaction=showIndividual&entitY_id=3523&source_type=A

Rate this book: 1 – 2 – 3   4 – 5 – 6   7 – 8 – 9

Fiction
Drama

A Man for All Seasons
by Robert Bolt (1990) 192p, ISBN-13: 978-0679728221

Standard book equivalent: 0.7
First published: 1960

Bolt (1924 – 1995) was a British playwright. *A Man for All Seasons* is a play based on the historical figure of Thomas More and his death by King Henry VIII. More was the Chancellor of England in the 16th century. The king wanted More to endorse his divorce from wife Catharine of Aragon (who was the first of King Henry's six wives). More refused on principle and his enemies used that to their political advantage.

Keywords: British author, biography (men), Thomas More, England, politics, religion

Websites:
http://www.sparknotes.com/lit/amanforallseasons/
http://www.law.umkc.edu/faculty/projects/ftrials/more/morebiography.html
http://www.catholiceducation.org/articles/politics/pg0078.html

Rate this book: 1 – 2 – 3   4 – 5 – 6   7 – 8 – 9

Fiction
Drama

Miss Julie
by August Strindberg (1992) 64p, ISBN-13: 978-0486272818

Standard book equivalent: 0.4
First published: 1888

Strindberg (1849 – 1912) was a Swedish author. *Miss Julie* is a play with three speaking parts: Miss Julie, a nobleman's daughter; Jean, a young valet; and Christine, a cook in the household. The title character's behavior is both bold and flirtatious. She initiates an affair with a commoner, which leads to controversy. *Miss Julie,* together with Ibsen's *A Doll House,* provides a glimpse into a society that was rigidly ordered around class stratification, gender roles, and sexual conduct. This play looks at the consequences people face when they resist that rigid order.

Keywords: Swedish author, feminism, social class

Websites:
http://www.cummingsstudyguides.net/MissJulie.html#top
http://www.sparknotes.com/drama/missjulie/
http://www.theatredatabase.com/20th_century/august_strindberg_004.html

Rate this book: 1 – 2 – 3   4 – 5 – 6   7 – 8 – 9

Fiction
Drama

Murder in the Cathedral
by T. S. Eliot (1964) 96p, ISBN-13: 978-0156632775

Standard book equivalent: 0.4
First published: 1935

Eliot (1888 – 1965) was an American author who won the 1948 Nobel Prize in Literature. *Murder in the Cathedral* is a play written in verse. It is about the martyrdom of Thomas Becket, the 12th century Archbishop of Canterbury who had a falling out with King Henry II. His martyrdom was for the sake of establishing the Church as the supreme ruler. This event was an early fight between the English crown and the church, a fight that continued with Henry VIII's execution of Thomas More in the 16th century.

Keywords: American author, biography (men), England, Nobel Prize (Literature), religion, politics, Thomas Becket

Websites:
http://www.historic-uk.com/HistoryUK/England-History/ThomasBecket.htm
http://www.bookrags.com/Murder_in_the_Cathedral
http://www.kirjasto.sci.fi/tseliot.htm

Rate this book: 1 – 2 – 3   4 – 5 – 6   7 – 8 – 9

Fiction
Drama

'night, Mother **
by Marsha Norman (1983) 92p, ISBN-13: 978-0374521387

Standard book equivalent: 0.4
First published: 1982

Norman (b. 1947) is an American playwright and a 1983 Pulitzer Prize winner for *'night, Mother*. The play opens with Jessie stating that she will be dead by morning because she plans to commit suicide that night. Intense dialogues between Mother and daughter Jessie, but filled with poor communication and inadequate listening, are unable to bridge the separateness between them. The play examines the issue of loss of self-identity as a cause of suicide. Compare to *Doll House* and the novel *Joys of Motherhood*.

Keywords: American author, woman author, death, depression, family, Pulitzer Prize, mental illness, motherhood, suicide

Websites:
http://www.fb10.uni-bremen.de/anglistik/kerkhoff/ContempDrama/Norman.htm
http://www.storyispromise.com/night.htm
http://www.theatrescene.net/ts%5Carticles.nsf/(Levy)/3C639612851B239E85256F520054EAE9?OpenDocument

Rate this book: 1 – 2 – 3   4 – 5 – 6   7 – 8 – 9

Fiction
Drama

No Exit and Three Other Plays **
by Jean Paul Sartre (1989) 288p, ISBN-13: 978-0679725169

Standard book equivalent: 1.1
First published: 1944

Sartre (1905 – 1980) was a French author and philosopher. *No Exit* is a one-act modern morality play. There are only four characters: the valet, Garcin, Estelle, and Inez. The valet brings the three damned souls into a room in which the entire play takes place. The three were condemned to hell because of crimes against humanity and have been placed in the room to make each other miserable. The central theme is "hell is other people." The three other plays in the book are *The Flies*, *Dirty Hands* and *The Respectful Prostitute*.

Keywords: French author, morality, philosophy

Websites:
http://www.sparknotes.com/lit/noexit/index.html
http://www.bookrags.com/No_Exit
http://www.theatrehistory.com/french/sartre002.html

Rate this book: 1 – 2 – 3   4 – 5 – 6   7 – 8 – 9

Fiction
Drama

Our Town *
by Thornton Wilder (1998) 128p, ISBN-13: 978-0060929848

Standard book equivalent: 0.5
First published: 1938

Wilder (1897 – 1975) was an American author and won the 1938 Pulitzer Prize for *Our Town*. This play takes place in the fictional small village of Grover's Corners, New Hampshire. It is about the interactions of ordinary people in an ordinary American small town. The play is in three acts. The first act describes the town and daily life in it. The second act takes place three years later and is about the marriage of Emily and John, two of the townspeople. The third act is about Emily's death.

Keywords: American author, marriage, New England, Pulitzer Prize

Websites:
http://www.sparknotes.com/lit/ourtown/index.html
http://www.pbs.org/wgbh/masterpiece/americancollection/ourtown/synopsis.html
http://www.cliffsnotes.com/WileyCDA/LitNote/id-186,pageNum-1.html

Rate this book: 1 – 2 – 3   4 – 5 – 6   7 – 8 – 9

Fiction
Drama

The Piano Lesson *
by August Wilson (1990) 128p, ISBN-13: 978-0452265349

Standard book equivalent: 0.5
First published: 1987

Wilson (1945 – 2005) was an American playwright who won the 1986 Pulitzer Prize for *The Piano Lesson*. It is set in 1930s Pittsburgh at the home of an African American family. The conflict centers on a piano (carved to show family history) that long ago was traded by the family's white master for two of the family's ancestors. Boy Willie and Berniece, the siblings who inherited the piano, argue about whether or not to sell it. This is one of Wilson's ten plays about African American families, each set in a different decade of the twentieth century.

Keywords: American author, African American author, African American experience, family, Great Depression, Pittsburgh, Pulitzer Prize

Websites:
http://www.sparknotes.com/drama/piano/index.html
http://www.washingtonpost.com/wp-dyn/content/article/2005/10/03/AR2005100301734.html
http://www.dartmouth.edu/~awilson/bio.html

Rate this book: 1 – 2 – 3   4 – 5 – 6   7 – 8 – 9

Fiction
Drama

A Raisin in the Sun *
by Lorraine Hansberry (1994) 160p ISBN-13: 978-0679755333

Standard book equivalent: 0.6
First published: 1959

Hansberry (1930 – 1965) was an American playwright. *A Raisin in the Sun* is set in Chicago during the 1950s. It is based on the author's own experiences growing up in Chicago. This three-act play explores the struggles of ordinary people to achieve their desires. The Younger family, a working-class African American family pursuing the American dream of owning a home, encounters racism and must decide what is really important in life. Additionally, the play depicts the stresses poverty imposes on a family.

Keywords: African American author, American author, woman author, African American experience, Chicago, family, prejudice, racism

Websites:
http://www.sparknotes.com/lit/raisin/
http://www.bookrags.com/notes/rai/
http://www.kirjasto.sci.fi/corhans.htm

Rate this book: 1 – 2 – 3   4 – 5 – 6   7 – 8 – 9

Fiction
Drama

Saint Joan
by George Bernard Shaw, Dan H. Laurence (editor) (2001)
160p, ISBN-13: 978-0140437911

Standard book equivalent: 0.6
First published: 1923

Shaw (1856 – 1950) was an Irish author and 1925 Nobel Prize in Literature recipient. *Saint Joan* consists of six acts and an epilogue. It is a historical representation of Joan of Arc. Shaw's interest in Ireland's independence can be found in the themes of nationalism, and the conflict between Protestantism and Catholicism. The character Joan is a champion of feminism. She leads the fight to drive the English out of her native France, and insists on direct communication with her God instead of through the intercession of Catholic priests. She refuses to dress, speak, or act according to traditional norms of feminine behavior.

Keywords: Irish author, biography (women), feminism, Joan of Arc, Nobel Prize (Literature), power, religion, war

Websites:
http://www.bookrags.com/Saint_Joan_%28play%29
http://www.litencyc.com/php/sworks.php?rec=true&UID=2287
http://www.seniornet.org/php/readerguide.php?GuideID=51&Version=0&Font=1

Rate this book: 1 – 2 – 3   4 – 5 – 6   7 – 8 – 9

Fiction
Drama

A Streetcar Named Desire
by Tennessee Williams (1986) 144p, ISBN-13: 978-0451167781

Standard book equivalent: 0.6
First published: 1947

Williams (1911 – 1983) was an American playwright who won the 1948 Pulitzer Prize for *A Streetcar Named Desire*. It is among the most admired plays of the twentieth century. It is about the mental and moral breakdown of Southern belle Blanche DuBois. Her neurotic and pretentious behaviors are exposed as frail and delicate defenses by the verbal onslaughts of her brutish brother-in-law, Stanley Kowalski. An important theme of the play is the conflict between reality and fantasy. Blanche exerts increasingly greater effort to hide the reality that is at odds with her fantasy of a genteel existence.

Keywords: American author, family, New Orleans, Pulitzer Prize

Websites:
http://www.sparknotes.com/lit/streetcar/
http://www.bookrags.com/notes/snd/
http://www.gradesaver.com/classicnotes/titles/desire/

Rate this book: 1 – 2 – 3   4 – 5 – 6   7 – 8 – 9

Fiction
Drama

Waiting for Godot **
by Samuel Beckett (2004) 128p, ISBN-13: 978-0521549387

Standard book equivalent: 0.5
First published: 1952

Beckett (1906 – 1989) was an Irish author who won the 1969 Nobel Prize in Literature. *Waiting for Godot* is a classic tragicomedy that symbolizes the tedium and meaninglessness of human life. It is known for its lack of plot—two old tramps beneath a single tree make jokes to pass the time and reflect on the state of human existence while they wait for Godot, who never comes. Neither the identity of Godot, nor the nature of their business with Godot is revealed.

Keywords: Irish author, absurdism, Nobel Prize (Literature)

Websites:
http://www.theatrehistory.com/french/beckett002.html
http://www.sparknotes.com/lit/godot/
http://www.gradesaver.com/classicnotes/titles/waitingforgodot/

Rate this book: 1 – 2 – 3   4 – 5 – 6   7 – 8 – 9

Fiction
Drama

Who's Afraid of Virginia Woolf? **
by Edward Albee (2006) 272p. ISBN-13: 978-0451218599

Standard book equivalent: 1.0
First published: 1962

Albee (b. 1928) is an American playwright. This play is set on the campus of a small New England university. The plot centers on Martha and George, a bitter well-educated couple, who invite a new professor and his wife to their house after a party. There they continue drinking and engage in relentless verbal—and sometimes physical—abuse in front of the guests. The party turns into a nightmare and when it is done the guests leave George and Martha to pick up the pieces resulting from their game.

Keywords: American author, absurdism, alcoholism, marriage, New England

Websites:
http://www.sparknotes.com/lit/afraidofwoolf/
http://www.gradesaver.com/classicnotes/titles/woolf/about.html
http://www.gradesaver.com/classicnotes/authors/about_edward_albee.html

Rate this book: 1 – 2 – 3   4 – 5 – 6   7 – 8 – 9

FICTION
Narrative Poetry

Fiction
Narrative Poetry

Aeneid
by Vergil (1995) 256p, ISBN-13: 978-0486287492

Standard book equivalent: 1.0
Written in 1st century BC

Vergil (70BC – 19Bc) was a Roman poet. This edition is Charles J. Billson's 1906 English translation. Virgil traces the wanderings of Aeneas, a Trojan hero of the wars with Greece, as he makes his way to Italy and his destiny to found Rome. The poem may have been an attempt by Vergil to win favor with Emperor Augustus who came to power through violence. The poem foreshadows the reign of Augustus suggesting it was fate that brought him to power.

Keywords: Italian author, ancient, hero, Rome, Troy

Websites:
http://www.sparknotes.com/lit/aeneid/
http://classics.mit.edu/Virgil/aeneid.html
http://www.bookrags.com/Aeneid

Rate this book: 1 – 2 – 3   4 – 5 – 6   7 – 8 – 9

Fiction
Narrative Poetry

Beowulf
by Anonymous, Seamus Heaney (translator) (2001) 215p,
ISBN-13: 978-0393320978

Standard book equivalent: 0.8
First published (written): circa 1100 AD

Beowulf is an early heroic poem in Old English about the exploits of Beowulf. He is a young nobleman of the Geats, a people of southern Sweden. He travels to Denmark to fight the monster Grendel and then returns home to become king. The setting of the poem is in the 5th or 6th century, about the time the Anglo-Saxons were settling in present day England. This narrative combines mythical elements, Christian and pagan symbolism, and actual historical figures and events. Heaney is an Irish poet, and writer. He was awarded the 1995 Nobel Prize in Literature.

Keywords: Irish author, Denmark, hero, Nobel Prize (Literature)

Websites:
http://www.sparknotes.com/lit/beowulf/
http://www.bookrags.com/notes/beo/
http://www.cliffsnotes.com/WileyCDA/LitNote/id-33.html

Rate this book: 1 – 2 – 3   4 – 5 – 6   7 – 8 – 9

Fiction
Narrative Poetry

Courtship of Miles Standish *
by Henry Wadsworth Longfellow (1992) 64p, ISBN-13: 978-0486272641

Standard book equivalent: 0.3
First published: 1858

Longfellow (1807 – 1882) was an American poet. This poem is set during the early days of the Plymouth Colony. It tells the story of a lover's triangle involving Mile's Standish, John Alden and Priscilla Mullens. The poem is famous for the line spoken by Priscilla—Words so tender and cruel: "Why don't you speak for yourself, John?" The poem is purely fictional although it is often mistakenly taken to be historically accurate. However, the main characters mentioned in the poem were real persons who lived in the Plymouth colony.

Keywords: American author, love, New England

Websites:
http://www.readbookonline.net/title/3077/
http://www.awerty.addr.com/courtshiphtml2.html
http://www.kirjasto.sci.fi/long.htm

Rate this book: 1 – 2 – 3   4 – 5 – 6   7 – 8 – 9

Fiction
Narrative Poetry

The Epic of Gilgamesh
by Anonymous, Andrew George (translator) (2003) 128p,
ISBN-13: 978-0140441000

Standard book equivalent: 1.2
First published (written): circa 7th cent BC

The original author of this epic poem from Babylonia is unknown. It is known to be a compilation of legends that date back to at least before 2000 BC and is considered the earliest example of extant literature. *Gilgamesh* is the story of a ruler, the title character, who was two-thirds god and one-third man and his friend a half-wild man named Enkidu. They go on many quests, but eventually Enkidu is killed, leaving Gilgamesh to mourn for him.

Keywords: ancient, Babylonia, hero

Websites:
http://www.sparknotes.com/lit/gilgamesh/
http://www.wsu.edu/~dee/MESO/GILG.HTM
http://gilgamesh.psnc.pl/

Rate this book: 1 – 2 – 3   4 – 5 – 6   7 – 8 – 9

Fiction
Narrative Poetry

Evangeline *
by Henry Wadsworth Longfellow (1995) 64p, ISBN-13: 978-0486282558

Standard book equivalent: 0.2
First published: 1847

Longfellow (1807 – 1882) was an American poet. *Evangeline* describes the dispersal by the British of whole communities of French Canadians from their homeland of Arcadia, Nova Scotia in 1755. Evangeline and Gabriel, on their wedding night, flee home separately for Louisiana and experience the pain of separation because Gabriel inadvertently keeps one step ahead of her during a major part of the story. They are finally reunited under tragic circumstances. A major theme of the epic poem is the beauty and strength of a woman's devotion.

Keywords: American author, Canada, loss, love

Websites:
http://www.cajunculture.com/Other/Evangeline.htm
http://www.theotherpages.org/poems/books/longfellow/evangeline00.html
http://bradley.bradley.edu/~dlb/sslngfel.html

Rate this book: 1 – 2 – 3   4 – 5 – 6   7 – 8 – 9

Fiction
Narrative Poetry

Idylls of the King
by Alfred Tennyson, W. J. Rolfe (editor) (2004) 304p,
ISBN-13: 978-0486437958

Standard book equivalent: 1.2
First published: 1885

Tennyson (1809 – 1892) was a British poet and Poet Laureate of the United Kingdom. He was a baron and held the title 'Lord'. The *Idylls of the King* is Tennyson's interpretation of the Arthurian myth based on Malory's *Le Morte d'Arthur* and is his most famous work. It consists of twelve poems that each recounts a different period of King Arthur's life. An important theme of *Idylls of the King* is the idea of fidelity and that unrepentant sin left to fester can destroy an ideal.

Keywords: British author, betrayal, England, fable, hero, King Arthur

Websites:
http://www.lib.rochester.edu/Camelot/auth/Tennyson.htm
http://www.online-literature.com/tennyson/idylls-of-the-king/
http://www.kirjasto.sci.fi/tennyson.htm

Rate this book: 1 – 2 – 3   4 – 5 – 6   7 – 8 – 9

Fiction
Narrative Poetry

The Poem of the Cid: Dual Language Edition
by Anonymous, Rita Hamilton (translator), Janet Perry (translator) (1985) 256p, ISBN-13: 978-0140444469

Standard book equivalent: 1.0
First published: circa 12th century

The author is unknown. The poem is based on the true story of Rodrigo Díaz de Vivar, also know as El Cid. He married the cousin of King Alphonso VI and then went onto fight the Spanish Moors. His heroism resulted in the liberation of Valencia. The poem combines fact with fiction to depict El Cid as the perfect Christian warrior. A major theme of the poem is the contrast of honor and courage with cowardice and brutality.

Keywords: Spanish author, El Cid, hero, Spain

Websites:
http://www.bookrags.com/studyguide-cantardemiocidelcid/
http://www.newadvent.org/cathen/03769a.htm
http://www.mythencyclopedia.com/Ca-Cr/Cid-El.html

Rate this book: 1 – 2 – 3   4 – 5 – 6   7 – 8 – 9

Fiction
Narrative Poetry

The Saga of the Volsungs
by Anonymous, Jesse L. Byock (translator) (2000) 160p, ISBN-13: 978-0140447385

Standard book equivalent: 0.6
First published: circa 13th century

The author is unknown. *The Saga of the Volsungs* is from Iceland and tells the story of two families, the Volsungs and the Nibelungs. The first part of the poem is about Sigurd's ancestors: his father Sigmund, his aunt Signy and his grandfather Volsung. The second part is about Sigurd and his exploits: slaying a dragon, winning the accursed gold, and his death by Brynhild. The third part is about Sigurd's wife, Gudrun, and his brothers-in-law, the Nibelungs. The saga inspired and was the basis for J. R. R. Tolkien's *Lord of the Rings* and for Richard Wagner's Ring cycle.

Keywords: betrayal, hero, Iceland, Nibelungs, Volsungs

Websites:
http://omacl.org/Volsunga/
http://www.thetroubleshooters.com/viking/Volsunga0001.html
http://www.enotes.com/classical-medieval-criticism/volsunga-saga

Rate this book: 1 – 2 – 3   4 – 5 – 6   7 – 8 – 9

Fiction
Narrative Poetry

The Song of Roland
by Anonymous, Dorothy L. Sayers (translator) (2001)
160p, ISBN-13: 978-0375757112

Standard book equivalent: 0.6
First published: circa 11th century

The author is unknown. *The Song of Roland* is the oldest extant French epic poem. It was inspired by an actual military disaster in 778 A.D. involving an ambush by the Basques on the rearguard of Charlemagne's army. The poem fictionalizes the story on several points. It substitutes the Saracens for the Basques and makes the title character a nephew of Charlemagne. The poem portrays Charlemagne as elderly though actually he was only 36 years-old at the time. It also describes Charlemagne's revenge, but this did not happen as the Basques had dispersed under the cover of darkness.

Keywords: hero, France, Roland

Websites:
http://omacl.org/Roland/
http://www.gradesaver.com/classicnotes/titles/roland/
http://www.sparknotes.com/lit/songofroland/

Rate this book: 1 – 2 – 3   4 – 5 – 6   7 – 8 – 9

Fiction
Narrative Poetry

Troilus and Criseyde
by Geoffrey Chaucer, Nevill Coghill (translator) (1998)
256p, ISBN-13: 978-0192832900

Standard book equivalent: 1.0
First published: the 14th century

Chaucer (c1343 – 1400) was a British poet and is often described as the father of English Literature. The tragedy *Troilus and Criseyde* is often listed as one of the greatest narrative poems in English literature. Set during the siege of Troy, it tells how the young knight Troilus, son of King Priam, falls in love with Criseyde, a beautiful widow. It is an example of 'courtly love' (typical of medieval literature, courtly love is idealized love in which a knight devotes himself to a noblewoman).

Keywords: British author, hero, Troy

Websites:
http://omacl.org/Troilus/
http://www.kirjasto.sci.fi/chaucer.htm
http://www.geocities.com/ladyisobelwren/chaucertroilus.html

Rate this book: 1 – 2 – 3   4 – 5 – 6   7 – 8 – 9

FICTION

Poetry, Collected Works

Fiction
Poetry, Collected Works

101 Great American Poems *
by The American Poetry & Literacy Project (editor) (1998)
96p, ISBN-13: 978-0486401584

Standard book equivalent: 0.4
First published: 1998

101 Great American Poems is an anthology of poems mostly from the 19th and 20th centuries written by various American authors. The collection includes Poe's "The Raven", Whitman's "I Hear America Singing", Longfellow's "Paul Revere's Ride", Langston Hughes' "Dream Deferred" as well as poems by Robert Frost, Langston Hughes, Emily Dickinson, T. S. Eliot, Marianne Moore, and many other notables. The American Poetry & Literacy Project was created by U.S. Poet Laureate Joseph Brodsky in 1993. A short biography of each of the poets precedes their poem.

Keywords: American author

Websites:
http://www.poets.org/page.php/prmID/301
http://www.kirjasto.sci.fi/brodsky.htm

Rate this book: 1 – 2 – 3   4 – 5 – 6   7 – 8 – 9

Fiction
Poetry, Collected Works

African-American Poetry: An Anthology, 1773-1927
by Joan R. Sherman (editor) (1997) 96p ISBN-13: 978-0486296043

Standard book equivalent: 0.4
First published: 1997

This volume of African American poetry contains seventy-four poems by twenty-five poets ranging from the religious and moral verse of Phillis Wheatley Peters (ca. 1753 – 1784) to 20th-century works of Langston Hughes and Countee Cullen. Other contributors include George Moses Horton, Francis Ellen Watkins Harper, Henrietta Cordelia Ray, Mary Weston Fordham, James Edwin Campbell, James Weldon Johnson, Paul Laurence Dunbar, and many others. The themes of the poems include slavery, literacy, religion, racial uplift, and folk culture.

Keywords: African American author, African American experience

Websites:
http://www.mtsu.edu/~vvesper/afampoet.htm
http://www.blackrefer.com/poetry.html
http://www.afropoets.net/

Rate this book: 1 – 2 – 3   4 – 5 – 6   7 – 8 – 9

Fiction
Poetry, Collected Works

American Primitive
by Mary Oliver (1983) 88p, ISBN-13: 978-0316650045

Standard book equivalent: 0.3
First published: 1983

Oliver (b. 1935) is an American poet whose anthology *American Primitive* won the 1984 Pulitzer Prize. It is a collection of fifty poems first published between 1978 and 1983 about American wildlife, with some poems about notable Americans. Recurrent themes of these poems include the natural world, cycle of life and the connectedness of all life. Many of the poems were inspired by the environs of her home in Provincetown, Massachusetts. Oliver is the winner of a Guggenheim Fellowship (1980) and a National Book Award (1992).

Keywords: American author, woman author, nature, Pulitzer Prize

Websites:
http://mclibrary.nhmccd.edu/lit/oliver.html
http://www.plagiarist.com/poetry/?aid=134
http://www.poets.org/poet.php/prmPID/265

Rate this book: 1 – 2 – 3   4 – 5 – 6   7 – 8 – 9

Fiction
Poetry, Collected Works

Mr. Cogito
by Zbigniew Herbert; John Carpenter, Bogdana Carpenter (translators) (1995) 100p, ISBN-13: 978-0880013819

Standard book equivalent: 0.4
First published: 1974

Herbert (1924 – 1998) was a Polish poet. He was active in the Polish resistance movement during World War II and an anti-communist after it. Herbert stated in an interview for the Manhattan Review (1984), "Writing—and in this I disagree with everybody—must teach men soberness: to be awake. To make people sober." This compilation contains most of the early Mr. Cogito poems. Mr. Cogito was a character that represented an Everyman in modern society. Each poem presents a simple question or issue and is deceptively plainspoken.

Keywords: Polish author, Cogito

Websites:
http://www.complete-review.com/reviews/herbertz/mrcogito.htm
http://www.ap.krakow.pl/nkja/literature/polpoet/herbert1.htm
http://www.culture.pl/en/culture/artykuly/os_herbert_zbigniew

Rate this book: 1 – 2 – 3   4 – 5 – 6   7 – 8 – 9

Fiction
Poetry, Collected Works

The Collected Songs of Cold Mountain
by Cold Mountain (Han-Shan) (2000) 272p, ISBN-13: 978-1556591402

Standard book equivalent: 1.0
First published: circa 8th century

Han-Shan (8th or 9th century) is a legendary Chinese figure to whom a collection of poems is usually attributed. Han-Shan is likely based on a real hermit who is reputed to have been eccentric, enjoying practical jokes. He apparently was born into the privileged class but lost favor with the Emperor during a time of political turmoil. These poems were actually written over the span of three centuries and are celebrated for their clarity, directness, and lack of pretension.

Keywords: Chinese author, China

Websites:
http://www.hermitary.com/articles/han-shan.html
http://www.gardendigest.com/zen/hsind.htm
http://www.poetry-chaikhana.com/H/HanshanColdM/index.htm

Rate this book: 1 – 2 – 3   4 – 5 – 6   7 – 8 – 9

Fiction
Poetry, Collected Works

Great Love Poems
by Shane Weller (editor) (1992) 128p, ISBN-13: 978-0486272849

Standard book equivalent: 0.5
First published: 1992

Great Love Poems is a collection of over 150 familiar poems by seventy-seven English and American poets. It includes a selection of Shakespeare's sonnets, John Donne's "The Ecstasy," John Keats' "Bright Star, Would I Were Stedfast as Thou Art?" and William Blake's "The Garden of Love". Other poets include W. B. Yeats, Emily Dickinson, Walt Whitman, Elizabeth Barrett Browning, John Milton, Edgar Allen Poe, D.H. Lawrence, Robert Frost and many more. These poems cover four centuries of literature.

Keywords: love

Websites:
http://www.pddoc.com/poems/
http://www.eromance.com/inspiration/poems/
http://www.poetry-online.org/copyright.htm

Rate this book: 1 – 2 – 3   4 – 5 – 6   7 – 8 – 9

Fiction
Poetry, Collected Works

Holocaust Poetry
by Hilda Schiff (editor) (1996) 256p, ISBN-13: 978-0312143572

Standard book equivalent: 1.0
First published: 1995

A collection of 59 poets and 119 poems are presented in this volume. The poems were either originally in English or translated into it from various languages. The works of Wiesel, Fink, Yevtushenko, Auden, and Sachs are included. Schiff points out that for historical accounts to be compelling they must document the facts and numbers. However a poem, like a story, makes us imagine how an experience felt for one person. For that reason, poems provide a different, but important, documentation of human experience. These poems are stark and unadorned about a human experience that was grim and tragic.

Keywords: Jewish experience, holocaust

Websites:
http://cghs.dadeschools.net/ib_holocaust2001/Ghettoes/education_culture/poetry_of_the_holocaust.htm
http://cte.jhu.edu/techacademy/web/2000/baczkowski/intro.htm
http://www.teachnlearn.org/HolTeachingGuide.htm

Rate this book: 1 – 2 – 3   4 – 5 – 6   7 – 8 – 9

Fiction
Poetry, Collected Works

The Metamorphoses: Selected Stories in Verse
by Ovid (2003) 80p, ISBN-13: 978-0486427584

Standard book equivalent: 0.3
Written before the 1st cent

Ovid (43 BC – 18 AD) was a Roman poet. This selection of 30 stories is from the verse translation by F. A. Wright of Ovid's *The Metamorphoses*. All of the tales involve a form of transformation and are populated by the gods, demigods, and mortals of classical mythology. Ovid's epic poem begins with a creation story and ends with Augustus' reign. The Metamorphoses is often divided into four parts: Gods in Love, Avenging Gods, Pathos of Love, and the History of Rome.

Keywords: ancient, mythology, Rome

Websites:
http://classics.mit.edu/Ovid/metam.html
http://www.bookrags.com/Metamorphoses_%28poem%29
http://books.guardian.co.uk/reviews/classics/0,6121,114758
    2,00.html

Rate this book: 1 – 2 – 3   4 – 5 – 6   7 – 8 – 9

Fiction
Poetry, Collected Works

Metaphysical Poetry: An Anthology **
by Paul Negri (editor) (2002) 224p, ISBN-13: 978-0486419169

Standard book equivalent: 0.9
First published: 17th century

Metaphysical poetry is represented in this anthology by such works as John Donne's "Death, Be Not Proud," and Andrew Marvell's "To His Coy Mistress." It also includes works by George Herbert, Henry Vaughan, Richard Crashaw, Francis Quarles, Thomas Traherne, and others. Metaphysical poets were 17th century British poets whose subjects often had to do with explaining the nature of the world. Their poetry typically attempted to answer such questions as "What is reality?" and "Is there a God?"

Keywords: metaphysics

Websites:
http://www.luminarium.org/sevenlit/metaphysical.htm
http://www.websyte.com/alan/metamul.htm
http://www.newadvent.org/cathen/10226a.htm

Rate this book: 1 – 2 – 3   4 – 5 – 6   7 – 8 – 9

Fiction
Poetry, Collected Works

Poems and Songs
by Robert Burns (1991) 96p, ISBN-13: 978-0486268637

Standard book equivalent: 0.4
First published: 1991

Burns (1759 – 1796) was a British poet from Scotland. His most popular work may be "Auld Lang Syne", which is often heard during New Year's celebrations. This volume collects 43 of his works including: "The Cotter's Saturday Night," "To a Mountain Daisy," "To a Mouse," "To a Louse," "Tam o' Shanter," "Comin' Thro' the Rye," "I'm Oe'r Young to Marry Yet," "O, Lay Thy Loof in Mine, Lass," "Scots, Wha Hae," "Highland Mary," and "O, Wert Thou in the Cauld Blast."

Keywords: British author, Burns

Websites:
http://www.it-serve.co.uk/poetry/Burns/burnshome.php
http://www.worldwideschool.org/library/books/lit/poetry/PoemsandSongsofRobertBurns/Chap0.html
http://www.robertburns.org.uk/

Rate this book: 1 – 2 – 3   4 – 5 – 6   7 – 8 – 9

Fiction
Poetry, Collected Works

The Poetry of Arab Women
by Nathalie Handal (editor) (2000) 355p, ISBN-13: 978-1566563741

Standard book equivalent: 1.4
First published: 2000

Handal is a Palestinian-American author who teaches at Columbia University. This volume collects the poetry of eighty-two Arab women poets from all over the world, including Syria, Saudi Arabia, Lebanon, Yemen, Gaza and the U.S. The Palestinian struggle for self-determination is woven throughout this book, and so, many of the poems have a strong political flavor. The book was financed with the help of Radius of Arab-American Writers, Inc. and Arab-American newspapers and journals such as *Al Jadid*.

Keywords: Arab author, woman author, Arab experience

Websites:
http://www.nathaliehandal.com/
http://www.pifmagazine.com/SID/53/
http://www.literati-magazine.com/magazine_features/fall05/readingroom/nathalie-handal.html

Rate this book: 1 – 2 – 3   4 – 5 – 6   7 – 8 – 9

Fiction
Poetry, Collected Works

Selected Poems
by Walt Whitman (1991) 128p, ISBN-13: 978-0486268781

Standard book equivalent: 0.5
First published: 1991

Whitman (1819 – 1892) was an American poet. This volume is a sampling of 24 of Whitman's poems from his book *Leaves of Grass*, including: "I Hear America Singing," "I Sing the Body Electric," "Song of the Open Road," "Out of the Cradle Endlessly Rocking," "When Lilacs Last in the Dooryard Bloom'd" and "O Captain! My Captain!" Whitman self-published *Leaves of Grass* in 1855 and continued to revise it until his death in 1892. At first it was poorly received, but it became well-known overseas and this stimulated interest at home.

Keywords: American author

Websites:
http://www.whitmanarchive.org/
http://www.kirjasto.sci.fi/wwhitman.htm
http://etext.virginia.edu/toc/modeng/public/Whi91LG.html

Rate this book: 1 – 2 – 3   4 – 5 – 6   7 – 8 – 9

Fiction
Poetry, Collected Works

Turtle Island
by Gary Snyder (1974) 114p, ISBN-13: 978-0811205467

Standard book equivalent: 0.4
First published: 1974

Snyder (b. 1930) is an American poet and winner of the 1975 Pulitzer Prize for *Turtle Island*. He is a student and practitioner of Buddhism, formerly affiliated with the Beat Generation, and professor emeritus of English at the University of California—Davis. This is a collection of his poems with themes heavily influenced by his strong sense of environmental responsibility and ecological stewardship. The title comes from a Native American term for the continent of North America.

Keywords: American author, nature, Pulitzer Prize

Websites:
http://www.wildlandsprojectrevealed.org/htm/turtle.htm
http://www.english.uiuc.edu/maps/poets/s_z/snyder/chronology.htm
http://www.cyberoz.net/city/sekine/paradaise.htm

Rate this book: 1 – 2 – 3   4 – 5 – 6   7 – 8 – 9

NONFICTION

History / Biography / Social Science

Nonfiction
History / Biography / Social Science

1831: Year of Eclipse
by Louis P. Masur (2002) 272p, ISBN-13: 978-0809041190

Standard book equivalent: 1.0
First published: 2001

Masur is an American author and professor of American Studies at Trinity College in Hartford, Connecticut. His book *1831* traces a fascinating year in American history that began with a solar eclipse. The year following that eclipse foreshadowed the coming Civil War and was set apart from others by events that include: Nat Turner's rebellion, violent congressional arguments over slavery and tariffs, religious revivalism in the North, the identity-shaping observations of Tocqueville, and Andrew Jackson's harsh policies toward the Cherokee.

Keywords: American author, American history, politics, Nat Turner's Rebellion, religion, slavery

Websites:
http://alumni.buffalo.edu/drpl/node/532
http://www.bookpage.com/0103bp/nonfiction/1831.html
http://www.boston.com/news/globe/ideas/articles/2004/10/31/remember_1831/

Rate this book: 1 – 2 – 3   4 – 5 – 6   7 – 8 – 9

Nonfiction
History / Biography / Social Science

African Genesis: Folk Tales and Myths of Africa
by Leo Frobenius, Douglas C. Fox (1999) 256p, ISBN-13: 978-0486409115

Standard book equivalent: 1.0
First published: 1937

Frobenius (1873 – 1938) was a German ethnologist and author. He published this collection of African folk tales and legends in 1937, a year before his death. The book includes 29 stories divided into sections for each of three different ethnic groups: the Berbers, the Sudanese, and the Southern Rhodesians. Léopold Sédar Senghor said that Frobenius' work had "given Africa back its dignity and identity." Aimé Césaire quoted Frobenius praising African people as being "civilized to the marrow of their bones".

Keywords: German author, Africa, anthropology, fable

Websites:
http://www.litencyc.com/php/speople.php?rec=true&UID=11722

Rate this book: 1 – 2 – 3   4 – 5 – 6   7 – 8 – 9

Nonfiction
History / Biography / Social Science

And Keep Your Powder Dry: An Anthropologist Looks at America **
by Margaret Mead (2000) 214p, ISBN-13: 978-1571812179

Standard book equivalent: 0.8
First published: 1942 and revised in 1965

Mead (1901 – 1978) was an American anthropologist and author. *And Keep Your Powder Dry* is a sketch of American culture and a classic of social anthropology. The research for the book was funded by the National Research Council's Committee on Food Habits. It offers a view of American society in the 40s, 50s, and 60s. "Keep your powder dry" is an idiom that means "be prepared". It is an allusion to gunpowder which soldiers had to keep dry in order to be ready to fight when required.

Keywords: American author, anthropology, culture, United States

Websites:
http://www.kirjasto.sci.fi/mmead.htm
http://www.webster.edu/~woolflm/margaretmead.html
http://www.greatwomen.org/women.php?action=viewone&id=109

Rate this book: 1 – 2 – 3   4 – 5 – 6   7 – 8 – 9

Nonfiction
History / Biography / Social Science

Anne Frank: The Diary of a Young Girl *
by Anne Frank (1993) 304p, ISBN-13: 978-0553296983

Standard book equivalent: 1.2
First published: 1947

Frank (1929 – 1945) was a Holocaust victim born in Germany but raised in The Netherlands. Her diary begins during World War II when she was 13 years of age and the Jews were already wearing yellow stars in Amsterdam. The Franks went into hiding from the Nazis with the Van Daan family in July 1942. They hid in a small room concealed above Otto Frank's old workplace, aided by faithful friends and employees. They were betrayed and arrested two years later in August 1944. Anne died in a concentration camp, having fallen ill during a typhus epidemic.

Keywords: Dutch author, biography (women), Anne Frank, betrayal, Jewish experience, holocaust, war, WWII

Websites:
http://www.ushmm.org/museum/exhibit/online/af/htmlsite/
http://www.annefrank.com/
http://www.annefrank.org/content.asp?pid=1&lid=2

Rate this book: 1 – 2 – 3   4 – 5 – 6   7 – 8 – 9

Nonfiction
History / Biography / Social Science

The Autobiography of Benjamin Franklin *
by Benjamin Franklin (1996) 144p, ISBN-13: 978-0486290737

Standard book equivalent: 0.6
First published: 1791

Franklin (1706 – 1790) was an American polymath—scientist, inventor, diplomat, author and more. He is well-known for his wit and quotable sayings (e.g., "Fish and visitors smell in three days" and "Never leave that till tomorrow which you can do today"). He wrote his autobiography as a letter to his 40 year-old son. It only covers the first half of his amazing life. Franklin describes his family's modest life in England and their move to Boston. He was among the youngest of a very large family, and eventually found his way to Philadelphia to work as a printer.

Keywords: American author, biography (men), Franklin

Websites:
http://www.earlyamerica.com/lives/franklin/
http://www.sparknotes.com/lit/franklinautobio/
http://www.litencyc.com/php/sworks.php?rec=true&UID=6475

Rate this book: 1 – 2 – 3   4 – 5 – 6   7 – 8 – 9

Nonfiction
History / Biography / Social Science

Behind the Scenes in the Lincoln White House: Memoirs of an African-American Seamstress *
by Elizabeth Keckley (2006) 160p, ISBN-13: 978-0486451220

Standard book equivalent: 0.6
First published: 1868

Keckley (1818 – 1907) was an American slave who purchased her freedom and went onto work in the Whitehouse as a seamstress. Elizabeth Keckley's narrative describes life in the White House during the Lincoln administration in careful detail. *Behind the Scenes in the Lincoln White House* became very controversial shortly after publication and Mary Lincoln's son Robert forced the book's removal from publication. Keckley died in poverty at the Home for Destitute Women and Children in Washington, D.C.

Keywords: American author, woman author, African American author, African American experience, American history, biography (women), Elizabeth Keckley, Lincoln, slavery

Websites:
http://lkwdpl.org/wihohio/keck-eli.htm
http://www.historymatters.gmu.edu/d/6223/
http://www.aaregistry.com/african_american_history/26/Elizabeth_Keckley_Mary_Todds_maid

Rate this book: 1 – 2 – 3   4 – 5 – 6   7 – 8 – 9

Nonfiction
History / Biography / Social Science

Black Elk Speaks: Being the Life Story of a Holy Man of the Oglala Sioux
by Black Elk, and John G. Neihardt (2000) 230p, ISBN-13: 978-0803261709

Standard book equivalent: 0.9
First published: 1932

Black Elk (1863 – 1950), or Hehaka Sapa, was a Holy Man of the Oglala Lakota Sioux. He took part in the Battle of Little Big Horn (1876) and was present at the Wounded Knee Massacre (1890). This is his autobiography, narrated to Neihardt in 1930. Black Elk's spiritual visions also are described in detail in the book. He was baptized a Catholic in 1903 with the name Nicolas Black Elk and, together with his Christian faith, continued to embrace the culture of his ancestors.

Keywords: Native American author, American history, biography (men), Black Elk, Native American experience

Websites:
http://blackelkspeaks.unl.edu/
http://www.peace.mb.ca/00.Native/nlrnz02.htm
http://www.heroesofhistory.com/page89.html

Rate this book: 1 – 2 – 3   4 – 5 – 6   7 – 8 – 9

Nonfiction
History / Biography / Social Science

Black Gold of the Sun: Searching for Home in Africa and Beyond
by Ekow Eshun (2006) 240p, ISBN-13: 978-0375424182

Standard book equivalent: 0.9
First published: 2005

Eshun (b. 1968), a journalist and author, is the son of Ghanaian nationals. He was born and raised in London after a coup prevented his parents from returning to Ghana. Eshun journeyed home in 2001, at the age of 33, to reconnect with his roots. This narrative chronicles that effort and the feeling of estrangement he felt in both his adopted homeland and Ghana. It also describes his reaction to the unexpected westernization of Ghanaian culture, e.g. the presence of a materialistic hip-hop culture in Ghana.

Keywords: Ghanaian author, Africa, assimilation, biography (men), cross-cultural, Ekow Eshun, England, Ghana, London

Websites:
http://www.thenation.com/doc/20060911/rowley/3
http://www.bbc.co.uk/africalives/myafrica/blogs/005075/
http://www.hindu.com/lr/2005/12/04/stories/2005120400130300.htm

Rate this book: 1 – 2 – 3   4 – 5 – 6   7 – 8 – 9

Nonfiction
History / Biography / Social Science

Black Hawk: An Autobiography
by Black Hawk, and Donald Jackson (editor) (2006) 128p,
ISBN-13: 978-1599869612

Standard book equivalent: 0.7
First published: 1833

Black Hawk (1767 – 1837) was a Native American Chief of the Sauk ethnic group. The Sauk's refusal in 1832 to abandon their village led to the last "Indian War" in Illinois. They—men, women and children—were massacred on the banks of the Mississippi. Black Hawk surrendered and was taken to meet President Jackson in Washington. He dictated his autobiography to a half Native American interpreter, Antoine Le Claire, who translated it into English. It then was edited by an Illinois newspaperman named John B. Patterson, who put it into publishable form.

Keywords: Native American author, American history, biography (men), Black Hawk, cross-cultural, Native American experience, war

Websites:
http://lincoln.lib.niu.edu/blackhawk/index.html
http://www.mtholyoke.edu/acad/intrel/black.htm
http://library.thinkquest.org/J0110072/famous/black_hawk.
    htm

Rate this book: 1 – 2 – 3   4 – 5 – 6   7 – 8 – 9

Nonfiction
History / Biography / Social Science

A Border Passage: From Cairo to America—A Woman's Journey
by Leila Ahmed (2000) 336p, ISBN-13: 978-0140291834

Standard book equivalent: 1.3
First published: 1999

Ahmed (b. 1940) is an Egyptian American author and professor of Women Studies at Harvard University. *A Border Passage* describes her life in Egypt during the 1940s and 1950s and the struggles she faced becoming acclimated to life in the West. She is critical of Arab nationalism, remarks on the racism and prejudice against Muslims she faced in the U.S., and addresses issues of gender in Muslim-led cultures. She also is the author of *Women and Gender in Islam.*

Keywords: Egyptian author, American author, woman author, assimilation, biography (women), colonialism, cross-cultural, Egypt, feminism, Islam, Leila Ahmed, Muslim experience

Websites:
http://www.sparknotes.com/lit/borderpassage/
http://us.penguingroup.com/static/rguides/us/border_passage.html
http://www.nytimes.com/books/first/a/ahmed-border.html?_r=1&oref=slogin

Rate this book: 1 – 2 – 3   4 – 5 – 6   7 – 8 – 9

Nonfiction
History / Biography / Social Science

Confessions of Lady Nijo
by Lady Nijo, Karen Brazell (translator) (1976) 320p,
ISBN-13: 978-0804709309

Standard book equivalent: 1.2
First published (written): 1307

Nijo (b. 1258) was a concubine in the Japanese royal imperial court. *Confessions of Lady Nijo* is a translation of a manuscript, found in 1940, that had been undiscovered for more than six centuries. It contains the thoughts and reflections of Lady Nijo during the years 1271 to 1306. Her autobiography reveals her strong personality and ambition for a higher position that provoked her dismissal. She subsequently traveled throughout the country as a Buddhist nun. *Confessions of Lady Nijo* provides a glimpse into the personalities, culture and politics of a distant world.

Keywords: Japanese author, Woman author, biography (women), Japan, Nijo, women

Websites:
http://www.bookrags.com/Lady_Nijo
http://www.gotterdammerung.org/books/reviews/c/confessions-of-lady-nijo.html
http://lrc.cornell.edu/asian/graduate/EAL/faculty

Rate this book: 1 – 2 – 3   4 – 5 – 6   7 – 8 – 9

Nonfiction
History / Biography / Social Science

The Conquest of Gaul
by Julius Caesar, Jane F. Gardner (Introduction), S. A. Handford (Translator) (1983) 272p, ISBN-13: 978-0140444339

Standard book equivalent: 1.0
First published: 51 BC

Caesar (100 BC – 44 BC) was a Roman general and dictator (49 BC – 44 BC). His 7 book memoir (*Commentarii de Bello Gallico*) was written in his winter quarters in Gaul, after the capture of Alesia in 52 BC. It describes the nine year campaign that took place mostly in what is now part of France, Belgium, and Britain. The first book deals primarily with the Helvetian War in 58 BC. In it, Caesar describes Gaul and the campaign against the Helvetii, a tribe located in what is now Switzerland. His memoir includes the earliest extant description of Britain.

Keywords: Italian author, ancient, biography (men), Caesar, Gaul, genocide, history, Rome, war

Websites:
http://www.livius.org/caa-can/caesar/caesar04.html
http://www.associatedcontent.com/article/35955/overview_
    of_julius_caesars_conquest.html
http://www.gutenberg.org/etext/18837

Rate this book: 1 – 2 – 3   4 – 5 – 6   7 – 8 – 9

Nonfiction
History / Biography / Social Science

Crossing Over: A Mexican Family on the Migrant Trail by Ruben Martinez (2002) 352p, ISBN-13: 978-0312421236

Standard book equivalent: 1.4
First published: 2001

Martinez is a Mexican-American author and journalist. His book was motivated by the tragedy of Mexican immigrants who died in a car crash while evading the U.S. Border Patrol. He writes about the forces that drive Mexicans to risk their lives crossing the border illegally. He also describes what they find when they arrive. Martinez writes a sentiment echoed in Eshun's *Black Gold of the Sun*, "We are Mexicans in America, Americans in Mexico: we are neither, we are both."

Keywords: American author, American history, assimilation, cross-cultural, immigrants, Mexico, poverty

Websites:
http://savvytraveler.publicradio.org/show/features/2002/20020222/interview2.shtml
http://zonezero.com/magazine/articles/ziff/ruben.html
http://www.imdiversity.com/villages/hispanic/arts_culture_media/archives/amoruso_crossing_over.asp

Rate this book:　　1 – 2 – 3　　4 – 5 – 6　　7 – 8 – 9

Nonfiction
History / Biography / Social Science

The Cruelest Miles: The Heroic Story of Dogs and Men in a Race against an Epidemic
by Gay Salisbury, Laney Salisbury (2005) 303p, ISBN-13: 978-0393325706

Standard book equivalent: 1.2
First published: 2003

Gay and Laney Salisbury are American cousins. In 1925 a diphtheria epidemic threatened the remote town of Nome, Alaska. Much discussion ensued about how to get the needed serum to the town. Traditionalists favored the use of the well-tested dog sled. Others demanded that an airplane be used. The proponents of flying were unsuccessful in a test flight. The governor weighed the arguments and went with the well-proven dog sled. It was successful, but at the cost of many deaths. The dogs, with their selfless determination and spirit, are the real heroes in the book.

Keywords: American author, Alaska, American history, dogs, medicine, Nome, winter

Websites:
http://www.nationalgeographic.com/adventure/0308/online extra.html
http://www.mpr.org/books/titles/salisbury_cruelestmiles.shtml
http://query.nytimes.com/gst/fullpage.html?res=9F04E6D71730F934A2575BC0A9659C8B63

Rate this book: 1 – 2 – 3   4 – 5 – 6   7 – 8 – 9

Nonfiction
History / Biography / Social Science

Crusades through Arab Eyes
by Amin Maalouf (1989) 352p, ISBN-13: 978-0805208986

Standard book equivalent: 1.4
First published: 1983

Maalouf (b. 1949) is a Lebanese author who writes in French. This book draws on various writings by Arab historians and diarists from the time of the Crusades to re-tell that story from the Arab point of view. The Arab viewpoint is that the Crusades were a barbaric invasion, but the book is evenhanded and not anti-Western. Barbarity on both sides is pointed out. The squabbling among allies, on both sides, often resulted in military failures.

Keywords: Lebanese author, Arab experience, Crusades, history, Islam, medieval, Muslim experience, war

Websites:
http://www.kirjasto.sci.fi/maalouf.htm
http://www.leoafricanus.com/bibliography/bibliography_Maalouf.html
http://www.wnd.com/news/article.asp?ARTICLE_ID=24918

Rate this book: 1 – 2 – 3   4 – 5 – 6   7 – 8 – 9

Nonfiction
History / Biography / Social Science

Curry: A Tale of Cooks and Conquerors
by Lizzie Collingham (2006) 304p, ISBN-13: 978-0195172416

Standard book equivalent: 1.2
First published: 2006

British historian Collingham tells how successive invasions of the Indian subcontinent contributed new ingredients and cooking techniques that combined into what is now recognized as classic Indian cuisine. Early invasions from the northwest brought rice, and Persian pilau became Hindustani biryani. Portuguese sailors imported pork and Brazilian chili peppers to create vindaloo. She then shows how Indian food has spread around the world and has become popular in such places as London, Tokyo, and New York where one can find a kosher Indian restaurant.

Keywords: British author, Woman author, curry, food, history, India

Websites:
http://www.nytimes.com/2006/02/01/books/01grim.html?ex=1296450000&en=bd24a96b9babda9b&ei=5088&partner=rssnyt&emc=rss
http://www.time.com/time/asia/magazine/article/0,13673,501060327-1174750,00.html
http://books.guardian.co.uk/review/story/0,12084,1556478,00.html

Rate this book: 1 – 2 – 3   4 – 5 – 6   7 – 8 – 9

Nonfiction
History / Biography / Social Science

Days of Grace
by Arthur Ashe and Arnold Rampersad (1994) 368p,
ISBN-13: 978-0345386816

Standard book equivalent: 1.4
First published: 1993

Ashe (1943 – 1993) was an American tennis champion and social activist. He won three tennis Grand Slam titles. He was the first African American to be selected to a U.S. Davis Cup team. Ashe founded the National Junior Tennis League and was one of the founders of the Association of Tennis Professionals. In 1988, Ashe contracted AIDS through blood transfusions he received for surgery. In the last year of his life he became a leading spokesman for AIDS research and medical care. He completed *Days of Grace* less than a week before he died on February 6, 1993.

Keywords: American author, African American author, AIDS, African American experience, Arthur Ashe, biography (men), inspirational, sports, tennis

Websites:
http://library.thinkquest.org/10615/no-frames/games/arthurarticle.html
http://espn.go.com/classic/biography/s/Ashe_Arthur.html
http://sportsillustrated.cnn.com/tennis/features/1997/arthurashe/profile.html

Rate this book: 1 – 2 – 3   4 – 5 – 6   7 – 8 – 9

Nonfiction
History / Biography / Social Science

Decisive Day: The Battle for Bunker Hill
by Richard M. Ketchum (1999) 288p, ISBN-13: 978-0805060997

Standard book equivalent: 1.1
First published: 1999

Ketchum is an American author and historian. He has written several best-selling books about the American Revolution. *Decisive Day* explores the factors that made that bloody skirmish decisive. Ketchum examines the deteriorating relationships between New England and Britain during the months before the battle. He describes how both the British and American commanders were still seeking ways to make peace as the guns began to fire. However, inflexibility on the part of British policymakers in London made conflict inevitable.

Keywords: American author, American history, American Revolution, Bunker Hill, New England, war

Websites:
http://www.historyofwar.org/articles/battles_bunkerhill.html
http://www.vermontmagazine.com/in_print.html
http://www.americanheritage.com/articles/magazine/ah/1991/7/1991_7_5.shtml

Rate this book: 1 – 2 – 3   4 – 5 – 6   7 – 8 – 9

Nonfiction
History / Biography / Social Science

The Declaration of Independence and Other Great Documents of American History 1775-1865
by John Grafton (editor) (2000) 64p, ISBN-13: 978-0486411248

Standard book equivalent: 0.2
First published: various dates 1775 to 1865

Thirteen influential documents of American history: Declaration of Independence (1776); Constitution of the United States (1787); James Madison's The Federalist (1787); George Washington's 1st Inaugural Address (1789); George Washington's Farewell Address (1796); Thomas Jefferson's 1st Inaugural Address (1801); James Monroe's Monroe Doctrine (1823); William Lloyd Garrison's The Liberator (1831, inaugural edition) ; Andrew Jackson's Veto of the Bank Bill (1832); Lincoln's 1st Inaugural Address (1861); Lincoln's Emancipation Proclamation (1863); Lincoln's Gettysburg Address (1863); Lincoln's 2nd Inaugural Address (1865).

Keywords: American history, Federalist, Jefferson, Lincoln, Washington

Websites:
http://www.ourdocuments.gov/index.php?flash=true&
http://www.let.rug.nl/usa/D/index.htm
http://www.loc.gov/rr/program/bib/ourdocs/NewNation.html

Rate this book: 1 – 2 – 3   4 – 5 – 6   7 – 8 – 9

Nonfiction
History / Biography / Social Science

Diary of an Early American Boy: Noah Blake 1805
by Eric Sloane (2004) 128p, ISBN-13: 978-0486436661

Standard book equivalent: 0.5
Written in 1805

Sloane (1905 – 1985) was an American painter and author. He discovered Noah Blake's diary at a library book sale in Warren, Connecticut. It was an account of New England farm life in 1805 by a fifteen year-old boy. Sloane added 72 informative drawings and commentary to the diary, and had it published in 1962. It became his best known book. The diary describes the everyday things that occupied farmers of the period, including how weather shaped their lives and the rhythm of activity set by the changing seasons.

Keywords: American author, American history, biography (men), Blake, farming, New England

Websites:
http://www.ericsloane.com/
http://alamo.nmsu.edu/~peidenba/sloane.html
http://store.cumberlandbooks.com/diaryofanearlyamericanboy.html

Rate this book: 1 – 2 – 3   4 – 5 – 6   7 – 8 – 9

Nonfiction
History / Biography / Social Science

Down on Parchman Farm: The Great Prison in the Mississippi Delta **
by William Banks Taylor (1999) 255p, ISBN-13: 978-0814250235

Standard book equivalent: 1.0
First published: 1999

Taylor is an American author and professor of criminal justice. This is a greatly revised version of *Brokered Justice*, first published in 1993. Parchman Farm was a prison built in 1900 in Mississippi. The Farm was operated for 70 years in a fashion similar to that of a Southern plantation. Taylor gives an account of its operations and how and why it was eventually replaced by a modern correctional facility. However, he is not convinced the modern facility is an improvement. Read *Worse than Slavery* by Oshinsky for a contrasting viewpoint.

Keywords: American author, American history, civil rights, Parchman Farm, poverty, prison, racism, the South

Websites:
http://www.h-net.org/reviews/showrev.cgi?path=28119981054292http://www.forewordmagazine.com/reviews/viewreviews.aspx?reviewID=356
http://www.sciencesbookreview.com/Down_on_Parchman_Farm_The_Great_Prison_in_the_Mississippi_Delta_0814250238.html

Rate this book: 1 – 2 – 3   4 – 5 – 6   7 – 8 – 9

Nonfiction
History / Biography / Social Science

Down These Mean Streets
by Piri Thomas (1997) 352p, ISBN-13: 978-0679781424

Standard book equivalent: 1.4
First published: 1967

Thomas (b. 1928) is a Puerto Rican-Cuban author. *Down These Mean Streets* is his autobiography. It tells the story of growing up as a dark-skinned Puerto Rican in New York City. The book chronicles his life from 1941 when he was twelve years-old and living with his family in Spanish Harlem, New York. The narrative describes his growth into manhood including his use of illegal drugs, his transformation into a violent criminal, time spent in prison, and eventual redemption.

Keywords: Puerto Rican author, biography (men), cross-cultural, drugs, immigrants, New York City, poverty, prejudice, prison, Puerto Rico, racism, Thomas

Websites:
http://www.cheverote.com/texts/30thed.html
http://www.mosaec.com/mosaec/books/books_thomas.htm
http://www.highbeam.com/doc/1G1-121647131.html

Rate this book: 1 – 2 – 3   4 – 5 – 6   7 – 8 – 9

Nonfiction
History / Biography / Social Science

Einstein on Race and Racism
by Fred Jerome, Rodger Taylor (2005) 206p, ISBN-13: 978-0813539522

Standard book equivalent: 0.8
First published: 2005

Jerome and Taylor are American authors and journalists. This book tells the story of Einstein's (1879 – 1955) role in the civil rights movement. An example of Einstein's views can be found in his 1946 address at Lincoln University (Pennsylvania) in which he said, "Segregation is a disease of white people not black people." His friends and colleagues of the civil rights movement included Paul Robeson, W.E.B. Du Bois and Marian Anderson. He co-chaired, with Paul Robeson, the American Crusade to End Lynching. This book includes many of Einstein's civil rights letters, speeches and published writings.

Keywords: American author, American history, civil rights, Einstein, racism

Websites:
http://www.logosjournal.com/issue_4.3/jerome_taylor.htm
http://66.70.33.220/JeromeTaylor_EinsteinRace.asp
http://www.drexel.edu/coas/ask/news/einstein-racism.asp

Rate this book: 1 – 2 – 3   4 – 5 – 6   7 – 8 – 9

Nonfiction
History / Biography / Social Science

The Essential Gandhi: An Anthology of His Writings on His Life, Work, and Ideas
by Mahatma Gandhi, Louis Fischer (editor), (2002) 368p,
ISBN-13: 978-1400030507

Standard book equivalent: 1.4
First published: 1962

Gandhi (1869 – 1948) was an Indian political and spiritual leader. This anthology of his writings forms an autobiography covering all phases of his life: childhood, marriage at young age, time in South Africa, role in the independence movement in India, and more. One can see his evolution from being an anglophile, to the radicalization he underwent when he witnessed the cruelty with which British soldiers repressed rebellion, to his spiritual transformation and acceptance of pacifism.

Keywords: Indian author, biography (men), Gandhi, India, Nobel Prize (Peace), South Africa

Websites:
http://www.mkgandhi.org/
http://www.sscnet.ucla.edu/southasia/History/Gandhi/gandhi.html
http://nobelprize.virtual.museum/nobel_prizes/peace/articles/gandhi/index.html

Rate this book: 1 – 2 – 3   4 – 5 – 6   7 – 8 – 9

Nonfiction
History / Biography / Social Science

Execution by Hunger: The Hidden Holocaust
by Miron Dolot (1987) 231p, ISBN-13: 978-0393304169

Standard book equivalent: 0.9
First published: 1985

Dolot is the pen name of a Ukrainian-born American author. *Execution by Hunger* is a riveting eyewitness account of Stalin's intentionally induced famine in the Ukraine. The author, a survivor of the famine, was 15 years-old during that winter of 1932-33. He clearly describes decisive actions taken by the communist regime against the Ukrainian peasants. The Soviets confiscated crops and searched houses for hidden food stores. By winter, people were starving and even resorting to cannibalism.

Keywords: American author, Ukrainian author, dictatorship, famine, genocide, history, Russia, Stalinism, Ukraine

Websites:
http://www.vho.org/GB/Journals/JHR/7/2/Ward229-231.html
http://umanitoba.ca/manitoban/2003-2004/1126/nf_02.html
http://www.artukraine.com/famineart/famine07.htm

Rate this book: 1 – 2 – 3   4 – 5 – 6   7 – 8 – 9

Nonfiction
History / Biography / Social Science

The Fall of Constantinople 1453
by Steven Runciman (1990) 270p, ISBN-13: 978-0521398329

Standard book equivalent: 1.0
First published: 1965

Runciman (1903 – 2000) was a British historian and author. *The Fall of Constantinople 1453* begins with the Ottoman advance into Europe in the 14th century and ends with the City's capture in 1453. Runciman describes how the last Byzantine Emperors desperately tried, to no avail, to convince Western leaders to help them. Conflicts among Christian kingdoms in the Balkans polarized them to such an extent that the Ottoman sultans were able to conquer territories one at a time until Constantinople was isolated and indefensible.

Keywords: British author, Constantinople, Crusades, history, Islam

Websites:
http://www.byzantium.ac.uk/frameset_spbsnews.htm?spbsnews_obituaries
http://www.thenagain.info/WebChron/EastEurope/FallConstantin.html
http://www.geocities.com/egfrothos/FourthCrusade.html

Rate this book: 1 – 2 – 3   4 – 5 – 6   7 – 8 – 9

Nonfiction
History / Biography / Social Science

Flu: The Story of the Great Influenza Pandemic of 1918 and the Search for the Virus That Caused It
by Gina Kolata (1999) 256p, ISBN-13: 978-0374157067

Standard book equivalent: 1.0
First published: 1999

Kolata is an American science journalist for the *New York Times*. This book describes the 1918 pandemic and discusses what can be done to prevent a repeat occurrence. From the back cover "…in 1918 the Great Flu Epidemic killed an estimated 40 million people virtually overnight. If such a plague returned today, taking a comparable percentage of the U.S. population with it, 1.5 million Americans would die." Kolata begins the story describing how rumors quickly spread that the flu was a deadly form of germ warfare perpetrated by the Germans.

Keywords: American author, woman author, disease, flu, history, medicine

Websites:
http://www.nature.com/nm/journal/v6/n1/full/nm0100_12.html;jsessionid=16131A648CCACE3377B81834B1A267AC
http://www.cnn.com/books/beginnings/9911/flu/index.html
http://www.webmd.com/content/article/1/1707_50029.htm

Rate this book: 1 – 2 – 3   4 – 5 – 6   7 – 8 – 9

Nonfiction
History / Biography / Social Science

For Cause and Comrades: Why Men Fought in the Civil War
by James M. McPherson (1998) 256 p, ISBN-13: 978-0195124996

Standard Book Equivalent: 1.0
First published: 1997

McPherson (b. 1936) is an American historian and professor emeritus at Princeton University. *For Cause and Comrades* addresses the question of what motivated men—many of them married with families—during the Civil War to enlist in the military (and stay once enlisted). McPherson examined more than 1,000 diaries and letters from Union and Confederate soldiers to answer that question. A surprisingly large number of soldiers were motivated by noble ideals of duty and honor. Most of the book consists of excerpts from soldiers' letters with McPherson providing commentary.

Keywords: American author, American history, Civil War, war

Websites:
http://www.ess.uwe.ac.uk/genocide/reviewsw6.htm
http://www.nytimes.com/books/first/m/mcpherson-comrades.html?_r=1&oref=slogin
http://www.strategypage.com/bookreviews/50.asp
http://www.nytimes.com/books/97/03/23/reviews/970323.23weiglet.html

Rate this book: 1 – 2 – 3   4 – 5 – 6   7 – 8 – 9

Nonfiction
History / Biography / Social Science

Founding Brothers: The Revolutionary Generation
by Joseph J. Ellis (2002) 304p, ISBN-13: 978-0375705243

Standard book equivalent: 1.2
First published: 2000

Ellis (b. 1943) is an American author and historian who won a 2001 Pulitzer Prize for *Founding Brothers*. It focuses on six decisive moments in the founding of the new nation at the end of the 18th century: Burr and Hamilton's duel; Hamilton, Jefferson and Madison's secret dinner during which the location of the seat of government was determined; Franklin's petition to end slavery; Washington's Farewell Address; Adams' difficult term as President; and Adam's and Jefferson's renewed correspondence at the end of their lives.

Keywords: American author, Adams, American history, American Revolution, Franklin, Jefferson, Pulitzer Prize, Washington

Websites:
http://www.bookrags.com/studyguide-founding-brothers/
http://www.bookpage.com/0011bp/nonfiction/founding_br
    others.html
http://www.pbs.org/newshour/bb/media/jan-
    june01/ellis_04-18.html

Rate this book: 1 – 2 – 3   4 – 5 – 6   7 – 8 – 9

Nonfiction
History / Biography / Social Science

Friday Night Lights: A Town, a Team, and a Dream by H. G. Bissinger (2006) 357p, ISBN-13: 978-0306815294

Standard book equivalent: 1.4
First published: 1990

Bissinger (b. 1954) is an American journalist and author. *Friday Night Lights* chronicles the 1988 Permian High School football team's season and their attempt to make it to the Texas state championship game. Bissinger spent that season in Odessa, Texas following the team and recording their highs and lows. He also depicts the obsession the town has with their football team. The coach is vilified if they lose a game—for sale signs are put on his lawn and calls for his resignation flood radio talk shows. This book was made into a movie and a television series.

Keywords: American author, football, high school, sports

Websites:
http://www.fridaynightlightsbook.com/
http://www.gracecentered.com/friday_night_lights.htm
http://www.oaoa.com/specialsections/fridaylights/author.htm

Rate this book: 1 – 2 – 3   4 – 5 – 6   7 – 8 – 9

Nonfiction
History / Biography / Social Science

The Game
by Ken Dryden (1999) 280p, ISBN-13: 978-0771576737

Standard book equivalent: 1.1
First published: 1983

Dryden (b. 1947) is a Canadian politician, author and former National Hockey League (NHL) player. He holds a BA degree in history from Cornell University and a law degree from McGill University. He was an NHL goalie from 1970 to 1979 and elected to the Hockey Hall of Fame in 1983. *The Game* describes the 1979 season of the champion Montreal Canadiens, what it means to be a goalie in the NHL, and what hockey means to Canadians. It is an intelligent and reflective look at life in hockey.

Keywords: Canadian author, hockey, Montreal Canadiens, sports

Websites:
http://www.kendryden.ca/
http://www.legendsofhockey.net:8080/LegendsOfHockey/jsp/LegendsMember.jsp?mem=P198301#photo

Rate this book: 1 – 2 – 3   4 – 5 – 6   7 – 8 – 9

Nonfiction
History / Biography / Social Science

The Game They Played
by Stanley Cohen (2001) 256p, ISBN-13: 978-0786708215

Standard book equivalent: 1.0
First published: 1977

Cohen is an American author and journalist and also author of *The Man in the Crowd*. *The Game They Played* is about the point shaving scandal of the 1949-50 college basketball season. The unranked City College (CUNY) team ("five street kids from the City of New York-three Jews and two blacks") won both the NCAA championship and National Invitation Tournament. However, the scandal that followed ended with the indictment of twenty players and left New York without big-time college basketball.

Keywords: American author, American history, basketball, CUNY, New York City, sports, sports scandal

Websites:
http://www.gopherhole.com/modules.php?name=News&file=article&sid=582
http://collegeresearchonline.com/BooksOfOurTime/37%20Books%20of%20Our%20Times%20The%20Game%20They%20Played.htm
http://www.aafla.org/SportsLibrary/JSH/JSH1981/JSH0801/jsh0801o.pdf

Rate this book: 1 – 2 – 3   4 – 5 – 6   7 – 8 – 9

Nonfiction
History / Biography / Social Science

Gauntlet: Five Friends, 20,000 Enemy Troops, & the Secret That Could Have Changed the Course of the Cold War
by Barbara Masin (2006) 382p, ISBN-13: 978-1591145158

First published: 2006
Masin (b. 1967) is an American author. The five friends of *Gauntlet* include the author's father, uncle, and their three friends. This is the story of their daring attempt to free Czechoslovakia from communist control. They were Czech members of an anti-communist underground group during the 1950s. Their plan was to escape to West Berlin by crossing through Communist East Germany with the goal of joining the U.S. Army. They hoped to become part of a U.S. invasion force that, unfortunately, never materialized. It is estimated that 20,000 Communist-Block troops were hunting them down during their flight.

Keywords: American author, woman author, communism, Czechoslovakia, cold war

Websites:
http://www.gauntletinfo.com/
http://www.murdoconline.net/archives/004427.html
http://www.praguepost.com/P03/2006/Art/0810/tempo1.php

Rate this book: 1 – 2 – 3   4 – 5 – 6   7 – 8 – 9

Nonfiction
History / Biography / Social Science

The Good Man of Nanking: The Diaries of John Rabe
by John Rabe (2000) 320p, ISBN-13: 978-0375701979

Standard book equivalent: 1.2
First published: 1998

Rabe (1882 – 1950) was a German businessman in Nanking during the massacre of 1937-1938. He saved thousands of Chinese from brutality and certain death. Yet, he also was an ardent Nazi. He was a complicated man and perhaps naïve about his politics. He returned to Germany in 1938 and wrote to Hitler asking him to intervene on behalf of China to stop Japan's aggression. Instead, Rabe was questioned by the Gestapo and told to stop speaking about Nanking. His diaries provide a rare first-hand account of what happened in Nanking.

Keywords: German author, biography (men), China, Germany, massacre, Nanking, war, John Rabe, WW II

Websites:
http://www.nytimes.com/books/98/12/13/reviews/981213.1
       3wudunnt.html?_r=1&oref=slogin
http://www.atimes.com/japan-econ/BC10Dh01.html
http://www.asiamedia.ucla.edu/article.asp?parentid=16772

Rate this book: 1 – 2 – 3   4 – 5 – 6   7 – 8 – 9

Nonfiction
History / Biography / Social Science

Having Our Say: The Delany Sisters' First 100 Years
by Sarah and A. Elizabeth Delaney, with Amy Hill Hearth
(1994) 324p, ISBN-13: 978-0440220428

Standard book equivalent: 1.2
First published: 1992

Sarah (1889 – 1999) and Elizabeth (1891-1995) were two American sisters and authors. Daughters of former slaves, in *Having Our Say* they recount their experiences and observations of growing up during the 20th century. They were raised in North Carolina, but as adults lived in Harlem and Mount Vernon, New York. Both were professionals, Sarah (Sadie) was a teacher in New York and Elizabeth (Bessie) a dentist. They were intimately involved with the civil rights movement, especially during the Harlem Renaissance and rubbed elbows with Paul Robeson, Langston Hughes and Cab Calloway.

Keywords: American author, African American author, woman author, African American experience, biography (women), civil rights, Delaney, prejudice, racism

Websites:
http://www.sparknotes.com/lit/havingoursay/
http://www.amyhillhearth.com/work1.htm
http://havingoursay.com/home.htm

Rate this book: 1 – 2 – 3   4 – 5 – 6   7 – 8 – 9

Nonfiction
History / Biography / Social Science

Here I Stand
by Paul Robeson (1998) 160p, ISBN-13: 978-0807064450

Standard book equivalent: 0.6
First published: 1958

Robeson (1898 – 1976) was a multi-lingual American actor, athlete, concert singer, writer, and civil rights activist who, because of his socialist political views, became entangled in the Red Scare of the McCarthy era. In the first few pages of his book he clearly informs the reader that it is not an autobiography. And it is not a biography, although it does deal with facets of his life. The book focuses more on exploring how Paul Robeson came to hold his strong political beliefs.

Keywords: African American author, American author, African American experience, McCarthyism, politics, prejudice, Robeson

Websites:
http://www.pbs.org/wnet/americanmasters/database/robeson_p.html
http://www.spartacus.schoolnet.co.uk/USArobeson.htm
http://www.scc.rutgers.edu/njh/PaulRobeson/index.htm

Rate this book: 1 – 2 – 3   4 – 5 – 6   7 – 8 – 9

Nonfiction
History / Biography / Social Science

Hip Hop Matters: Politics, Pop Culture, and the Struggle for the Soul of a Movement
by S. Craig Watkins (2006) 304p, ISBN-13: 978-0807009864

Standard book equivalent: 1.2
First published: 2005

Watkins is a professor of sociology, and African American Studies at the University of Texas, Austin. In *Hip Hop Matters* he chronicles the history and meaning of Hip Hop music, describes the Hip Hop subculture and discusses the impact it has on the larger American culture. Watkins covers the major artists, the details of how the music industry operates and the interrelationships between Hip Hop and politics. In an epilogue he discusses both the successes and failures of Hip Hop as an industry and a culture.

Keywords: American author, American history, hip hop, music

Websites:
http://rtf.utexas.edu/faculty/watkins/
http://www.utexas.edu/features/archive/2003/hiphop.html
http://www.hiphoplinguistics.com/reviews/books/hiphopmatters.php

Rate this book: 1 – 2 – 3   4 – 5 – 6   7 – 8 – 9

Nonfiction
History / Biography / Social Science

Hiroshima
by John Hersey (1989) 160p, ISBN-13: 978-0679721031

Standard book equivalent: 0.6
First published: 1946, last chapter in 1985

Hersey (1914 – 1993) is an American author and journalist. *Hiroshima* grew from a story he did for *New Yorker* magazine in August 1946. It is about the effects of the atomic bomb dropped on Hiroshima. Hersey records the reflections of six survivors on the aftermath of the first atomic bomb. The book's first four chapters describe these survivors over the course of one year following the bombing. Chapter 5 was added in 1985 and traces the long-term consequences the bombing had on the lives of these six people and the world at large.

Keywords: American author, American history, atomic bomb, Japan, war, WWII

Websites:
http://www.sparknotes.com/lit/hiroshima/index.html
http://www.herseyhiroshima.com/
http://www.spartacus.schoolnet.co.uk/2WWhersey.htm

Rate this book: 1 – 2 – 3   4 – 5 – 6   7 – 8 – 9

Nonfiction
History / Biography / Social Science

How to Read Literature like a Professor: a Lively and Entertaining Guide to Reading Between the Lines **
by Thomas Foster (2003) 336p, ISBN-13: 978-0060009427

Standard book equivalent: 1.3
First published: 2003

Foster is an American author and professor at the University of Michigan, Flint. This book explains what it means to be a critical reader. From the back cover of the book, "What does it mean when a fictional hero takes a journey? Shares a meal? Gets drenched in a sudden rain shower? Often, there is much more going on in a novel or poem than is readily visible on the surface…" However, more than describing "how to read between the lines", this book shows what it means to study literature, both as a university student and literature professor.

Keywords: American author, literature, reading

Websites:
http://www.bookreporter.com/reviews/006000942X.asp
http://www.worldlearnerschool.com/wls/Content.asp?Nav=
    home&ContentID=9
http://www.harpercollins.ca/global_scripts/product_catalog
    /book_xml.asp?isbn=006000942X&tc=ae

Rate this book: 1 – 2 – 3   4 – 5 – 6   7 – 8 – 9

Nonfiction
History / Biography / Social Science

I Know Why the Caged Bird Sings
by Maya Angelou (1997) 304p, ISBN-13: 978-0553380019

Standard book equivalent: 1.2
First published: 1969

Angelou (b. 1928) is an American author, poet and civil rights activist. This autobiography describes her coming-of-age in Arkansas. It is quite graphic and discusses issues of rape, racism and sexism the author experienced as a child. It is often placed on lists of banned books because it deals with those issues. However, it is also frequently found on high school required reading lists because of the sensitivity with which it portrays those issues. The title comes from Paul Dunbar's poem 'Sympathy'.

Keywords: American author, African American author, Woman author, abuse, African American experience, Angelou, biography (women), , inspirational, prejudice, racism

Websites:
http://www.sparknotes.com/lit/cagedbird/index.html
http://www.gradesaver.com/classicnotes/titles/caged/about.html
http://www.cliffsnotes.com/WileyCDA/LitNote/id-24.html

Rate this book: 1 – 2 – 3   4 – 5 – 6   7 – 8 – 9

Nonfiction
History / Biography / Social Science

I Never Had It Made: An Autobiography of Jackie Robinson
by Jackie Robinson, Alfred Duckett (2003) 304p, ISBN-13: 978-0060555979

Standard book equivalent: 1.2
First published: 1972

Robinson (1919 – 1972) was an American professional baseball player and civil rights leader. This autobiography is about the life of a man who played a major role in the civil rights movement. He tells of his accomplishments at UCLA and his time in the army, where he was court-martialed for refusing to move to the back of a bus. Robinson reminisces about playing in the Negro Leagues for the Kansas City Monarchs before becoming the first African American to play in the majors in 1947. He also describes the appalling abuse he suffered for doing so.

Keywords: American author, African American author, African American experience , baseball, biography (men), Brooklyn Dodgers, civil rights, Jackie Robinson, prejudice, sports

Websites:
http://www.usatoday.com/sports/bbw/2001-04-04/2001-04-04-archive-robinson.htm
http://www.sportingnews.com/archives/jackie/rawlings.html
http://afgen.com/jackie_robinson.html

Rate this book: 1 – 2 – 3   4 – 5 – 6   7 – 8 – 9

Nonfiction
History / Biography / Social Science

I Write What I Like: Selected Writings
by Steve Biko, Aelred Stubbs (editor) (2002) 240p, ISBN-13: 978-0226048970

Standard book equivalent: 0.9
First published: 1978

Biko (1946 – 1977) was a black South African journalist and anti-apartheid activist. He was tortured and killed in prison. *I Write What I Like* is a selection of Biko's writings from 1969 to 1972, when he was prohibited from publishing. His speeches and interviews are also included. Chapter titles include "What is Black Conciousness?", "Black Consciousness and the Quest for a True Humanity", "Our Strategy for Liberation", "White Racism and Black Consciousness", and "On Death". A memoir is included that was written by Father Aelred Stubbs, Biko's longtime pastor and friend.

Keywords: South African author, Africa, apartheid, Biko, civil rights, racism, South Africa, violence

Websites:
http://www.press.uchicago.edu/cgi-bin/hfs.cgi/00/14833.ctl
http://www.sbf.org.za/index.htm?e-shop.htm~main
http://www.polity.org.za/html/govdocs/speeches/2002/sp0322a.html

Rate this book: 1 – 2 – 3   4 – 5 – 6   7 – 8 – 9

Nonfiction
History / Biography / Social Science

In the Heart of the Sea: The Tragedy of the Whaleship Essex
by Nathaniel Philbrick (2001) 320p, ISBN-13: 978-0141001821

Standard book equivalent: 1.2
First published: 2000

Philbrick is an American author and historian who won the 2001 National Book Award for *In the Heart of the Sea*. It tells the tale of the *Essex*, an American whale ship that in 1819 in the South Pacific was rammed and sunk by an enraged sperm whale. The story is told from the point of view of the 14 year-old cabin boy, Thomas Nickerson. Philbrick's primary source was Nickerson's notebook, which he wrote in 1875 but had been lost until 1980.

Keywords: American author, American history, National Book Award, Pacific Ocean, sea, whaling

Websites:
http://www.bookreporter.com/reviews/0670891576.asp
http://www.reasontofreedom.com/Heart_of_Sea_Tragedy_of_Whaleship_Essex.html
http://www.bookbrowse.com/reviews/index.cfm?book_number=535

Rate this book: 1 – 2 – 3   4 – 5 – 6   7 – 8 – 9

Nonfiction
History / Biography / Social Science

In These Girls, Hope is a Muscle *
by Madeleine Blais (1996) 272p, ISBN-13: 978-0446672108

Standard book equivalent: 1.0
First published: 1995

Madeleine Blais is an American journalist and professor at the University of Massachusetts, Amherst. *In These Girls, Hope is a Muscle* is about the '92-'93 State Championship season of the Amherst High School Lady Hurricanes basketball team. They made it to the playoffs each of the previous five seasons but fell short of winning the championship. Blais tagged along the following season and recorded their progress for a New York Times article (April 1993) that she expanded into this book. The title was inspired from a line in the Emily Dickenson poem 'Hope' (Hope is the thing with feathers…).

Keywords: American author, woman author, basketball, high school, New England, sports

Websites:
http://teenink.com/Past/1997/8553.html
http://findarticles.com/p/articles/mi_m1295/is_n1_v59/ai_16038859
http://ballin.editthispage.com/stories/storyReader$148

Rate this book: 1 – 2 – 3   4 – 5 – 6   7 – 8 – 9

Nonfiction
History / Biography / Social Science

Incidents in the Life of a Slave Girl
by Harriet Jacobs, Nellie Y. McKay (editor), Frances Smith Foster (editor) (2001) 176p, ISBN-13: 978-0486419312

Standard book equivalent: 0.7
First published: 1861

Jacobs (1813 – 1897) was an American slave who escaped to freedom. *Incidents in the Life of a Slave Girl* is one of the first narratives by a slave and one of the few written by a woman. She was a slave in North Carolina and suffered at the hands of a ruthless abusive owner. She made several failed attempts to escape before successfully making her way to the North, though it was slow progress taking years of hiding.

Keywords: American author, woman author, African American author, abuse, African American experience, biography (women), Jacobs, slavery, violence

Websites:
http://xroads.virginia.edu/~Hyper/JACOBS/hjhome.htm
http://www.spartacus.schoolnet.co.uk/Sjacobs.htm
http://afroamhistory.about.com/library/bljacobs_contents.htm

Rate this book: 1 – 2 – 3   4 – 5 – 6   7 – 8 – 9

Nonfiction
History / Biography / Social Science

The Irish Famine: An Illustrated History
by Helen Litton (2003) 144p, ISBN-13: 978-0863279126

Standard book equivalent: 0.6
First published: 1994

Litton's *The Irish Famine* describes events that took place in Ireland between 1845 and 1850. The death toll may be close to one million people. She provides an evenhanded account of the famine and addresses questions such as, "Why did millions of starving people seem to accept their fate without rebelling?" and "Why did people starve beside seas and rivers stocked with plenty of fish?" Litton uses quotes from first-hand accounts, and information from numerous studies and sources. It is a concise introduction to a complicated period.

Keywords: woman author, famine, farming, food, history, Ireland, potatoes

Websites:
http://www.nde.state.ne.us/SS/irish/irish_pf.html
http://www.siu.edu/~ebl/leaflets/blight.htm
http://www.emsc.nysed.gov/nysssa/gif/famnature2.pdf

Rate this book: 1 – 2 – 3   4 – 5 – 6   7 – 8 – 9

Nonfiction
History / Biography / Social Science

Johnstown Flood
by David McCullough (1987) 304p, ISBN-13: 978-0671207144

Standard book equivalent: 1.2
First published: 1968

McCullough (b. 1933) is an American historian and author. This is an account of the tragic 1889 dam failure in Johnstown, Pennsylvania. McCullough's narrative, using eyewitness accounts, tells the story of the town and the forces of nature that came together that day. From McCullough's book, "The wave kept on coming straight toward him, heading for the very heart of the city. Stores, houses, trees, everything was going down in front of it, and the closer it came, the bigger it seemed to grow... The height of the wall of water was at least thirty-six feet at the center..."

Keywords: American author, American history, flood, Pennsylvania

Websites:
http://www.electriceggplant.com/davidmccullough/flood.htm
http://www.nps.gov/archive/jofl/histiography.htm
http://www.bookreporter.com/authors/au-mccullough-david.asp

Rate this book: 1 – 2 – 3   4 – 5 – 6   7 – 8 – 9

Nonfiction
History / Biography / Social Science

Kaffir Boy: The True Story of a Black Youth's Coming-of-age in Apartheid South Africa
by Mark Mathabane (1998) 368p, ISBN-13: 978-0684848280

Standard book equivalent: 1.4
First published: 1986

Mathabane (b. 1960) is a black South African tennis player and author. *Kaffir Boy* is an autobiography about his life under the South African apartheid regime. Mathabane begins his story when he is five years-old and he with his family faces the terror of the Peri-Urban, a local police squad. He describes how Arthur Ashe became his role-model with Ashe's victory over Jimmy Connors. Mathabane took up tennis and eventually won a scholarship to an American university.

Keywords: South African author, Africa, apartheid, biography (men), civil rights, coming-of-age, Mathabane, racism, South Africa, sports, tennis

Websites:
http://mathabane.com/
http://www.bookrags.com/Kaffir_Boy
http://www.classzone.com/novelguides/litcons/kaffir/guide.cfm

Rate this book: 1 – 2 – 3   4 – 5 – 6   7 – 8 – 9

Nonfiction
History / Biography / Social Science

The Lemon Tree: An Arab, a Jew, and the Heart of the Middle East
by Sandy Tolan (2006) 304p, ISBN-13: 978-1582343433

Standard book equivalent: 1.2
First published: 2006

Tolan is an American journalist, National Public Radio (NPR) correspondent and lecturer at the University of California, Berkeley. The book's title refers to a tree in the backyard of a house in Ramla, Israel. The house is currently owned by Dalia, a Jewish Holocaust survivor who emigrated from Bulgaria. However, before Israel gained its independence in 1948, the house was owned by the Palestinian family of Bashir. Bashir meets Dalia when he visits after the Six-Day War of 1967. Tolan traces the history of the Israeli-Palestinian conflict through the parallel stories of Dalia's and Bashir's families—all refugees seeking a home.

Keywords: American author, Arab experience, history, Jewish experience, Middle East, war

Websites:
http://www.bookpage.com/0605bp/nonfiction/lemon_tree.html
http://www.tomdispatch.com/index.mhtml?pid=100409
http://www.npr.org/templates/story/story.php?storyId=5405369

Rate this book: 1 – 2 – 3   4 – 5 – 6   7 – 8 – 9

Nonfiction
History / Biography / Social Science

Life along the Silk Road
by Susan Whitfield (2001) 253p, ISBN-13: 978-0520232143

Standard book equivalent: 1.0
First published: 1999

Whitfield is a British author and historian. *Life along the Silk Road* is a narrative history about trade across Central Asia. Each chapter introduces an inhabitant who lived on the Silk Road at the end of the 10th century. The chapters are titled: The Merchant's Tale; The Soldier's Tale; The Horsemen's Tale; The Monk's Tale; The Courtesan's Tale; The Nun's Tale; The Widow's Tale; The Official's Tale; and The Artist's Tale. Whitfield's approach makes the history of pre-Islamic central Asia personal, fleshing out the battles of conquest and trade with the details of everyday life.

Keywords: British author, woman author, central Asia, history, medieval, silk, trade

Websites:
http://books.guardian.co.uk/reviews/travel/0,,1873503,00.html
http://www.ucpress.edu/books/pages/9076.html
http://www.silk-road.com/toc/index.html

Rate this book: 1 – 2 – 3   4 – 5 – 6   7 – 8 – 9

Nonfiction
History / Biography / Social Science

The Life of Olaudah Equiano
by Olaudah Equiano (1999) 192p, ISBN-13: 978-0486406619

Standard book equivalent: 0.7
First published: 1789

Equiano (c.1745 – 1797) was a slave who purchased his freedom. He was captured from what is now Nigeria. This autobiography traces his journey beginning with his boyhood as an Igbo prince. He recounts his enslavement in the New World, service in the Seven Years War with General Wolfe in Canada, voyages to the Arctic with the Phipps expedition of 1772–73, and time spent among the Miskito Indians in Central America. After purchasing his freedom he wrote his autobiography as a strong abolitionist statement against slavery.

Keywords: African author, Africabiography (men), Equiano, history, Nigeria, slavery

Websites:
http://www.brycchancarey.com/equiano/
http://www.princeton.edu/~howarth/304.Projects/Erera/Pages/Main.htm
http://docsouth.unc.edu/neh/equiano1/menu.html

Rate this book: 1 – 2 – 3   4 – 5 – 6   7 – 8 – 9

Nonfiction
History / Biography / Social Science

A Long Way Gone: Memoirs of a Boy Soldier
by Ishmael Beah (2007) 240p, ISBN-13: 978-0374105235

Standard book equivalent: 0.9
First published: 2007

Beah (b. 1980) is a Sierra Leonean author who was a child soldier during Sierra Leone's civil war (1991 – 2000). That war is infamous for the atrocities committed on the civilian population. His memoirs describe his experiences before the war and abduction into a rebel army when he was 12 years-old. His life as a soldier centered on drugs, killing and pillage. He lived that life until the age of 15 when he was sent to a rehabilitation center. Eventually, he made his way to the United States and Oberlin College where he graduated in 2004.

Keywords: Sierra Leonean author, abuse, Africa, child soldier, drugs, Sierra Leone, war

Websites:
http://www.alongwaygone.com/
http://www.nytimes.com/2007/01/14/magazine/14soldier.t.html?ei=5089&amp;amp;amp;amp;amp;amp;amp;amp;amp;en=18db63db3854257e&ex=1326430800&adxnnl=1&partner=rssyahoo&emc=rss&adxnnlx=
http://www.iht.com/articles/2007/02/23/features/IDLEDE24.php?page=1

Rate this book: 1 – 2 – 3   4 – 5 – 6   7 – 8 – 9

Nonfiction
History / Biography / Social Science

The Lost German Slave Girl: The Extraordinary True Story of Sally Miller and Her Fight for Freedom in Old New Orleans
by John Bailey (2006) 288p, ISBN-13: 978-0802142290

Standard book equivalent: 1.1
First published: 2003

Bailey (b. 1944) is an Australian author. *The Lost German Slave Girl* is the story of a mystery that gripped New Orleans from 1843 until 1849. A community of German immigrants claimed that a young slave woman had sailed with them from Holland years earlier and therefore should not be a slave. The girl and her sister had been sent off to become indentured servants after their parents died. Lawyers were brought in as the case quickly changed from a simple matter of establishing proper identification to questioning the honor of the slave owner.

Keywords: Australian author, American history, Miller, New Orleans, slavery

Websites:
http://www.jbailey.info/index.html
http://www.washingtonpost.com/wp-dyn/articles/A22519-2005Jan19.html
http://www.aalbc.com/reviews/lostgermanslavegirl.htm

Rate this book: 1 – 2 – 3   4 – 5 – 6   7 – 8 – 9

Nonfiction
History / Biography / Social Science

A Love Supreme: The Making of John Coltrane's Masterpiece **
by Ashley Kahn (2003) 288p, ISBN-13: 978-0142003527

Standard book equivalent: 1.0
First published: 2002

Kahn is an American journalist and music historian. *A Love Supreme* is about the making of the same-titled John Coltrane album in 1964. It describes how the album was made, where it was made, and why it is so important. That album is noted for the broad audience it reached. It is one of the top-selling jazz albums of all time. Kahn's book is filled with anecdotes from Bono, Phil Lesh, and Alice Coltrane (Coltrane's widow). It features a foreword written by the late Jazz drummer Elvin Jones, who was a close colleague and friend of Coltrane.

Keywords: American author, American history, Coltrane, jazz, music

Websites:
http://www.jerryjazzmusician.com/mainHTML.cfm?page=kahn-als.html
http://www.brothersjudd.com/index.cfm/fuseaction/reviews.detail/book_id/1292/
http://www.alovesupremethebook.com/

Rate this book: 1 – 2 – 3   4 – 5 – 6   7 – 8 – 9

Nonfiction
History / Biography / Social Science

Madness: A Brief History **
by Roy Porter (2003) 256p, ISBN-13: 978-0192802675

Standard book equivalent: 1.0
First published: 2002

Porter (1946 – 2002) was a British historian and author. *Madness: A Brief History* provides a concise but sweeping description of the concept of madness through the ages. It focuses on the question, "What is meant when we say, madness?" Porter examines the wide range of possibilities this question covers, from witches to electric shock therapy to Prozac. He concludes that psychiatry has not progressed nearly enough in its diagnosis, understanding of the biological basis, and treatment of madness.

Keywords: British author, history, medicine, mental illness, psychology

Websites:
http://books.guardian.co.uk/reviews/healthmindandbody/0,
    6121,647617,00.html
http://www.scielosp.org/scielo.php?script=sci_arttext&pid=
    S0042-96862002000700015
http://www.sfms.org/AM/Template.cfm?Section=Home&T
    EMPLATE=/CM/HTMLDisplay.cfm&SECTION=
    Article_Archives&CONTENTID=1841

Rate this book: 1 – 2 – 3   4 – 5 – 6   7 – 8 – 9

Nonfiction
History / Biography / Social Science

The Man Who Would Be King: The First American in Afghanistan
by Ben MacIntyre (2005) 368p, ISBN-13: 978-0374529574

Standard book equivalent: 1.4
First published: 2004

MacIntyre is a British journalist and author who covered Afghanistan for the London Times from 1989 to 1991. *The Man Who Would Be King* is about the life of Josiah Harlan, a 19th century maverick who likely was the first American to ever visit Afghanistan. His exploits were as amazing as the fictional character in Kipling's short story of the same title. In 1838, Harlan was crowned king of the fierce Hazara people, although the British overthrow of the sitting Afghan ruler soon ended his reign.

Keywords: British author, adventure, Afghanistan, biography (men), colonialism, Harlan, history, war

Websites:
http://www.curledup.com/manwhowo.htm
http://www.desijournal.com/book.asp?articleid=135
http://news.bbc.co.uk/2/hi/south_asia/3750931.stm

Rate this book: 1 – 2 – 3   4 – 5 – 6   7 – 8 – 9

Nonfiction
History / Biography / Social Science

Man's Search for Meaning
by Viktor E. Frankl (2006) 193p, ISBN-13: 978-0807014295

Standard book equivalent: 0.7
First published: 1945

Frankl (1905 – 1997) was an Austrian psychiatrist, author, and holocaust survivor. His book is divided into two parts. The first part describes his horrific experiences during five years in the Auschwitz Death Camp. The second part describes his theory of logotherapy which grew out of those experiences. Its basis is that our primary motivation for existence is a search for meaning in life. As long as our ability to search for meaning remains intact we can weather even the basest experiences.

Keywords: Austrian author, Auschwitz, holocaust, logotherapy, psychology

Websites:
http://www.firstthings.com/ftissues/ft9504/scully.html
http://www.rjgeib.com/thoughts/frankl/frankl.html
http://www.ship.edu/~cgboeree/frankl.html

Rate this book: 1 – 2 – 3   4 – 5 – 6   7 – 8 – 9

Nonfiction
History / Biography / Social Science

Marathon Woman: Running the Race to Revolutionize Women's Sports
by Katherine Switzer (2007) 320p, ISBN-13: 978-0786719679

Standard book equivalent: 1.2
First published: 2007

Switzer (b. 1947) is an American author and the first woman to officially run in the Boston Marathon (1967). She won instant fame when a photograph was published showing Boston Marathon official Jock Semple attempting to physically remove her from the race while she was competing. Semple thought she was making a mockery of the prestigious event. They later became good friends. Switzer went on to run in 35 marathons and won the 1974 New York City Marathon. She became a successful author and leading advocate for both feminism and fitness.

Keywords: American author, woman author, biography (women), Boston, feminism, marathon, running, sports, Switzer

Websites:
http://www.katherineswitzer.com/
http://www.coolrunning.com/engine/6/6_1/marathon-woman-running-th.shtml
http://www.runwashington.com/features/misckateswitzer.html

Rate this book: 1 – 2 – 3   4 – 5 – 6   7 – 8 – 9

Nonfiction
History / Biography / Social Science

Memoirs of Fray Servando Teresa de Mier
by Fray Servando Teresa De Mier, Helen Lane (translator)
(1998) 304p, ISBN-13: 978-0195106749

Standard book equivalent: 1.2
First published about 1827

Servando (1765 – 1827) was a Spanish Mexican priest. On December 12, 1794, Fray Servando preached a sermon in Mexico City supporting the native peoples, which the Spanish authorities deemed subversive. He was exiled to Spain by the Inquisition, but escaped prison and spent ten years wandering around Europe and North America in the guise of a French priest. This autobiography details his adventures and is critical of a so-called civilized European society that viewed native peoples as savages.

Keywords: Mexican author, biography (men), colonialism, history, Mexico, religion, Spain

Websites:
http://www.questia.com/PM.qst;jsessionid=FcqMX18B6W
    FvnhFLgkPJnp0FkfY7mj3QPkCT7xXcmMjp3LD
    mJ5vf!67577388?a=o&d=79016688
http://www.elbalero.gob.mx/pages_kids/history/biographie
    s/fray_kids.html
http://www.nytimes.com/books/98/10/25/reviews/981025.2
    5luciant.html

Rate this book: 1 – 2 – 3   4 – 5 – 6   7 – 8 – 9

Nonfiction
History / Biography / Social Science

My Land and My People: The Original Autobiography of His Holiness the Dalai Lama of Tibet
by The Dalai Lama (1997) 256p, ISBN-13: 978-0446674218

Standard book equivalent: 1.0
First published: 1962

The Dalai Lama (b. 1935), Tenzin Gyatso, is the head of Tibetan Buddhism. Tenzin Gyatso became the 14th Dalai Lama in 1950; a line of leaders that stretches back to the 14th century. He went into exile in 1959. This autobiography describes the search that identified him as the reincarnated leader of his country as well as the way of life for Tibetan Buddhists. Also described is the occupation of Tibet, his exile and struggle to free Tibet once again.

Keywords: Tibetan author, biography (men), Buddhism, Dalai Lama, Nobel Prize (Peace), religion, Tibet

Websites:
http://www.questia.com/PM.qst?a=o&d=22951217
http://www.tibet.ca/en/wtnarchive/1998/1/5_1.html
http://nobelprize.org/nobel_prizes/peace/laureates/1989/lama-bio.html

Rate this book: 1 – 2 – 3   4 – 5 – 6   7 – 8 – 9

Nonfiction
History / Biography / Social Science

My Journey to Lhasa
by Alexandra David-Neel (1993) 310p, ISBN-13: 978-0807059036

Standard book equivalent: 1.2
First published: 1927

David-Neel (1868 – 1969) was a French author, pioneer feminist, and explorer fluent in Tibetan language. She was raised in a strict Victorian society but escaped that mold by traveling to exotic places. In 1923 she became the first Western woman to visit the Tibetan Forbidden City of Lhasa. She made the almost 1-year trek from China to Lhasa on foot with her adopted Tibetan son. They disguised themselves as pilgrims and traveled at night to avoid detection. *My Journey to Lhasa* is her travelogue of that trip. It is part adventure story and part ethnography.

Keywords: French author, woman author, Buddhism, China, David-Neel, Tibet, travel

Websites:
http://www.alexandra-david-neel.org/index_anim.htm
http://www.awakenedwoman.com/david_neel.htm
http://www.trivia-library.com/b/biography-of-female-explorer-and-adventurer-alexandra-david-neel-part-2.htm

Rate this book: 1 – 2 – 3   4 – 5 – 6   7 – 8 – 9

Nonfiction
History / Biography / Social Science

Naked Economics: Undressing the Dismal Science **
by Charles Wheelan (2003) 388p, ISBN-13: 978-0393324860

Standard book equivalent: 1.5
First published: 2002

Wheelan is an American author and economist. He writes in an irreverent style without resorting to math or jargon to explain economics. In *Naked Economics*, he demystifies basic economic concepts and applies them to everyday life situations, explaining everything from interest rates to free markets to the World Bank and the International Monetary Fund. Wheelan's book focuses on the big picture rather than getting bogged down in the details and is suitable for the lay person with no prior knowledge of economics.

Keywords: American author, economics

Websites:
http://www.nakedeconomics.com/
http://www.blackstarreview.com/rev-0114.html
http://brionews.com/cont/a_naked_economics.php

Rate this book: 1 – 2 – 3   4 – 5 – 6   7 – 8 – 9

Nonfiction
History / Biography / Social Science

Narrative of my captivity among the Sioux Indians. By Fanny Kelly. With a brief account of General Sully's Indian expedition in 1864, bearing upon events occurring in my captivity *
by Michigan Historical Reprint Series (2006) 310p, ISBN-13: 978-1425529444

Standard book equivalent: 1.2
First published: 1871

Kelly (1845 – 1904) was an American pioneer from Kansas. She and her family were part of a small wagon train headed for Idaho when it was attacked by the Sioux in Wyoming. She was taken captive and spent five months traveling with her nomadic captors. Her story provides a glimpse into the harsh life of pioneers and harsher life of Native Americans. Her commentary is balanced though somewhat colored by the prejudices of the times. Particularly sad is the revenge sequences of both the Native Americans and United States military.

Keywords: American author, woman author, American history, biography (women), cross-cultural, Kelly, Midwest, Native American experience, Sioux

Websites:
http://www.hti.umich.edu/cgi/t/text/text-idx?c=moa;idno=ABB5283
http://www.dickshovel.com/sittingbull.html
http://wyoshpo.state.wy.us/trailsdemo/kelly-larimer.htm

Rate this book: 1 – 2 – 3   4 – 5 – 6   7 – 8 – 9

Nonfiction
History / Biography / Social Science

Narrative of the Life of Frederick Douglass
by Frederick Douglass (2004) 96p, ISBN-13: 978-1580495769

Standard book equivalent: 0.4
First published: 1845

Douglass (1818 – 1895) was an American abolitionist and author. He wrote *Narrative* twenty years before the end of the Civil War. His autobiography tells of his struggle to gain freedom and it became a 19th century national bestseller. The publication of his book forced Douglass into exile to England for two years to avoid capture by slave traders. British supporters eventually bought his freedom allowing Douglass to return to the United States and live in freedom.

Keywords: African American author, American author, African American experience, American history, biography (men), Douglas, slavery

Websites:
http://www.history.rochester.edu/class/douglass/home.html
http://www.americaslibrary.gov/cgi-bin/page.cgi/aa/activists/douglass
http://sunsite.berkeley.edu/Literature/Douglass/Autobiography/

Rate this book: 1 – 2 – 3   4 – 5 – 6   7 – 8 – 9

Nonfiction
History / Biography / Social Science

Never Die Easy: The Autobiography of Walter Payton *
by Walter Payton, Don Yaeger (2001) 288p, ISBN-13: 978-0375758218

Standard book equivalent: 1.1
First published: 2001

Payton (1954 – 1999) was an American professional football player. He died of liver cancer at the age of 44. His coach, Mike Ditka, called him the greatest player he had ever seen. Payton was not only a great football player, but he also lived his life commensurate with being a role model for youth. *Never Die Easy* shows him to be a man of compassion. Moreover, commentary from his wife, children, brother, and sister are included.

Keywords: African American author, African American experience, biography (men), cancer, Chicago, Chicago Bears, football, inspirational, Peyton, sports

Websites:
http://www.payton34.com/
http://www.bearshistory.com/lore/walterpayton.aspx
http://slam.canoe.ca/FootballNFLWalterPayton/nov3_bio.html

Rate this book: 1 – 2 – 3   4 – 5 – 6   7 – 8 – 9

Nonfiction
History / Biography / Social Science

News of a Kidnapping
by Gabriel Garcia Marquez, Edith Grossman (translator)
(1998) 304p, ISBN-13: 978-0140269444

Standard book equivalent: 1.2
First published: 1996

Marquez (b. 1928) is a Colombian author and journalist who won the Nobel Prize in Literature in 1982. Marquez is known for his works of fiction, e.g., *One Hundred Years of Solitude* (1967), which are often rich in magical realism. However, this is a nonfiction work, written using his skills as a journalist. It is the story of the kidnapping of ten Colombian citizens by drug lords attempting to avoid capture and extradition to the United States. It takes place during the time of drug lord Pablo Escobar.

Keywords: Colombian author, Colombia, drugs, history, kidnapping, Nobel Prize (Literature)

Websites:
http://www.spikemagazine.com/0404gabrielgarciamarquez.php
http://www.bookrags.com/studyguide-newskidnapping/
http://www.chron.com/cgi-bin/auth/story/content/chronicle/features/books/archives/97/june/marquez.html

Rate this book: 1 – 2 – 3   4 – 5 – 6   7 – 8 – 9

Nonfiction
History / Biography / Social Science

The Only Girl in the Car
by Kathy Dobie (2004) 240p, ISBN-13: 978-0385318839

Standard book equivalent: 0.9
First published: 2003

Dobie is an American author and journalist. *The Only Girl in the Car* is a story that portrays many parents' worst nightmare. It shows how naiveté and youthful indiscretions can result in tragic decisions. This memoir shows how Dobie's awareness that she could attract men and boys simply by being provocative was too much for her to handle. In the end, it led her down a path with costs she did not foresee. Fortunately, she was able to reconstruct her life. However, her writing makes it clear that she could have faced even more serious consequences.

Keywords: American author, woman author, biography (women), coming-of-age

Websites:
http://www.arlindo-correia.com/020703.html
http://dir.salon.com/story/books/review/2003/03/19/dobie/index.html
http://www.npr.org/templates/story/story.php?storyId=1207702

Rate this book: 1 – 2 – 3   4 – 5 – 6   7 – 8 – 9

Nonfiction
History / Biography / Social Science

Ordinary Men: Reserve Police Battalion 101 and the Final Solution in Poland
by Christopher R. Browning (1998) 271p, ISBN-13: 978-0060995065

Standard Book Equivalent: 1.0
First published: 1992

Browning (b. 1944) is an American author and history professor at the University of North Carolina—Chapel Hill. He used archived war crime documents to follow the activity of a 500 man German police battalion in 1942 as they took part in the massacre of Jews in Poland. Browning discovered that at the beginning of 1942, about 75% of all victims of the holocaust were still alive; eleven months later that figure dropped to about 25%. He found that ordinary people acting out of peer pressure, not fanatical racists, were responsible for much of the killing.

Keywords: American Author, Germany, history, holocaust, Jewish experience, Poland, war, WWII

Websites:
http://www.spectacle.org/295/ordinary.html
http://query.nytimes.com/gst/fullpage.html?res=9E0CE3DA123BF931A25757C0A964958260
http://books.guardian.co.uk/reviews/history/0,6121,1222639,00.html

Rate this book: 1 – 2 – 3   4 – 5 – 6   7 – 8 – 9

Nonfiction
History / Biography / Social Science

The Pact *
by Sampson Davis, George Jenkins, Rameck Hunt, and Lisa Frazier Page (2003) 272p, ISBN-13: 978-1573229890

Standard book equivalent: 1.0
First published: 2002

Sampson, Jenkins and Hunt (all b. 1973) are American doctors. They came from a rough section of Newark, New Jersey. They had nothing special going for them except loving mothers (one of whom was a drug user), above-average intelligence, and most importantly, tremendous self-motivation. A recruitment presentation about Seton Hall University rekindled George's dream of becoming a dentist. George convinced his two friends to go to college with him and they made a pact to help each other through to the end.

Keywords: African American author, African American experience, biography (men), friendship, inspirational, medicine

Websites:
http://threedoctorsfoundation.org/
http://www.icommag.com/july-2005/july-page-2.html
http://www.mc.vanderbilt.edu/reporter/index.html?ID=300
6

Rate this book: 1 – 2 – 3   4 – 5 – 6   7 – 8 – 9

Nonfiction
History / Biography / Social Science

Polio: An American Story
by David M. Oshinsky (2006) 368p, ISBN-13: 978-0195307146

Standard book equivalent: 1.5
First published: 2005

Oshinsky is an American author who won a Pulitzer Prize in 2006 for *Polio: An American Story*. Oshinsky's book chronicles the search for a polio vaccine. American communities of all sizes were griped in fear during the 1940s and 1950s. The culprit was polio, an unseen threat that seemed to attack randomly. This book describes the breakthroughs and rivalries, the innovations in reaching out to philanthropists for funding, and the innovations in research. Albert Sabin and Jonas Salk are featured in this story as they competed, using different strategies for vaccine development.

Keywords: American author, disease, history, medicine, polio, Pulitzer Prize, vaccines

Websites:
http://www.utexas.edu/research/profiles/oshinsky.html
http://www.pbs.org/newshour/bb/health/jan-june06/polio_4-24.html
http://hnn.us/roundup/entries/11357.html

Rate this book: 1 – 2 – 3   4 – 5 – 6   7 – 8 – 9

Nonfiction
History / Biography / Social Science

Red Legs and Black Sox: Edd Roush and the Untold Story of the 1919 World Series
by Susan Dellinger (2006) 320p, ISBN-13: 978-1578602292

Standard book equivalent: 1.2
First published: 2006

Dellinger is an American author and psychologist. She is the granddaughter of Edd Roush who played in the 1919 World Series for the Cincinnati Reds and was their star player. That World Series resulted in eight members of the White Sox being banned from the game for life. However unlike other books on the topic, Susan Dellinger focuses on the series from the Cincinnati Reds' perspective. She shows that the story is far more complicated than popularly believed, involving fixes on both teams and corruption by league officials themselves.

Keywords: American author, woman author, American history, baseball, "Black" Sox, Cincinnati Reds, Edd Roush, sports, sports scandal, World Series

Websites:
http://www.redlegsandblacksox.com/index.html
http://www.studio10.tv/category/entertainment/segment.aspx/40640/Red_Legs_and_Black_Sox
http://108mag.typepad.com/extra_bases/2006/08/book_review_red.html

Rate this book: 1 – 2 – 3   4 – 5 – 6   7 – 8 – 9

Nonfiction
History / Biography / Social Science

The Right Stuff
by Tom Wolfe (1980) 367p, ISBN-13: 978-0553381351

Standard book equivalent: 1.4
First published: 1979

Wolfe (b. 1931) is an American author and journalist. He is best known for his book, *The Electric Kool-Aid Acid Test*, a literary journalism novel. *The Right Stuff* is the story of post-World War II American test pilots and the first American astronauts. It is both a candid and entertaining account of their lives and accomplishments. Wolfe puts human faces to the heroes and dispels the myths surrounding Chuck Yeager, John Glenn, Alan Shepard and others. He portrays them honestly, with both their shortcomings and heroics.

Keywords: American author, American history, aviation, pilots, U.S. Air force

Websites:
http://www.tomwolfe.com/RightStuff.html
http://www.bookideas.com/reviews/index.cfm?fuseaction=
    displayReview&id=269
http://www.sci.fi/~fta/the_right_stuff.htm

Rate this book: 1 – 2 – 3   4 – 5 – 6   7 – 8 – 9

Nonfiction
History / Biography / Social Science

Rough Riders
by Theodore Roosevelt (2006) 144p, ISBN-13: 978-0375754760

Standard book equivalent: 0.6
First published: 1899

Roosevelt (1858 – 1919) was the 26th President of the United States. *Rough Riders* tells the story of his exploits during the Spanish-American War. In 1898, Roosevelt put together an assorted regiment—the Rough Riders—of Ivy Leaguers, cowboys, Native Americans, African Americans, and Western Territory land speculators. They trained for four weeks in the Texas desert before heading for Cuba. Roosevelt developed this book from the detailed diary he kept chronicling the entire experience. The *Rough Riders* was published to instant praise and greatly increased his popularity.

Keywords: American author, American history, biography (men), Cuba, Roosevelt, Spanish-American war, war

Websites:
http://www.loc.gov/rr/hispanic/1898/roughriders.html
http://www.bartleby.com/51/
http://www.theodoreroosevelt.org/life/Rough_Riders.htm

Rate this book: 1 – 2 – 3   4 – 5 – 6   7 – 8 – 9

Nonfiction
History / Biography / Social Science

The Sixteenth Round: From Number 1 Contender To #45472
by Rubin Carter (2005) 368p, ISBN-13: 978-0140149296

Standard book equivalent: 1.4
First published: 1974

Carter (b. 1937) is an American former middleweight boxer. *The Sixteenth Round* was written from prison chronicling the events that took him from the world of boxing to his life sentence as the accused murderer of three people in a New Jersey bar. Celebrities such as Joan Baez, Muhammad Ali and Roberta Flack took up his cause protesting his innocence. However, it was the hard work of Canadians Sam Chaiton and Terry Swinton that resulted in the charges finally being dropped.

Keywords: African American author, American author, African American experience, biography (men), boxing, Carter, prison, prejudice, racism, sports

Websites:
http://www.njboxinghof.org/cgi-bin/henryseehof.pl?57
http://www.salon.com/people/feature/1999/12/24/hurricane carter/index.html
http://transcripts.cnn.com/TRANSCRIPTS/0001/21/lkl.00.html

Rate this book: 1 – 2 – 3   4 – 5 – 6   7 – 8 – 9

Nonfiction
History / Biography / Social Science

Some Survived: An Eyewitness Account of the Bataan Death March and the Men Who Lived Through It *
by Manny Lawton, John Toland (2004) 320p, ISBN-13: 978-1565124349

Standard book equivalent: 1.2
First published: 1984

Manny Lawton (b. 1919) was a twenty-three-year-old U.S. Army captain on April 8, 1942 when orders came to surrender to the Japanese forces invading the Philippine Islands. This was after the three-month Battle of Bataan. The next day, the American and Filipino prisoners were forced to make the infamous Bataan Death March. It was a six-day, sixty-mile trek under a sweltering sun. More than ten thousand of the seventy five thousand men died: bayoneted, clubbed, shot, or from exhaustion.

Keywords: American author, American history, Asia, Bataan Death March, biography (men), Japan, Philippines, war, WWII

Websites:
http://history.acusd.edu/gen/st/~ehimchak/death_march.html
http://connections.smsd.org/veterans/baraan_death_march.htm
http://www.nationalmuseum.af.mil/factsheets/factsheet.asp?id=3667

Rate this book: 1 – 2 – 3   4 – 5 – 6   7 – 8 – 9

Nonfiction
History / Biography / Social Science

The Spirit Catches You and You Fall Down
by Anne Fadiman (1998) 352p, ISBN-13: 978-0374525644

Standard book equivalent: 1.4
First published: 1997

Fadiman is an American author. *The Spirit Catches You and You Fall Down* is the story of a Hmong family in Merced, California and their struggles with cross-cultural communication. The language barrier and different cultural perceptions between the Hmong and Americans exacerbate an already difficult medical situation. This book reveals that even casual conversations are loaded with unseen assumptions that can lead to miscommunication. The issue has become so important that some medical schools now make this book required reading.

Keywords: American author, woman author, Asia, California, Cambodia, cross-cultural, disease, medicine

Websites:
http://www.hmongnet.org/publications/spirit_review.html
http://members.aol.com/hmongstudiesjrnl/HSJ-
        v2n2_Yang_Frames.html
http://www.beatrice.com/interviews/fadiman/

Rate this book: 1 – 2 – 3   4 – 5 – 6   7 – 8 – 9

Nonfiction
History / Biography / Social Science

Stolen Harvest: The Hijacking of the Global Food Supply
by Vandana Shiva (2000) 150p, ISBN-13: 978-0896086074

Standard book equivalent: 0.6
First published: 1999

Shiva (b. 1952) is an Indian author, physicist and environmental activist. *Stolen Harvest* contrasts corporate large-scale food production with the small farmer agriculture common in developing economies. She strongly argues that small-holder agriculture is superior to the large agri-business model. A central theme of the book is that biotechnology leads to a vertically integrated industry, which leads to tenant farming. This book's focus is Indian agriculture but much of the argument can, and has, been applied to American agriculture.

Keywords: Indian author, woman author, agriculture, biotechnology, crops, farming, India

Websites:
http://www.greens.org/s-r/23/23-19.html
http://www.vshiva.net/
http://www.mindfully.org/WTO/Stolen-Harvest-Intro.htm

Rate this book: 1 – 2 – 3   4 – 5 – 6   7 – 8 – 9

Nonfiction
History / Biography / Social Science

The Story of My Life *
by Helen Keller (1996) 80p, ISBN-13: 978-0486292496

Standard book equivalent: 0.9
First published: 1902

Keller (1880 – 1968) was a blind and deaf American author. *The Story of My Life* is Keller's memoir of her early life and relationship with her teacher Anne Sullivan. Sullivan, herself partially blind, was suggested as Keller's teacher by Alexander Graham Bell. Keller wrote these memoirs while a student at Radcliffe College and then became the first blind and deaf person to ever receive a college degree. This book was first published when she was only 22 years old. Keller went on to become a famous lecturer, author, Socialist and political activist.

Keywords: American author, woman author, biography (women), blind, Keller

Websites:
http://www.afb.org/MyLife/book.asp?ch=HK-intro
http://www.gutenberg.org/etext/2397
http://www.spartacus.schoolnet.co.uk/USAkeller.htm

Rate this book: 1 – 2 – 3   4 – 5 – 6   7 – 8 – 9

Nonfiction
History / Biography / Social Science

The Supreme Court
by William H. Rehnquist (2002) 336p, ISBN-13: 978-0375708619

Standard book equivalent: 1.3
First published: 1987

Rehnquist (1924 – 2005) was Chief Justice of the United States Supreme Court (1986 – 2005) and noted for his conservative outlook. *The Supreme Court* traces the history of the court beginning with *Marbury v. Madison* (1803) and ending with a chapter about the role of the court in its third century. Although important cases are described, the discussion is kept light enough to maintain the interest of casual readers and important personalities are described. However, it is more concerned with describing the workings of the court than controversial issues such as abortion rights.

Keywords: American author, Supreme Court, American history

Websites:
http://massbar.org/for-attorneys/publications/massachusetts-law-review/2001/v87-n3/book-reviewthe-supreme-court
http://atheism.about.com/od/bookreviews/fr/RhenSupCourt.htm
http://news.bbc.co.uk/1/hi/world/americas/4682369.stm

Rate this book: 1 – 2 – 3   4 – 5 – 6   7 – 8 – 9

Nonfiction
History / Biography / Social Science

The Sweet Science
by A.J. Liebling (2004) 288p, ISBN-13: 978-0374272272

Standard book equivalent: 1.1
First published: 1956

Liebling (1904 – 1963) was an American author and journalist with the *New Yorker*. In this collection of Liebling's classic New Yorker pieces on the "sweet science" of boxing he brings to life the boxing world of a time now past. It covers the period from June 1951 to September 1955. The great events of boxing are presented: Sugar Ray Robinson's dramatic comeback, Rocky Marciano's rise to prominence, and Joe Louis's unfortunate decline. A characteristic of Liebling's writing is the atmosphere he evokes while describing the main event.

Keywords: American author, American history, boxing, sports

Websites:
http://www.doghouseboxing.com/Chhim/Chhim010805.htm
http://journalism.nyu.edu/portfolio/books/book250.html
http://dir.salon.com/story/books/review/2004/09/23/liebling/index.html

Rate this book: 1 – 2 – 3   4 – 5 – 6   7 – 8 – 9

Nonfiction
History / Biography / Social Science

Tell Them Who I Am: The Lives of Homeless Women **
by Elliot Liebow (1995) 368p, ISBN-13: 978-0140241372

Standard book equivalent: 1.4
First published: 1993

Liebow (1925 – 1994) was an American author and ethnographer. He is the author of *Tally's Corner* (1967), a study of black street-corner life that is still read by college students; here, he uses the same participant-observer technique. *Tell Them Who I Am* is the story of several homeless women living in homeless shelters. In 1984 Elliot Liebow learned he had terminal cancer. He left his position to work for the soup kitchens and shelters of a small city outside of Washington, D.C. This book is the result of those experiences and details the trials of homelessness in America.

Keywords: American author, anthropology, homeless, poverty, women, Washington D.C.

Websites:
http://www.bsos.umd.edu/socy/vanneman/socy498/books.html
http://www.takingfive.com/saint_homeless.htm
http://librarydust.typepad.com/library_dust/2004/11/the_shelter_of_.html

Rate this book: 1 – 2 – 3   4 – 5 – 6   7 – 8 – 9

Nonfiction
History / Biography / Social Science

There Are No Children Here: The Story of Two Boys Growing Up in Urban America
by Alex Kotlowitz (1992) 336p, ISBN-13: 978-0385265560

Standard book equivalent: 1.3
First published: 1991

Kotlowitz is an American author and journalist. *There Are No Children Here* is the story of 9 year-old Lafayette and 11 year-old Pharoah Rivers and their family as they struggle to survive in one of Chicago's worst housing projects, Henry Horner Homes. It housed 6,000 residents in 1987, two-thirds of whom were children. This book follows Lafayette and Pharoah for two years giving a human face to poverty and issues of race relations. This book is a good companion to *Tell them Who I Am*.

Keywords: American author, Chicago, children, family, poverty

Websites:
http://alexkotlowitz.com/
http://www.chron.org/tools/viewart.php?artid=759
http://query.nytimes.com/gst/fullpage.html?res=9D0CEED6163FF936A25757C0A967958260

Rate this book: 1 – 2 – 3   4 – 5 – 6   7 – 8 – 9

Nonfiction
History / Biography / Social Science

To Destroy You Is No Loss: The Odyssey of a Cambodian Family
by Joan D. Criddle and Teeda Butt Mam (1998) 293p,
ISBN-13: 978-0963220516

Standard book equivalent: 1.1
First published: 1987

Criddle (b. 1935) is an American author. *To Destroy You Is No Loss* is the story of Teeda, a fourteen year-old Cambodian girl, and her well-to-do family when the ruthless Khmer Rouge came to power; the family was soon reduced to slave-like living. Their plan for survival was basic. Never be the first to ask for help or to do anything. If someone else does it first and it goes well for them, then it is safe for you to do, also. Many people were slaughtered simply for asking the wrong question. This book describes the many horrors they endured.

Keywords: American author, Cambodian author, Asia, biography (women), Cambodia, genocide, history, violence, war

Websites:
http://www.nytimes.com/books/first/p/pran-cambodia.html
http://query.nytimes.com/gst/fullpage.html?res=9B0DE0D
　　C143DF931A3575BC0A961948260
http://query.nytimes.com/gst/fullpage.html?res=9B0DE0D
　　C143DF931A3575BC0A961948260&sec=&pagewant
　　ed=1

Rate this book:　　1 – 2 – 3　　4 – 5 – 6　　7 – 8 – 9

Nonfiction
History / Biography / Social Science

The True History of Chocolate
by Sophie D. Coe, Michael D. Coe (2000) 280p, ISBN-13: 978-0500282298

Standard book equivalent: 1.1
First published: 1996

The Coes, a married couple both of whom were anthropologists with a culinary bent, write about the history of chocolate showing how their subject relates to the cultures it touches. The history stretches back 4000 years, beginning with the Mayans and passing through much intrigue along the way. The Spanish obtained chocolate from the Mayans and brought it to Europe where it was first only used by the nobility. The history in Europe is chronicled and the authors include a chapter on the mass production of chocolate.

Keywords: American author, woman author, anthropology, chocolate, food, history

Websites:
http://news.nationalgeographic.com/news/2002/07/0717_02 0717_TVchocolate.html
http://wwwchem.uwimona.edu.jm:1104/lectures/cocoa.html
http://www.psu.edu/dept/cccrg/bookreview.html

Rate this book: 1 – 2 – 3   4 – 5 – 6   7 – 8 – 9

Nonfiction
History / Biography / Social Science

The Twentieth Train: The True Story of the Ambush of the Death Train to Auschwitz
by Marion Schreiber (2005) 320p, ISBN-13: 978-0802141859

Standard book equivalent: 1.2
First published: 2000

Schreiber (b. 1942) is a German author and journalist. *The Twentieth Train: The True Story of the Ambush of the Death Train to Auschwitz* was previously published as *Silent Rebels*. It tells the story of Belgian resistance fighter Youra Livchitz and two friends who conspired to ambush a Nazi deportation train in Belgium on April 19, 1943. They rescued 17 men and women using only three pairs of pliers, a hurricane lamp covered in red paper and a pistol.

Keywords: German author, Auschwitz, Belgium, Germany, holocaust, Jewish experience, war, WWII

Websites:
http://www.buzzle.com/editorials/6-19-2003-41883.asp
http://www.bookfinder.us/review0/0802141854.html
http://www.largeprintreviews.com/schreiber.html

Rate this book: 1 – 2 – 3   4 – 5 – 6   7 – 8 – 9

Nonfiction
History / Biography / Social Science

Up from Slavery: An Autobiography
by Booker T. Washington (2006) 140p, ISBN-10: 1406923400

Standard book equivalent: 0.5
First published: 1901

Washington (1856 – 1915) was an American educator and author. He was born into slavery in Virginia. Washington worked menial jobs after emancipation while acquiring an education, eventually graduating from a normal school for teachers. He then became the first head of the Tuskegee Institute, and built up its endowment from $2,000 to $12 million. He did this by befriending wealthy industrialists. Washington's emphasis on an industrial education for blacks contrasted with WEB Dubois emphasis on classical education and the two became heated rivals. Overworked, Washington died of a hypertension related disease at the age of 59.

Keywords: African American author, American author, African American experience, biography (men), slavery, Tuskegee, Washington

Websites:
http://www.bookrags.com/ebooks/2376/
http://www.spartacus.schoolnet.co.uk/USAbooker.htm
http://www.pbs.org/wgbh/pages/frontline/shows/race/etc/road.html

Rate this book: 1 – 2 – 3   4 – 5 – 6   7 – 8 – 9

Nonfiction
History / Biography / Social Science

A Vietcong Memoir: An Inside Account of the Vietnam War and Its Aftermath
by Truong Nhu Tang (1986) 368p, ISBN-13: 978-0394743097

Standard book equivalent: 1.4
First published: 1984

Tang was a founder of the National Front for the Liberation of Vietnam (NLF) and the Provisional Revolutionary Government of South Vietnam (PRG) Minister of Justice during the Vietnam War. *A Vietcong Memoir* is about the political developments during the war and a personal look at the lives of those who were fighting against South Vietnam. The author traces his life from being a student in Paris and meeting Ho Chi Minh to founding the NLF to his disillusionment with the North Vietnamese and exile to Paris. The book's focus is on politics and personalities rather than guerrilla tactics.

Keywords: Vietnamese author, Asia, biography (men), Paris, politics, Tang, Vietcong, Vietnam, war

Websites:
http://query.nytimes.com/gst/fullpage.html?res=9D05E4DB1639F935A15756C0A963948260&sec=&pagewanted=print
http://www.pbs.org/battlefieldvietnam/guerrilla/index.html
http://www.spartacus.schoolnet.co.uk/VNnlf.htm

Rate this book: 1 – 2 – 3   4 – 5 – 6   7 – 8 – 9

Nonfiction
History / Biography / Social Science

We Took to the Woods
by Louise Rich (1970) 322p, ISBN-13: 978-0892720163

Standard book equivalent: 1.2
First published: 1942

Rich (1904 – 1991) was an American author. *We Took to the Woods* is the best-selling memoir about the Richs' decision to leave behind the amenities of modern 1930s America and live in a cabin in the wilderness of northern Maine, near Upton along the Rapid River. Their only neighbors were lumberjacks. Rich's book is filled with anecdotes romanticizing the trials and tribulations as well as the joys of chucking it all away and living in the woods. She once spent four years straight without venturing back into civilization. Her summers were busy and winters housebound.

Keywords: American author, woman author, nature, New England, roughing-it

Websites:
http://www.mountainwomanguideservice.com/woodstour.html
http://travel2.nytimes.com/2006/08/04/travel/escapes/04Canoe.html?pagewanted=print
http://dll.umaine.edu/welcome/wom/lewis.htm

Rate this book: 1 – 2 – 3   4 – 5 – 6   7 – 8 – 9

Nonfiction
History / Biography / Social Science

We Wish to Inform You That Tomorrow We Will be Killed with Our Families: Stories from Rwanda
by Philip Gourevitch (1999) 368p, ISBN-13: 978-0312243357

Standard book equivalent: 1.4
First published: 1998

Gourevitch (b. 1961) is an American author, journalist and editor of the *Paris Review*. This is a story of the genocide of Hutus by Tutsis. As many as one million were killed in a 100-day period during 1994. Gourevitch traveled to Rwanda between 1995 and 1998 and interviewed people from a broad range of perspectives: government officials, UN personnel, military men and ordinary citizens. He examines how it happened, why it happened and what the outcome is. The Rwandan genocide was not unique to Africa, nor was it based on longstanding ethnic conflict; Gourevitch shows that it could happen anywhere.

Keywords: American author, Africa, massacre, genocide, Rwanda, war

Websites:
http://www.pbs.org/wgbh/pages/frontline/shows/evil/interviews/gourevitch.html
http://archive.salon.com/special/1998/12/bookawards/21sba_gourevitch.html
http://www.historyplace.com/pointsofview/rwanda.htm

Rate this book: 1 – 2 – 3   4 – 5 – 6   7 – 8 – 9

Nonfiction
History / Biography / Social Science

Why Sinatra Matters
by Pete Hamill (2003) 192p, ISBN-13: 978-0316738866

Standard book equivalent: 0.7
First published: 1998

Hamill (b. 1935) is an American author and journalist. *Why Sinatra Matters* tells the Sinatra story, from someone who knew and admired Sinatra. Hamill draws on years of personal contact and conversations with Sinatra to describe his music and how he came to sing the way he did. Hamill explains the environment that produced Sinatra, including the intense prejudice against Italians. He describes Sinatra's growth and the evolution of his fan base from female bobbysoxers to mature men drawn to the Sinatra's image of toughness, gentleness and loneliness.

Keywords: American author, biography (men), music, Sinatra

Websites:
http://www.jazzsingers.com/PeteHamill/
http://www.jazzsingers.com/Sinatra1/
http://www.icf.org/dec04book.html

Rate this book: 1 – 2 – 3   4 – 5 – 6   7 – 8 – 9

Nonfiction
History / Biography / Social Science

Winterdance: The Fine Madness of Running the Iditarod *
by Gary Paulsen (1995) 272p, ISBN-13: 978-0156001458

Standard book equivalent: 1.0
First published: 1994

Paulsen (b. 1939) is an American author. *Winterdance* is Paulsen's account of his experiences participating in the Iditarod—an 1150-mile winter sled-dog race between Anchorage and Nome. What he lacked in knowledge and experience he made up for in determination. However, the author's life had prepared him for offbeat experiences. He ran away from home at the age of 14 and traveled with a carnival, working as everything from a construction worker to a ranch hand to a sailor. Read as a companion to the *Cruelest Miles*.

Keywords: American author, Alaska, dogs, Iditarod, nature, Nome, sports, winter

Websites:
http://www.randomhouse.com/features/garypaulsen/about.html
http://www.bookpage.com/9711bp/firstperson2.html
http://www.npr.org/templates/story/story.php?storyId=1139537

Rate this book: 1 – 2 – 3   4 – 5 – 6   7 – 8 – 9

Nonfiction
History / Biography / Social Science

With Santa Anna in Texas: A Personal Narrative of the Revolution
by Jose Enrique de la Pena, Carmen Perry (editor) (1997)
237p, ISBN-13: 978-0890965276

Standard book equivalent: 1.0
Written in 1836

de la Pena (1805 – 1841) was an officer in the Mexican military and fought with Santa Ana at the Alamo in 1836. This wartime diary of the Mexican army officer, written several months after the battle, includes a description of the fall of the Alamo. The diary contradicts popular legend by stating that Davy Crockett was captured and subsequently executed. The author was an anti-Santa Ana agitator and found himself in and out of prison beginning in 1838.

Keywords: Mexican author, Alamo, American history, biography (men), history, Mexico, Santa Ana

Websites:
http://www.chapala.com/chapala/may2000.htm
http://www.thealamo.org/myths.html
http://www.cah.utexas.edu/exhibits/Pena/translation.html

Rate this book: 1 – 2 – 3   4 – 5 – 6   7 – 8 – 9

Nonfiction
History / Biography / Social Science

The Woman Warrior: Memoirs of a Girlhood Among Ghosts
by Maxine Hong Kingston (1989) 224p, ISBN-13: 978-0679721888

Standard book equivalent: 0.9
First published: 1976

Kingston (b. 1940) is an American writer of Chinese ancestry. *The Woman Warrior* is about growing up Chinese American in Stockton, California. The memoirs reveal the conflict immigrants to America face between their old culture and the new one in which they find themselves. Kingston retells the lessons of her mother's compelling "talk-story" tales of China. These are stories that remind the listener girls are worthless, tradition is held high, and only a strong, clever woman can succeed. The ghost in the title refers both to White Americans and the ghosts of past ancestors.

Keywords: American author, woman author, assimilation, China, biography (women), cross-cultural, feminism, immigrants, women

Websites:
http://www.cliffsnotes.com/WileyCDA/LitNote/id-162.html
http://www.edwardsly.com/kingsto.htm
http://www.berkeley.edu/news/media/releases/97legacy/09_29_97b.html

Rate this book: 1 – 2 – 3   4 – 5 – 6   7 – 8 – 9

Nonfiction
History / Biography / Social Science

Worse than Slavery: Parchman Farm and the Ordeal of Jim Crow Justice **
by David M. Oshinsky (1997) 320p, ISBN-13: 978-0684830957

Standard book equivalent: 1.2
First published: 1996

Oshinsky is an American author who won a Pulitzer Prize in 2006 for *Polio: An American Story*. *Worse than Slavery* is a study of crime and punishment in America in the context of a racially segregated society. It focuses on Parchman Penitentiary located in Mississippi. He places the story in historical context by tracing the penitentiary's development from a labor farm of the Old South up to its present status. Read *Down on Parchman* for a contrasting viewpoint.

Keywords: American author, American history, Parchman Farm, poverty, Pulitzer Prize, prison, racism, the South

Websites:
http://www.washingtonpost.com/wp-srv/style/longterm/books/chap1/worsethanslavery.htm
http://www.h-net.org/reviews/showrev.cgi?path=22500870194459
http://www.nytimes.com/books/97/05/25/nnp/19465.html

Rate this book: 1 – 2 – 3   4 – 5 – 6   7 – 8 – 9

Nonfiction
History / Biography / Social Science

Zimmermann Telegram
by Barbara W. Tuchman (2001) 256p, ISBN-13: 978-1842122792

Standard book equivalent: 1.0
First published: 1958

Tuchman (1912 – 1989) was an American author and historian. The Zimmermann Telegram was a message sent by the German Foreign Minister to the Mexican Government in early 1917. It was an attempt to make Mexico a German ally in the event of the US entering World War I on the side of the Allies. The motivating factor was the possibility of Mexico reclaiming Texas, New Mexico, and Arizona. However, British Intelligence intercepted and decoded the telegram. They made certain that the US government and public heard about it.

Keywords: American author, woman author, American history, Germany, Mexico, war, WWI, Zimmerman

Websites:
http://www.kirjasto.sci.fi/tuchman.htm
http://www.pittstate.edu/services/scied/Staff/Shoberg/History/wwi/zimmer.htm
http://ergo-sum.us/Members/cmcurtin/zimtel/view

Rate this book: 1 – 2 – 3   4 – 5 – 6   7 – 8 – 9

NONFICTION

Science / Math

Nonfiction
Science / Math

The Antibiotic Paradox: How the Misuse of Antibiotics Destroys Their Curative Powers **
by Stuart B. Levy (2002) 296p, ISBN-13: 978-0738204406

Standard book equivalent: 1.1
First published: 1992

Levy is an American physician and professor of medicine and molecular genetics at Tufts University. *The Antibiotic Paradox* combines the history of antibiotic discovery and the mechanisms of microbial resistance with a discussion of how antibiotic abuse destroys their effectiveness. Although challenging reading, the writing is clear and free of jargon making it suitable for general readers. The book begins with the early history of antibiotic development and then discusses microorganisms, genetic resistance, and the use of antibiotics in agriculture. He concludes the book with a chapter on future prospects for antibiotics.

Keywords: American author, antibiotics, biology, germs, history, medicine, science

Websites:
http://www.medscape.com/viewarticle/472308
http://healthresources.caremark.com/topic/brantibiotic
http://www.journals.uchicago.edu/CID/journal/issues/v36n2/021002/021002.html

Rate this book: 1 – 2 – 3   4 – 5 – 6   7 – 8 – 9

Nonfiction
Science / Math

At the Fringes of Science: With a New Epilogue **
by Michael W. Friedlander (1998) 202p, ISBN-13: 978-0813390604

Standard book equivalent: 0.8
First published: 1998

Friedlander is an American professor of physics at Washington University in St Louis. Where does science end and pseudo-science begin? Friedlander answers this question with a discussion of what science is and how to identify 'good science'. His examples begin with the infamous cold-fusion experiments and then he covers such far-ranging topics as ESP, creationism, and medical fraud. He demonstrates the communal nature of science and discusses the strengths and weaknesses that come with that nature. He also explains the workings of scientific journals and conferences where science gets formulated for public consumption.

Keywords: American author, science

Websites:
http://www.uow.edu.au/arts/sts/bmartin/pubs/95BRmetascience.html
http://members.aol.com/steamdoc/writings/friedlander95.html
http://www.findarticles.com/p/articles/mi_m2843/is_n1_v20/ai_17849151

Rate this book: 1 – 2 – 3   4 – 5 – 6   7 – 8 – 9

Nonfiction
Science / Math

Blue Frontier: Saving America's Living Seas
by David Helvarg (2006) 333p, ISBN-13: 978-1578051571

Standard book equivalent: 1.3
First published: 2001

Helvarg (b. 1951) is an American journalist and environmental activist. *Blue Frontier* won the 2001 *LA Times* Book of the Year Award. Helvarg's book is an expedition to what he calls America's last great frontier— the ocean wilderness. America lays claim to a 200-mile Exclusive Economic Zone of ocean along its coastline. That area is larger than the area occupied by the continental United States. Helvarg's writing is lively and humorous as he describes both the animals and peoples that live, work and play in this zone.

Keywords: American author, ecology, environment, nature, Pacific Ocean, sea

Websites:
http://ucsdnews.ucsd.edu/newsrel/science/sio_helvarg06.asp
http://www.latimes.com/news/opinion/commentary/la-op-catastrophe11sep11,0,3174876.story?coll=la-news-comment-opinions
http://www.bluefront.org/aboutus/aboutus.php?recordID=1

Rate this book: 1 – 2 – 3   4 – 5 – 6   7 – 8 – 9

Nonfiction
Science / Math

The Botany of Desire: A Plant's-Eye View of the World
by Michael Pollan (2001) 304p, ISBN-13: 978-0375760396

Standard book equivalent: 1.2
First published: 2001

Pollan (b. 1955) is an American author and journalist. *The Botany of Desire* traces the evolution of apples, tulips, cannabis and potatoes —in four chapters titled sweetness, beauty, intoxication and control—to demonstrate the complex, reciprocal relationships between humans and the natural world. His thesis is that it is not easy to say whether humans exploit plants or the other way around. After all, many species of plants get what they need only from human intervention—offspring to populate future generations.

Keywords: American author, apples, biology, botany, cannabis, potatoes, science, tulips

Websites:
http://www.pbs.org/newshour/conversation/jan-june01/botany_06-29.html
http://www.grist.org/news/maindish/2006/05/31/roberts/
http://michaelpollan.com/

Rate this book: 1 – 2 – 3   4 – 5 – 6   7 – 8 – 9

Nonfiction
Science / Math

A Briefer History of Time
by Stephen Hawking and Leonard Mlodinow (1999) 171p,
ISBN-13: 978-0716733898

Standard book equivalent: 0.7
First published: 2005

Hawking (b. 1942) is a British theoretical physicist and author, and Mlodinow (b. 1954) is an American physicist and author. This is an updated version of Hawking's *A Brief History of Time* (1988) that is rewritten to reach a wider audience. It is a summary of space-time physics written for non-scientific readers. It includes discussions about the mysterious dark matter of the universe, quantum mechanics and string theory. It also has a chapter on time travel, which the authors deem unlikely.

Keywords: British author, physics, science, time

Websites:
http://www.hawking.org.uk/
http://news.bbc.co.uk/1/hi/sci/tech/1599719.stm
http://books.guardian.co.uk/digestedread/story/0,6550,1579381,00.html

Rate this book: 1 – 2 – 3   4 – 5 – 6   7 – 8 – 9

Nonfiction
Science / Math

The Cartoon Guide to Genetics
by Larry Gonick, Mark Wheelis (1991) 224p, ISBN-13: 978-0062730992

Standard book equivalent: 0.9
First published: 1983

Gonick (b. 1946) is an American author and cartoonist, and Wheelis is a lecturer in microbiology at the University of California—Davis. *The Cartoon Guide to Genetics* covers the history of genetics and selective breeding, Mendelian genetics, molecular biology, and the basics of genetic engineering. Gonick's drawings are in true comic book form, ranging from a sketch of ribosomes in action to zany drawings of "personified peas" and "freakin' fruit flies". It is written in one piece without chapters or section breaks.

Keywords: American author, biology, DNA, genetics, graphic book, science

Websites:
http://larrygonick.com/
http://bancroft.berkeley.edu/Exhibits/Biotech/cartoon.html
http://www-tech.mit.edu/V116/N4/gonick.4n.html

Rate this book: 1 – 2 – 3   4 – 5 – 6   7 – 8 – 9

Nonfiction
Science / Math

Cats Are Not Peas: A Calico History of Genetics
by Laura L. Gould (1996) 228p, ISBN-13: 978-0387947969

Standard book equivalent: 0.9
First published: 1996

Gould is an American author. *Cats Are Not Peas* is a journey into genetics and its history. Gould began the journey with her companion, a cat named George. George was definitely male and definitely calico. But calico cats are always female. Gould tracks down why George is the exception. It turns out that calicos are better described as probably female, with a probability of male calicos being very small but definite. George happens to have an extra chromosome that enables him to have the calico coat color. It's a great genetics investigation by a non-geneticist.

Keywords: American author, woman author, biology, cats, DNA, genetics, science

Websites:
http://www.genomenewsnetwork.org/articles/10_00/cats_not_peas_review.php
http://www.newscientist.com/article/mg15220596.000-review--mendel-and-the-mixed-up-moggie.html
http://www.thecatsite.com/Snips/200/Calico-Cats.html

Rate this book: 1 – 2 – 3   4 – 5 – 6   7 – 8 – 9

Nonfiction
Science / Math

Complications: A Surgeon's Notes on an Imperfect Science
by Atul Gawande (2003) 288p, ISBN-13: 978-0312421700

Standard book equivalent: 1.1
First published: 2002

Gawande (b. 1965) is an American physician and author. *Complications* reveals medicine as an endeavor that is both complex and human. Gawande—a surgical resident, staff writer for the *New Yorker*, and former Rhodes Scholar—describes how the fallibility of medical practitioners drives them to constantly update their knowledge and skills. Gawande provides tense accounts of medical ordeals, physician's anxieties and the constant concern about burnout. He also covers medical mysteries, for example, his chapter titled "Full Moon Friday the Thirteenth."

Keywords: American author, biography (men), medicine, science

Websites:
http://www.hsph.harvard.edu/faculty/AtulGawande.html
http://www.popmatters.com/books/reviews/c/complications.shtml
http://www.slate.com/id/3729/

Rate this book: 1 – 2 – 3   4 – 5 – 6   7 – 8 – 9

Nonfiction
Science / Math

Damned Lies and Statistics: Untangling Numbers from the Media, Politicians, and Activists
by Joel Best (2001) 196p, ISBN-13: 978-0520228658

Standard book equivalent: 0.8
First published: 2001

Best is Professor and Chair of Sociology and Criminal Justice at the University of Delaware. *Damned Lies and Statistics* demonstrates how statistics are frequently misused and misunderstood, often to the point of reversing the direction of arguments. Has the number of children killed by guns doubled each year since 1950? Are 150,000 young American women dying each year from anorexia? Best answers with a clear "no" to both of these questions. He also shows why it is that many people would mistakenly answer "yes".

Keywords: American author, science, statistics

Websites:
http://www.udel.edu/soc/best.htm
http://chronicle.com/free/v47/i34/34b00701.htm
http://www.issues.org/18.2/br_moore.html

Rate this book:　　1 – 2 – 3　　4 – 5 – 6　　7 – 8 – 9

Nonfiction
Science / Math

The Double Helix: A Personal Account of the Discovery of the Structure of DNA
by James D. Watson (2001) 256p, ISBN-13: 978-0743216302

Standard book equivalent: 1.0
First published: 1968

Watson (b. 1928) is an American author and winner of the 1962 Nobel Prize in Physiology or Medicine. *The Double Helix* is about Watson's and Crick's discovery of the structure of DNA, and the personalities and rivalries behind the race to be the first to correctly publish it. Along the way Watson describes how science is done. Richard Feynman said of *The Double Helix*, "The history of a scientific endeavor, a true detective story that leaves the reader breathless from beginning to end."

Keywords: American author, biology, DNA, genetics, Nobel Prize (Physiology or Medicine), science

Websites:
http://www.brown.edu/Courses/BI0020_Miller/dh/guide.html
http://www.americanscientist.org/template/BookReviewTypeDetail/assetid/21921;jsessionid=aaa5LVF0
http://educ.queensu.ca/~science/main/profdev/books/PDBRJK.htm

Rate this book: 1 – 2 – 3   4 – 5 – 6   7 – 8 – 9

Nonfiction
Science / Math

Dr. Tatiana's Sex Advice to All Creation: the Definitive Guide to the Evolutionary Biology of Sex
by Olivia Judson (2003) 320p, ISBN-13: 978-0805063325

Standard book equivalent: 1.2
First published: 2002

Judson is a British author, journalist and evolutionary biologist at the Imperial College of London. *Dr. Tatiana's Sex Advice* is written in the style of a newspaper's advice column dealing with questions of sex (reproductive biology) for all manner of creatures great and small. It is an utterly painless way to learn some interesting biology. Among the critters 'writing-in' are manatees, honeybees, spiders, black vultures, green spoon worms, hyenas, and slime molds. Who knew the Animal Kingdom was in such dire need?

Keywords: British author, woman author, biology, sex

Websites:
http://www.drtatiana.com/
http://www.stanfordalumni.org/news/magazine/2005/janfeb/show/tatiana.html
http://www.nytimes.com/2005/01/23/opinion/23judson.html?ex=1264222800&en=703f9e273756ce4c&ei=5088&partner=rssnyt

Rate this book: 1 – 2 – 3   4 – 5 – 6   7 – 8 – 9

Nonfiction
Science / Math

Emotional Intelligence: 10th Anniversary Edition; Why It Can Matter More Than IQ **
by Daniel Goleman (2005) 384p, ISBN-13: 978-0553383713

Standard book equivalent: 1.5
First published: 1995

Goleman (b. 1946) is an American author and psychologist. *Emotional Intelligence* is divided into five sections. The first section, "The Emotional Brain", describes brain anatomy. The second section, "The Nature of Emotional Intelligence", defines emotional intelligence and illustrates the concept's usefulness. "Emotional Intelligence Applied" describes how to manage emotions and offers examples of such management in medicine. "Windows of Opportunity" is the fourth section and is about development issues and what happens when emotional development is interrupted. The fifth section, "Emotional Literacy", is an argument on the importance of understanding the role emotions play in our lives.

Keywords: American author, psychology

Websites:
http://www.danielgoleman.info/bio.html
http://www.shareguide.com/Goleman.html
http://www.americanscientist.org/template/InterviewTypeD
    etail/assetid/30504;jsessionid=aaa5LVF0

Rate this book: 1 – 2 – 3   4 – 5 – 6   7 – 8 – 9

Nonfiction
Science / Math

Five Quarts: A Personal and Natural History of Blood by Bill Hayes (2006) 304p, ISBN-13: 978-0345456885

Standard book equivalent: 1.2
First published: 2006

Hayes is an American author. *Five Quarts*, written in a manner suitable for general readers, is all about the five quarts of blood that the average human possesses. It is a personal look at an often misunderstood subject that starts with the author getting a cut. The topics cover leeches, bloodletting, and the inheritance of hemophilia with the extended family of royalty as guides. Hayes writes about blood banks and the AIDS epidemic. "Five quarts run through each of us, along some sixty thousand miles of arteries, veins, and capillaries."–from *Five Quarts*.

Keywords: American author, biology, blood, medicine, science

Websites:
http://www.sfbaytimes.com/index.php?sec=article&article_id=3433
http://www.enotalone.com/article/4660.html
http://www.sfgate.com/cgi-bin/article.cgi?file=/chronicle/archive/2005/01/11/DDGE5AN3SU1.DTL&type=books

Rate this book: 1 – 2 – 3   4 – 5 – 6   7 – 8 – 9

Nonfiction
Science / Math

The Genie in the Bottle: 64 All New Commentaries on the Fascinating Chemistry of Everyday Life *
by Joe Schwarcz (2002) 320p, ISBN-13: 978-0805071382

Standard book equivalent: 1.2
First published: 2001

Schwarcz is a Canadian author and professor of chemistry at McGill University. *The Genie in the Bottle* contains sixty-four short accounts of the sometimes humorous—and sometimes disastrous—applications of chemistry to everyday life. The chemistry of health and food is emphasized. The essays touch on a broad range of topics: drain cleaners, candies, stinky feet, spoon-bending, and the use of Thalidomide to treat morning sickness in pregnant women. However, all of the essays have in common the importance of using sound scientific reasoning in drawing conclusions.

Keywords: Canadian author, chemistry, science

Websites:
http://www.oss.mcgill.ca/schwarcz.php
http://www.umanitoba.ca/outreach/cm/vol10/no14/fascinatingchemistry.html
http://www.nist.gov/public_affairs/bestpractices/Schwarcz.htm

Rate this book: 1 – 2 – 3   4 – 5 – 6   7 – 8 – 9

Nonfiction
Science / Math

Gifted Hands: The Ben Carson Story *
by Ben Carson, Cecil Murphey (1996) 224p, ISBN-13: 978-0310214694

Standard book equivalent: 0.9
First published: 1996

Carson (b. 1951) is an American author and physician. *Gifted Hands* is the autobiography of a man who is one of today's leading neurosurgeons. However, he started out as a kid with low self-esteem who thought of himself as stupid. His autobiography chronicles the prejudice, negative peer pressure, and politics in getting a job. His sense of humor, faith in God, patience, and his belief in the work ethic are what carried him through. The last chapter gives recommendations to students on how to succeed in life.

Keywords: African American author, American author, biography (men), Carson, inspirational, medicine, science

Websites:
http://www.drbencarson.com/
http://www.cnn.com/SPECIALS/2001/americasbest/science.medicine/pro.bcarson.html
http://www.adventistreview.org/2002-1545/story1.html

Rate this book: 1 – 2 – 3   4 – 5 – 6   7 – 8 – 9

Nonfiction
Science / Math

Gorillas in the Mist
by Dian Fossey (2000) 352p, ISBN-13: 978-0618083602

Standard book equivalent: 1.4
First published: 1983

Fossey (1932 – 1985) was an American primatologist and author. *Gorillas in the Mist* is her memoir about researching mountain gorillas in the wild. The book covers the years 1963 through 1983, and gives us an intimate look into her life and her interactions with gorillas in the mountain forests of Rwanda. Known for her vigilant pursuit of poachers, Dr. Fossey made many enemies. She took advantage of the fact that the local people thought she was a witch and she played that role while interrogating poachers. Dr. Fossey was murdered in her hut on December 27, 1985.

Keywords: American author, woman author, biology, gorillas, nature, primates, Rwanda, science

Websites:
http://www.mnsu.edu/emuseum/information/biography/fghij/fossey_dian.html
http://www.dian-fossey.com/
http://www.gorillas.org/home/

Rate this book:　　1 – 2 – 3　　4 – 5 – 6　　7 – 8 – 9

Nonfiction
Science / Math

Heart of the Sound: An Alaskan Paradise Found and Nearly Lost
by Marybeth Holleman (2004) 210p, ISBN-13: 978-0874807912

Standard book equivalent: 0.8
First published: 2004

Holleman is an American author and conservationist. *Heart of the Sound* is the memoir of Holleman's relationship with Prince William Sound. It begins with her first experience of the sound by kayak in 1986 and continues through the Exxon Valdez oil spill tragedy in 1989 to the ongoing restoration process. It is a reflection on the beauty of nature and on her life's story. It is also a wakeup call to not accept the inevitability of environmental degradation.

Keywords: American author, woman author, Alaska, biology, conservation, environment, nature, Prince William Sound, science

Websites:
http://www.marybethholleman.com/
http://www.commondreams.org/views04/0322-04.htm
http://www.tidepool.org/original_content.cfm?articleid=111545

Rate this book: 1 – 2 – 3   4 – 5 – 6   7 – 8 – 9

Nonfiction
Science / Math

Hydrogen: The Essential Element **
by John S. Rigden (2003) 288p, ISBN-13: 978-0674012523

Standard book equivalent: 1.1
First published: 2002

Rigden is an American author and professor of physics at Washington University in St. Louis. The author uses the element Hydrogen to describe the developments of 20th century physics. It is written as twenty-three essays that begin with the creation of protons in the big bang and end with an essay that describes Positronium (an association between an electron and a 'positive electron'). Some of the material is challenging, but anyone with a good grasp of high school chemistry (especially atomic theory) will be able to get through those sections.

Keywords: American author, chemistry, hydrogen, physics, science

Websites:
http://www.aip.org/history/historymatters/rigden.htm
http://www.physicstoday.org/vol-56/iss-3/p69b.html
http://physicsweb.org/articles/review/16/6/1

Rate this book: 1 – 2 – 3   4 – 5 – 6   7 – 8 – 9

Nonfiction
Science / Math

In the Shadow of Man
by Jane Goodall (2000) 304p, ISBN-13: 978-0618056767

Standard book equivalent: 1.2
First published: 1971

Goodall (b. 1934) is a British primatologist and author. *In the Shadow of Man* describes Goodall's experiences studying chimpanzees in the Gombe Wildlife Reserve of Tanzania. The book is part memoir in that it begins with her first few days in Africa. It then focuses on her research with chimpanzees, describing her observations about their behavior and personalities as she follows their lives across multiple generations. One of her innovations is to provide names, instead of the conventional number identifications, for the chimpanzees. This increases the book's readability and makes it much more entertaining.

Keywords: British author, woman author, biology, chimpanzees, primates, nature, science

Websites:
http://www.janegoodall.org/
http://www.webster.edu/~woolflm/janegoodall.html
http://ecopsychology.athabascau.ca/0996/ecogoodall.html

Rate this book: 1 – 2 – 3   4 – 5 – 6   7 – 8 – 9

Nonfiction
Science / Math

Innumeracy: Mathematical Illiteracy and Its Consequences by John Allen Paulos (2001) 208p, ISBN-13: 978-0809058402

Standard book equivalent: 0.8
First published: 1989

Paulos is an American author and professor of mathematics at Temple University. *Innumeracy* is about mathematical illiteracy and examines its effects on personal decisions, government policies, and the acceptance of pseudoscience. Paulos states as a motivating factor for writing the book, "I'm distressed by a society which depends so completely on mathematics and science and yet seems too indifferent to the innumeracy and scientific illiteracy of so many of its citizens." His writing is filled with humorous and sometimes sarcastic barbs. Suggested companion books: *At the Fringes of Science* and *Damned Lies and Statistics*.

Keywords: American author, innumeracy, math, science

Websites:
http://www.math.temple.edu/~paulos/
http://www.complete-review.com/reviews/maths/paulosja.htm
http://abcnews.go.com/Technology/WhosCounting/story?id=997688

Rate this book: 1 – 2 – 3   4 – 5 – 6   7 – 8 – 9

Nonfiction
Science / Math

The Journey of Man: A Genetic Odyssey **
by Spencer Wells (2004) 240p, ISBN-13: 978-0812971460

Standard book equivalent: 0.9
First published: 2003

Wells (b. 1969) is an American author, geneticist and anthropologist. *The Journey of Man* describes how genetics can be used to trace the history of mankind. It is based on the facts that mitochondrial DNA can be traced through successive mother-daughter lines of inheritance, and that the same can be done for father-son lines using the Y-chromosome. These facts coupled with knowledge about mutation rates help us to unveil when and where early man emigrated out of Africa. Wells provides the details to understand how biology allows us to draw these inferences and describes some startling conclusions.

Keywords: American author, anthropology, biology, genetics, science

Websites:
http://www.pupress.princeton.edu/chapters/i7442.html
http://www.npr.org/templates/story/story.php?storyId=4597357
http://books.guardian.co.uk/reviews/scienceandnature/0,6121,845454,00.html

Rate this book: 1 – 2 – 3   4 – 5 – 6   7 – 8 – 9

Nonfiction
Science / Math

Last Breath: The Limits of Adventure
by Peter Stark, (2003) 320p, ISBN-13: 978-0330486972

Standard book equivalent: 1.2
First published: 2001

Stark is an American author and writer for *Outside* magazine. *Last Breath* is about extreme sports and why people participate in them. Each of its eleven chapters is a short story. They are based on fictional characters who each suffer a different medical crisis while participating in a wilderness/adventure activity. The crises include hypothermia, heatstroke, mountain sickness, scurvy, cerebral malaria and more. Stark delves into the characters thoughts as they come close to death and describes the physiology—superficially—that comes into play.

Keywords: American author, anthropology, medicine, science, sports

Websites:
http://www.bookreporter.com/authors/au-stark-peter.asp
http://www.booknoise.net/lastbreath/reviews/index.html
http://www.wemjournal.org/wmsonline/?request=get-document&issn=1080-6032&volume=013&issue=02&page=0178

Rate this book: 1 – 2 – 3   4 – 5 – 6   7 – 8 – 9

Nonfiction
Science / Math

The Lives of a Cell **
by Lewis Thomas (1978) 160p, ISBN-13: 978-0140047431

Standard book equivalent: 0.6
First published: 1973

Thomas (1913 – 1993) was an American physician and author who won the 1974 National Book Award for *The Lives of a Cell*. It originally appeared as a series of essays in the *New England Journal of Medicine* that explore various aspects of biology. The twenty essays examine the complex interdependence of all things in a world of hidden relationships with topics that range from computers, to language, and the possibilities of extra-terrestrial life. Although the essays are meant for the general reader, they do require an understanding of high school science.

Keywords: American author, biology, medicine, science

Websites:
http://www.vcu.edu/engweb/LewisThomas.htm
http://www.ias.ac.in/resonance/Feb2000/pdf/Feb2000Book
    Reviews.pdf
http://en.wikipedia.org/wiki/Lewis_Thomas

Rate this book: 1 – 2 – 3   4 – 5 – 6   7 – 8 – 9

Nonfiction
Science / Math

Looking for Earths: The Race to Find New Solar Systems
by Alan Boss (2000) 240p, ISBN-13: 978-0471379119

Standard book equivalent: 0.9
First published: 1998

Boss (b. 1951) is an American astrophysicist at the Carnegie Institution of Washington. *Looking for Earths* is a history of astronomers' quest to find planets outside this solar system (i.e. extrasolar planets or exoplanets). The first exoplanet was discovered in 1963. More than 200 have been discovered as of 2006. Those exoplanets that are similar to earth in size, density and distance from their star offer the best opportunities of finding an environment suitable for sustaining life. This book balances descriptions of science with politics and is geared towards general readers.

Keywords: American author, astronomy, exoplanets, science, solar system, space

Websites:
http://www.amazings.com/sbb/reviews/review0327.html
http://www.dtm.ciw.edu/boss/
http://findarticles.com/p/articles/mi_m1134/is_1_108/ai_53682797
http://exoplanets.org/

Rate this book: 1 – 2 – 3   4 – 5 – 6   7 – 8 – 9

Nonfiction
Science / Math

Lords of the Harvest: Biotech, Big Money, and the Future of Food
by Daniel Charles (2002) 368p, ISBN-13: 978-0738207735

Standard book equivalent: 1.4
First published: 2001

Charles is an American author and radio producer. He is also a former technology correspondent for National Public Radio and Washington correspondent for New Scientist. *Lords of the Harvest* is an even-handed account of the history of genetic engineering in crops starting from the early 1980s. It covers the surprise appearance of Starlink genes in taco shells, the Flavr Savr tomato, and the Terminator gene that would produce crops with sterile seeds. It also takes a close look at the strategy Monsanto followed during this period as it committed to embracing biotechnology.

Keywords: American author, agriculture, biology, biotechnology, crops, food, science

Websites:
http://www.npr.org/templates/story/story.php?storyId=2100329
http://danielcharles.com/
http://www.techsoc.com/harvest.htm

Rate this book: 1 – 2 – 3   4 – 5 – 6   7 – 8 – 9

Nonfiction
Science / Math

The Man Who Mistook His Wife for a Hat: And Other Clinical Tales
by Oliver Sacks (1998) 256p, ISBN-13: 978-0684853949

Standard book equivalent: 1.0
First published: 1985

Sacks (b. 1933) is an English-born American physician and author. A neurologist by training, in *The Man Who Mistook His Wife for a Hat* Sacks presents a series of clinical anecdotes from his medical practice. The book has four sections: "losses" of neurological function; "excesses"; "transports" involving reminiscence, altered perception, and imagination; and "the simple", or the world of the severely learning disabled. It is written in an informal style making it especially easy to sympathize with the patients and imagine what their lives must be like.

Keywords: British author, biology, medicine, mental illness, neurology, science

Websites:
http://www.oliversacks.com/
http://www.fortunecity.com/emachines/e11/86/duncan3.html
http://www.npr.org/programs/wesat/features/2001/sacks/011110.sacks.html

Rate this book: 1 – 2 – 3   4 – 5 – 6   7 – 8 – 9

Nonfiction
Science / Math

Mathematics, Magic and Mystery (Cards, Coins, and Other Magic)
by Martin Gardner (1956) 176p, ISBN-13: 978-0486203355

Standard book equivalent: 0.7
First published: 1956

Gardner (b. 1914) is an American mathematician and author. *Mathematics, Magic and Mystery* explains the math behind mystifying card tricks, stage "mind reading", coin and match tricks, counting out games, geometric dissections, and many more. There are nine chapters including three chapters on card tricks, a chapter of tricks with objects such as dice, and a chapter titled "Magic with Pure Numbers". He briefly explains basic probability, sets, and theory of numbers. He also explains how to do more than 400 tricks, guaranteed to work, to impress your family and friends.

Keywords: American author, card tricks, magic tricks, math, science

Websites:
http://www.csicop.org/si/9803/gardner.html
http://www.ams.org/notices/200506/fea-gardner.pdf
http://www.bookrags.com/Martin_Gardner

Rate this book: 1 – 2 – 3   4 – 5 – 6   7 – 8 – 9

Nonfiction
Science / Math

The Naked Ape
by Desmond Morris (1999) 256p, ISBN-13: 978-0385334303

Standard book equivalent: 1.0
First published: 1967

Morris (b. 1928) is a British author and zoologist. In *The Naked Ape*, Morris examines human behaviors (for example, child-rearing, exploratory habits, feeding, fighting, nonverbal communication, sex, and more) as he would the behavior of any primate. Relating humans to other primates emphasized the place of *Homo sapiens* in the Animal Kingdom, which made the book a bit controversial in 1967. The title refers to the fact that of the 193 primate species, man is the only one not covered with hair.

Keywords: American author, anthropology, primates

Websites:
http://www.desmond-morris.com/
http://news.bbc.co.uk/onthisday/hi/dates/stories/october/12/newsid_3116000/3116329.stm
http://www.bookrags.com/wiki/Desmond_Morris

Rate this book: 1 – 2 – 3   4 – 5 – 6   7 – 8 – 9

Nonfiction
Science / Math

A Natural History of the Senses
by Diane Ackerman (1991) 352p, ISBN-13: 978-0679735663

Standard book equivalent: 1.4
First published: 1990

Ackerman (b. 1948) is an American poet and naturalist. *A Natural History of the Senses* blends literature, biology, anthropology, history, art, and natural science into an investigation of the five senses. It is divided into five parts, one for each sense, and includes such stories as the evolution of the kiss, and the chemistry of pain. Ackerman states about our senses, "We live on the leash of our senses. They define the edges of consciousness."

Keywords: American author, woman author, anthropology, biology, science, senses

Websites:
http://www.dianeackerman.com/
http://www.januarymagazine.com/profiles/ackerman.html
http://www.nytimes.com/books/97/03/02/reviews/ackerman-senses.html?_r=1&oref=slogin

Rate this book: 1 – 2 – 3   4 – 5 – 6   7 – 8 – 9

Nonfiction
Science / Math

The New World of Mr. Tompkins **
by George Gamow, Russell Stannard (editor), (2001) 270p,
ISBN-13: 978-0521639927

Standard book equivalent: 1.0
First published: 1965

Gamow (1904 – 1968) was a Ukrainian-born American physicist and author. *Mr. Tompkins in Paperback* is a revision of *Mr. Tompkins in Wonderland* (1940) and *Mr. Tompkins Explores the Atom* (1945). *The New World of Mr. Tompkins* adds four new chapters to that text. Mr. Tompkins is a fictional bank clerk whose whimsical dreams and adventures lead him into a world inside the atom. Written in nineteen chapters, it provides an entertaining explanation of the central concepts of modern physics, including: atomic structure, relativity, quantum theory, fusion and fission.

Keywords: Ukrainian author, physics, science, time

Websites:
http://www.gwu.edu/~physics/gwmageh.htm
http://www.aps.org/units/fed/newsletters/fall2003/HobsonBookRev.cfm
http://www.physicstoday.org/pt/vol-54/iss-5/pdf/vol53no6p57.pdf

Rate this book: 1 – 2 – 3   4 – 5 – 6   7 – 8 – 9

Nonfiction
Science / Math

The Relaxation Response
by Herbert Benson and Miriam Z. Klipper, (2000) 240p, ISBN-13: 978-0380815951

Standard book equivalent: 0.9
First published: 1975

Benson is a physician and associate professor at Harvard Medical School. *The Relaxation Response* is based on research done at Boston's Beth Israel Hospital and Harvard Medical School that showed relaxation techniques such as meditation have significant physical benefits, from lowered blood pressure to a reduction in heart disease. *The Relaxation Response* explains why mantra meditation used in transcendental meditation works by discussing the physiological responses of the body to stress and anxiety. Also, it describes how the relaxation response can be learned and used to improve health.

Keywords: American Author, psychology, relaxation, science

Websites:
http://www.mbmi.org/home/
http://www.hno.harvard.edu/gazette/2004/03.04/11-stress.html
http://www.division42.org/MembersArea/Nws_Views/articles/Reviews_Books/relaxation_response.html

Rate this book: 1 – 2 – 3   4 – 5 – 6   7 – 8 – 9

Nonfiction
Science / Math

The Secret Life of Germs: What They Are, Why We Need Them, and How We Can Protect Ourselves Against Them by Philip M., Tierno Jr (2004) 320p, ISBN-13: 978-0743421881

Standard book equivalent: 1.2
First published: 2001

Tierno is an associate professor of microbiology at New York University. *The Secret Life of Germs* is the story of bacteria, viruses, and prions and their many effects on human beings. Tierno discusses such topics as toxic shock syndrome, Lyme disease, and diarrheal infections of the Third World. The book is divided into three parts: an introduction to the world of germs, how germs are spread, and themes of current interest. The last part includes discussions of the role of germs in ulcers and heart disease, and bioterrorism.

Keywords: American author, biology, germs, medicine, microbiology, science

Websites:
http://www.oprah.com/tows/booksseen/200404/tows_book_20040413_ptierno.jhtml
http://archives.cnn.com/2001/COMMUNITY/11/08/tierno.cnna/
http://www.infectioncontroltoday.com/articles/381feat1.html

Rate this book: 1 – 2 – 3   4 – 5 – 6   7 – 8 – 9

Nonfiction
Science / Math

The Selfish Gene **
by Richard Dawkins (2006) 384p, ISBN-13: 978-0199291144

Standard book equivalent: 1.5
First published: 1976

Dawkins (b. 1941) is an evolutionary biologist and British author. *The Selfish Gene* is about evolutionary biology with the central theme that evolution acts on genes (not individuals or populations) through selection. The word "selfish" is used to suggest that the organism is just a vehicle to ensure a gene's survival and propagation. This revised edition of Dawkins' book contains two new chapters: "Nice Guys Finish First" about the evolution of altruism, and "The Long Reach of the Gene", which is about his theory of the extended phenotype.

Keywords: British author, biology, DNA, genetics, science

Websites:
http://www.simonyi.ox.ac.uk/dawkins/WorldOfDawkins-archive/index.shtml
http://www.edge.org/3rd_culture/selfish06/selfish06_index.html
http://books.guardian.co.uk/review/story/0,12084,981412,00.html

Rate this book: 1 – 2 – 3   4 – 5 – 6   7 – 8 – 9

Nonfiction
Science / Math

Silent Thunder: In the Presence of Elephants
by Katy Payne (1999) 288p, ISBN-13: 978-0140285963

Standard book equivalent: 1.1
First published: 1998

Payne (b. 1937) is an American author and researcher in acoustic biology at Cornell University. *Silent Thunder* is both a memoir and a biology book about her field research on infrasonic (i.e., sound below the range of human hearing) communication among elephants. It describes her thirteen year study observing the social behaviors and family structures of African elephants. Especially interesting is her account of elephants digging wells. It is also a rich source of information about conservation issues.

Keywords: American author, woman author, biology, conservation, elephants, science

Websites:
http://www.npr.org/programs/re/archivesdate/2002/nov/index.html
http://www.awionline.org/pubs/Quarterly/Spring2000/SilentThunder.htm
http://www.nytimes.com/books/98/08/23/reviews/980823.23foutst.html

Rate this book: 1 – 2 – 3   4 – 5 – 6   7 – 8 – 9

Nonfiction
Science / Math

Stiff: The Curious Lives of Human Cadavers *
by Mary Roach (2004) 304p, ISBN-13: 978-0393324822

Standard book equivalent: 1.2
First published: 2003

Roach is an American author and journalist. *Stiff* explores how human cadavers have been used throughout history to benefit every aspect of human existence. Roach approaches the topic with a humorous writing style. It is written in twelve chapters with chapters about the use of cadavers by medical students, the process of decay in cadavers, cannibalism, using cadavers to test ammunition, and more. There is also the 1907 experiment of the physician who weighed his patients just before and after their moment of death with the notion of weighing their soul (his estimation—approximately ¾ ounce).

Keywords: American author, woman author, biology, cadavers, death, science

Websites:
http://www.identitytheory.com/interviews/roach_interview.html
http://www.blacktable.com/gallagher041027.htm
http://www.failuremag.com/arch_science_stiff.html

Rate this book:　　1 – 2 – 3　　4 – 5 – 6　　7 – 8 – 9

Nonfiction
Science / Math

Waiting for Aphrodite: Journeys into the Time Before Bones
by Sue Hubbell (200) 256p, ISBN-13: 978-0618056842

Standard book equivalent: 1.0
First published: 1999

Hubbell (b. 1935) is an American author. *Waiting for Aphrodite* is a book about the natural history of invertebrates. The title refers to *Aphrodite aculeata*, or sea mouse, for which she is waiting to observe. Hubbell is a keen naturalist and having moved to the coast of Maine was curious to learn about all such species in her new environs. She examines camel crickets, sea cucumbers, sponges, periwinkles, corals, horseshoe crabs, and many other creatures. Interspersed with her descriptions are discussions of Darwinian evolution and her personal evolution from Michigan to the Ozarks to Maine.

Keywords: American author, woman author, biology, invertebrates

Websites:
http://query.nytimes.com/gst/fullpage.html?res=9806E0DB163CF93BA35754C0A96F958260
http://en.wikipedia.org/wiki/Sue_Hubbell
http://www.answers.com/topic/sue-hubbell

Rate this book: 1 – 2 – 3   4 – 5 – 6   7 – 8 – 9

Nonfiction
Science / Math

Why Flip a Coin? The Art and Science of Good Decisions **

by H. W. Lewis (1998) 206p, ISBN-13: 978-0471296454

Standard book equivalent: 0.8
First published: 1997

Lewis is an American author and professor emeritus of physics at the University of California, Santa Barbara. In *Why Flip a Coin?* Lewis explains systematic procedures for organizing your thinking and making sound decisions. Optimal choices depend on understanding the consequences, probabilities, and preferences involved in a situation. He illustrates his strategy with dozens of examples. His first example concerns the best procedure for choosing a spouse (the metrics of mating). Other examples include how to increase your chances of winning a football pool, and whether you can make more money playing poker or in the stock market.

Keywords: American author, decision-making, math, science

Websites:
http://maxvalue.com/tip020.htm
http://www.bainvestor.com/why-flip-a-coin.html

Rate this book: 1 – 2 – 3   4 – 5 – 6   7 – 8 – 9

Nonfiction
Science / Math

Why We Love: The Nature and Chemistry of Romantic Love
by Helen Fisher (2004) 320p, ISBN-13: 978-0805077964

Standard book equivalent: 1.2
First published: 2004

Fisher (b. 1945) is an American author and research anthropologist at Rutgers University. Fisher, in *Why We Love*, argues that much of our romantic behavior is hard-wired and that it represents a brain system distinct from our sex drive. She bases her conclusions on brain scans, behavioral research into the effects of norepinephrine and dopamine, and the results of surveys. The book has nine chapters covering animal magnetism, the chemicals involved in love, the evolution of romantic love, and making romance last.

Keywords: American author, woman author, anthropology, biology, love, science

Websites:
http://helenfisher.com/
http://www.theswartzfoundation.org/mind-brain-2006.asp
http://thebestreviews.com/review20806

Rate this book: 1 – 2 – 3   4 – 5 – 6   7 – 8 – 9

Nonfiction
Science / Math

Zero: The Biography of a Dangerous Idea **
by Charles Seife (2000) 256p, ISBN-13: 978-0140296471

Standard book equivalent: 1.0
First published: 2000

Seife is an American author and science journalist. In this book he covers the historical, mathematical, and scientific aspects of the number zero. His style is lively, and entertaining. However, this is a challenging book dealing with some weighty topics. Seife describes the shift from the Roman numeral system to that of the Arabic system. He traces the life of zero through Descartes' coordinate system and the role of zero in the development of calculus. He ends with the modern age and the use of zero in string theory.

Keywords: American author, math, science, zero

Websites:
http://www.users.cloud9.net/~cgseife/
http://www.maa.org/reviews/zero2.html
http://archive.salon.com/books/review/2000/03/03/seife/index.html

Rate this book: 1 – 2 – 3   4 – 5 – 6   7 – 8 – 9

NONFICTION

Philosophy / Religion / Spirituality

Nonfiction
Philosophy / Religion / Spirituality

The Analects of Confucius **
by Arthur Waley (translator) (1989) 256p, ISBN-13: 978-0679722960

Standard book equivalent: 1.0
First published: 1938 (Waley's translation)

Confucius (551 – 479 BCE) was a Chinese social philosopher who greatly influenced Eastern thought and philosophy. *The Analects* are a record of the words and acts of Confucius and his disciples. They were probably written prior to the 2nd century BCE over a period of several decades by his followers. They are in the form of brief maxims. The Analects are grouped by themes into chapters but the chapters are arranged randomly. The Chinese title literally means "discussion over Confucius' words."

Keywords: Chinese author, China, Confucius, philosophy, religion

Websites:
http://www.confucius.org/main01.htm
http://plato.stanford.edu/entries/confucius/
http://www.iep.utm.edu/c/confuciu.htm

Rate this book: 1 – 2 – 3   4 – 5 – 6   7 – 8 – 9

Nonfiction
Philosophy / Religion / Spirituality

The Art of Loving
by Erich Fromm (2000) 144p, ISBN-13: 978-0060958282

Standard book equivalent: 0.6
First published: 1956

Fromm (1900 – 1980) was a German philosopher, psychologist and author. In *The Art of Loving* he states that if love is merely a pleasant sensation then there is little need to examine it. However, if love is an art then it requires knowledge and effort to master. Fromm argues the latter assertion. Learning to love demands practice, concentration, insight and understanding. He suggests that most of us have not developed our ability to love on the only level that really counts—a love that is composed of maturity, self-knowledge, and courage.

Keywords: German author, inspirational, love, philosophy, psychology, relationships

Websites:
http://www.ship.edu/~cgboeree/fromm.html
http://www.astro.princeton.edu/~msshin/minsu/erich_fromm.htm
http://www.cliftonunitarian.com/toddstalks/theartoflove.htm

Rate this book: 1 – 2 – 3   4 – 5 – 6   7 – 8 – 9

Nonfiction
Philosophy / Religion / Spirituality

Between Man and Man **
by Martin Buber (2002) 320p, ISBN-13: 978-0415278270

Standard book equivalent: 1.2
First published: 1947

Buber (1878 – 1965) was a Jewish theologian and philosopher from Austria. He defined three types of relationships humans can have: between man and things, between man and God, and between man and man. This book represents his views about the third type, which are our deepest encounters with human experience. In discussing these relationships Buber touches on the subjects of religious ethics, social philosophy, marriage, education, psychology and art. This book presents the reader with a challenge to re-evaluate their encounter with the world that surrounds them.

Keywords: Austrian author, Jewish author, Judaism, philosophy, relationships, religion

Websites:
http://www.emanuelnyc.org/bulletin/archive/34.html
http://web.ionsys.com/~remedy/Buber,%20Martin.htm
http://web.singnet.com.sg/~chlim/Chapter2.html

Rate this book: 1 – 2 – 3   4 – 5 – 6   7 – 8 – 9

Nonfiction
Philosophy / Religion / Spirituality

Confessions
by Saint Augustine, Henry Chadwick (translator) (2002)
319p, ISBN-13: 978-0486424668

Standard book equivalent: 1.2
First published: circa late 4th century

Augustine of Hippo (354 – 430) was a bishop born in what is now Algeria. His autobiography, *Confessions*, is often held as a model for religious biographers. It is among the earliest extant Western autobiographies. The book discusses Augustine's conversion from a hard-core hedonistic life-style to his faith up until about the age of 40 years. He describes the role his mother, St Monica, played in his conversion and touches on subjects such as the nature of friendship and the role of women in the Church.

Keywords: Augustine of Hippo, biography (men), Christianity, religion

Websites:
http://www.stoa.org/hippo/
http://www.cliffsnotes.com/WileyCDA/LitNote/id-166.html
http://www.sparknotes.com/philosophy/confessionsaug/index.html

Rate this book: 1 – 2 – 3   4 – 5 – 6   7 – 8 – 9

Nonfiction
Philosophy / Religion / Spirituality

The Essential Kabbalah: The Heart of Jewish Mysticism **
by Daniel C. Matt (1997) 221p, ISBN-13: 978-0785808701

Standard book equivalent: 0.9
First published: 1996

Matt is a former professor of Judaism at the University of California, Berkeley. *The Essential Kabbalah* is a selection of writings from the Kabbalah, a Jewish tradition in mysticism. The Kabbalah is deeply symbolic and deals with the mysteries of Jewish philosophy about the nature of God and the soul. Matt provides a clear overview of the history of the Kabbalah along with commentary on each passage. The author translated the passages from the original Hebrew and Aramaic texts.

Keywords: American author, Judaism, Kabbalah, mysticism, religion

Websites:
http://www.somethingjewish.co.uk/articles/576_daniel_c_matt.htm
http://mandox.blogspot.com/2005_09_01_mandox_archive.html
http://www.jwmag.org/articles/10Spring04/p24.asp

Rate this book: 1 – 2 – 3   4 – 5 – 6   7 – 8 – 9

Nonfiction
Philosophy / Religion / Spirituality

The Essential Mystics: Selections from the World's Great Wisdom Traditions **
by Andrew Harvey (1997) 256p, ISBN-13: 978-0062513793

Standard book equivalent: 1.0
First published: 1996

Harvey is an American author born in India and educated at Oxford. *The Essential Mystics* includes selections of mysticism from an array of religions including the Shamanism of indigenous peoples, Taoism, Buddhism, Judaism, Greek philosophy and goddess worship, Islamic Sufism, and Christianity. The selections from indigenous people include works of Maori, Native American, African, and Australian elders. Harvey gives a historical introduction to the selections from each tradition. A major theme of all of the selections is the importance of the divine mother in mystical experience.

Keywords: mysticism, religion

Websites:
http://www.newdawnbooks.info/Reviews/The_Essential_Mystics_Selections.html
http://www.andrewharvey.net/
http://www.anaflora.com/articles/inter-sharon/interv-andrew.html

Rate this book: 1 – 2 – 3   4 – 5 – 6   7 – 8 – 9

Nonfiction
Philosophy / Religion / Spirituality

Fakhruddin Iraqi: Divine Flashes
by William Chittick, Peter Wilson (translator), Seyyed Hossein Nasr (translator) (1982) 194p, ISBN-13: 978-0809123728

Standard book equivalent: 0.7
First published: the 13th century

Chittick is an American professor of religious studies at the State University of New York at Stony Brook. This is an English translation of the influential and classic Sufi text. Fakhruddin 'Iraqi (1213 – 1289) was born in what is now Iran. He was one of the foremost teachers of Sufi tradition and one of the greatest of Persian poets. *Divine Flashes* contains beautiful descriptions of "the mysteries of Union". The poems are classic expressions of Sufi love mysticism.

Keywords: Persian author, Islam, Persia, Sufism

Websites:
http://www.poetry-chaikhana.com/I/IraqiFakhrud/index.htm
http://www.buddhanet.net/mag_one.htm
http://www.theosophytrust.org/tlodocs/articlesTeacher.php?d=Iraqi.htm&p=63

Rate this book: 1 – 2 – 3   4 – 5 – 6   7 – 8 – 9

Nonfiction
Philosophy / Religion / Spirituality

Interior Castle
by St. Teresa of Avila, (2006) 214p, ISBN-13: 978-1600962912

Standard book equivalent: 1.0
First published: 1577

St. Teresa (1515 – 1582) was a Spanish mystic and major figure of the Catholic Reformation. *Interior Castle* compares the soul to a castle with many rooms. Each room is a stage of the soul's development, and one can progress into and out of each room. As the soul moves toward the center of this castle it conforms more to the will of God. God dwells in the interior-most room. This book is a map for the soul to make its way to that room. St. Teresa's tone is conversational and humble.

Keywords: Spanish author, woman author, Christianity, mysticism, religion

Websites:
http://www.intratext.com/X/ENG0033.htm
http://www.mcs.drexel.edu/~gbrandal/Illum_html/Teresa.html
http://www.themystica.com/mystica/articles/t/teresa_of_avila_st.html

Rate this book: 1 – 2 – 3   4 – 5 – 6   7 – 8 – 9

Nonfiction
Philosophy / Religion / Spirituality

Introduction to the Devout Life
by St. Francis De Sales (2002) 288p, ISBN-13: 978-0375725623

Standard book equivalent: 1.1
First published: 1609

St. Francis de Sales (1567 – 1622) was a French Jesuit priest during the Calvinist Reformation. *Introduction to the Devout Life* was written as a guide to devotion for lay people "living in the world". It consists of five books: (1) freeing the soul from all inclination to sin, (2) how to be united to God by prayer and the sacraments, (3) the practice of virtue, (4) strengthening the soul against temptation, and (5) how to form resolutions and persevere.

Keywords: French author, Christianity, religion

Websites:
http://www.garythomas.com/classics/desales.html
http://www.newadvent.org/cathen/06220a.htm
http://www.catholicity.com/devoutlife/

Rate this book: 1 – 2 – 3   4 – 5 – 6   7 – 8 – 9

Nonfiction
Philosophy / Religion / Spirituality

Islam: A Short History
by Karen Armstrong (2002) 272p, ISBN-13: 978-0812966183

Standard book equivalent: 1.0
First published: 2000

Armstrong (b. 1944) is a British author of Irish roots. *Islam: A Short History* is a concise political and religious history of the Muslim world from the Qur'anic revelation of Muhammad in 610AD through the present day. She covers the major events of Islamic history. Armstrong concludes with discussions of the influences of modern Western democracies on Islam, the nature of the modern Islamic state, and how Islamic perceptions of democracy differ from Western notions.

Keywords: British author, woman author, history, Islam, religion

Websites:
http://www.beliefnet.com/story/38/story_3813_1.html
http://www.pbs.org/now/transcript/transcript_armstrong.html
http://speakingoffaith.publicradio.org/programs/armstrong/index.shtml

Rate this book: 1 – 2 – 3   4 – 5 – 6   7 – 8 – 9

Nonfiction
Philosophy / Religion / Spirituality

New Seeds of Contemplation **
by Thomas Merton (1972) 297p, ISBN-13: 978-0811200998

Standard book equivalent: 1.1
First published: 1961

Merton (1915 – 1968) was an American Trappist monk and author. In *New Seeds of Contemplation* Merton writes about contemplation and how it can best be achieved using examples from both the Bible and from his own life. The book is written as a series of 39 independent essays with titles such as 'Everything That Is, Is Holy', 'A Body of Broken Bones', and 'Hell as Hatred'. Merton believed that, "Every moment and every event of every man's life on earth plants something in his soul." Contemplation cultivates those seeds so that the good might thrive.

Keywords: American author, Christianity, contemplation, religion

Websites:
http://www.merton.org/
http://www.hermitary.com/solitude/merton.html
http://www.crosscurrents.org/essays.htm

Rate this book: 1 – 2 – 3   4 – 5 – 6   7 – 8 – 9

Nonfiction
Philosophy / Religion / Spirituality

Pragmatism: A New Name for Some Old Ways of Thinking by William James (1995) 128p, ISBN-13: 978-0486282701

Standard book equivalent: 0.5
First published: 1907

James (1842 – 1910) was an American psychologist, philosopher and author. *Pragmatism* is his classic work of eight lectures he gave in 1906 and 1907. James defines pragmatism many ways but especially as a method of resolving philosophical disputes. "The pragmatic method…is to try to interpret each [theory] by tracing its respective practical consequences. If no practical difference [among theories] whatever can be traced, then the alternatives mean practically the same thing, and all dispute is idle." This book is suitable for high school students without a background in philosophy.

Keywords: American author, philosophy, pragmatism

Websites:
http://www.gutenberg.org/etext/5116
http://serendip.brynmawr.edu/sci_cult/philsci/s03/Bastani.html
http://www.philosophypages.com/ph/jame.htm

Rate this book: 1 – 2 – 3   4 – 5 – 6   7 – 8 – 9

Nonfiction
Philosophy / Religion / Spirituality

Shinto Norito - a Book of Prayers
by Ann Llewellyn Evans (translator) (2006) 168p, ISBN-13: 978-1553691389

Standard book equivalent: 0.6
First published: 2006

Evans is a Canadian author and Shinto priestess. *Shinto Norito* is a collection of 22 ancient Japanese Shinto prayers, provided in both English and Japanese. Shinto's focus is on the divinity of all creation, on living with gratitude and humility, and on purification of one's self and environment. In the Shinto tradition, prayer and ritual are a means to regain a divine state of being as an acknowledgement of what already exists. The purpose of ritual is to restore a sensitive awareness of our relationship to the universe.

Keywords: Japanese author, contemplation, religion, Shinto

Websites:
http://www.asahi-net.or.jp/~qm9t-kndu/shintoism.htm
http://www.shinto.nl/shinto_books/evans.htm
http://eos.kokugakuin.ac.jp/modules/xwords/

Rate this book: 1 – 2 – 3   4 – 5 – 6   7 – 8 – 9

Nonfiction
Philosophy / Religion / Spirituality

Teachings of the Hindu Mystics
by Andrew Harvey (2001) 192p, ISBN-13: 978-1570624490

Standard book equivalent: 0.7
First published: 2001

Harvey is an American author born in India and educated at Oxford. *Teachings of the Hindu Mystics* contains 71 short readings of ancient mystical texts from the Vedas, the Upanishads, Yoga Vasishtha, the Ashtavakra Gita, the devotional classic Bhagavad Gita, and more. It also contains the writings of individuals such as Mirabai (1498-1546), Aurobindo (1872-1950) and other contemporary sources. There is a glossary of Sanskrit names and terms at the end of the book.

Keywords: Indian author, Hinduism, mysticism, religion

Websites:
http://www.spiritualityandpractice.com/books/books.php?id=3880
http://www.eclectica.org/v10n2/palcewski.html
http://www.religioustolerance.org/hinduism.htm

Rate this book: 1 – 2 – 3   4 – 5 – 6   7 – 8 – 9

Nonfiction
Philosophy / Religion / Spirituality

Turning Points: Decisive Moments in the History of Christianity
by Mark A. Noll (2001) 352p, ISBN-13: 978-0801062117

Standard book equivalent: 1.4
First published: 1997

Noll (b. 1946) is an American author and was a professor at Wheaton College before transferring to Notre Dame University. *Turning Points* describes a dozen influential events that shaped Christianity. These events include the Fall of Jerusalem, Council of Nicaea, Council of Chalcedon, the beginning of Monasticism, the coronation of Charlemagne, the Great Schism of 1054, Diet of Worms, the English Act of Supremacy, the founding of the Jesuits, the conversion of the Wesleys, the French Revolution, the Edinburgh Missionary Conference, and the Twentieth Century.

Keywords: American author, Christianity, history, religion

Websites:
http://sojourners.com/index.cfm?action=magazine.article&issue=soj9809&article=980932a
http://www.cathyduffyreviews.com/bible/turning-points.htm
http://www.ignatiusinsight.com/features2005/marknoll_intvw_sept05.asp

Rate this book: 1 – 2 – 3   4 – 5 – 6   7 – 8 – 9

LONG BOOKS

Long Books

The Autobiography of Malcolm X *
by Malcolm X, with Alex Haley (1987) 496p, ISBN-13: 978-0345350688

Standard book equivalent: 1.9
First published: 1965

Malcolm X (1925 – 1965) was an African American civil rights activist and a leader of the Nation of Islam. He then converted to orthodox Islam after a pilgrimage to Mecca in 1964. This autobiography traces his transformation from street hustler to religious and national leader. It covers his boyhood, days in prison, conversion to the Nation of Islam, his trip to Mecca, and assassination. As with Gandhi, his outlook evolved from that of an angry man to that of a peacemaker.

Keywords: African American author, American author, biography (men), African American experience, civil rights, Islam, Nation of Islam, prejudice, prison, racism, religion

Websites:
http://www.sparknotes.com/lit/malcolmx/
http://www.cmgworldwide.com/historic/malcolm/index.htm
http://www.monthlyreview.org/0205simon.htm

Rate this book: 1 – 2 – 3   4 – 5 – 6   7 – 8 – 9

Long Books

Before the Fallout: From Marie Curie to Hiroshima
by Diana Preston (2005) 416p, ISBN-13: 978-0802714459

Standard book equivalent: 1.6
First published: 2005

Preston is a British author, historian and broadcaster. *Before the Fallout* brings together history, physics, politics and military strategies to show the great significance the development of the atomic bomb represented. The story begins with Curie's description of radioactivity in 1898 and traces the development of technology through the scientific achievements of Rutherford, Bohr, Einstein and Oppenheimer. Preston places this discussion in the context of the ethical and humanitarian implications of creating such a destructive and uncontrollable power.

Keywords: British author, woman author, atomic bomb, Einstein, Hiroshima, history, Marie Curie, Oppenheimer, politics, physics, science, technology, war

Websites:
http://www.timesonline.co.uk/article/0,,2102-1709951,00.html
http://seattletimes.nwsource.com/html/books/2002264044_preston08.html
http://www.atomicarchive.com/Reviews/0802714455.shtml

Rate this book: 1 – 2 – 3   4 – 5 – 6   7 – 8 – 9

Long Books

The Boys of Summer
by Roger Kahn (2006) 512p, ISBN-13: 978-0060883966

Standard book equivalent: 2.0
First published: 1971

Kahn (b. 1927) is an American sportswriter and journalist. *The Boys of Summer* is a memoir of his relationship with his father and their love for the Brooklyn Dodgers. He covered the Dodgers as a reporter for the *New York Herald Tribune*. The first part of the book is about those experiences during the time Jackie Robinson broke into the majors. Kahn—years later—sought out the players from that team and wrote about his interviews in the latter part of the book. It is a sobering account of what happens to great performers after they leave their chosen profession.

Keywords: American author, American history, baseball, Brooklyn Dodgers, New York City, Jackie Robinson, sports

Websites:
http://www.chronogram.com/issue/2004/07/bookshelf/
http://www.rogerkahn.com/
http://www.bookpage.com/9704bp/nonfiction/memoriesofsummer.html

Rate this book: 1 – 2 – 3   4 – 5 – 6   7 – 8 – 9

Long Books

Bury My Heart at Wounded Knee: An Indian History of the American West
by Dee Brown (2001) 512p, ISBN-13: 978-0805066692

Standard book equivalent: 2.0
First published: 1970

Brown (1908 – 2002) was an American author and historian. He is often mistakenly assumed to be of Native American ancestry. *Bury My Heart at Wounded Knee* is a narrative of the white man's conquest of the North American continent from the perspective of Native Americans. Most of the narrative deals with the period 1860 to 1890. He uses council records, autobiographies, and first-hand accounts from the Ute, Cheyenne, Sioux, Apache, Crow, Dakota and more to reconstruct the genocide of Native Americans. The final chapter is about the Wounded Knee Massacre of 1890.

Keywords: American author, American history, Native American experience, massacre, war

Websites:
http://www.bookrags.com/studyguide-woundedknee/
http://www.uneco.org/Bury_My_Heart.html
http://www.lastoftheindependents.com/wounded.htm

Rate this book: 1 – 2 – 3   4 – 5 – 6   7 – 8 – 9

Long Books

Catch 22 **
by Joseph Heller (1996) 464p, ISBN-13: 978-0684833392

Standard book equivalent: 1.8
First published: 1961

Heller (1923 – 1999) was an American author and satirist. This book coined the term 'catch 22' to mean a no-win situation, usually created by bureaucracy or circumstance. *Catch 22* is a novel set during World War II and is about the often humorous, but frustrating and absurd, actions and inactions of bureaucracies. It is also a strident anti-war novel. The main character is Captain John Yossarian of the U.S. Army Air Force. He eventually comes to fear American bureaucrats more than the enemy trying to shoot him down.

Keywords: American author, absurdism, bureaucracy, war, WWII

Websites:
http://www.sparknotes.com/lit/catch22/
http://www.cliffsnotes.com/WileyCDA/LitNote/id-176.html
http://www.bookrags.com/notes/c22/

Rate this book: 1 – 2 – 3   4 – 5 – 6   7 – 8 – 9

Long Books

Doctor Zhivago
by Boris Pasternak (1997) 592p, ISBN-13: 978-0679774389

Standard book equivalent: 2.3
First published: 1957 in Italy

Pasternak (1890 – 1960) was a Russian poet and novelist who won the 1958 Nobel Prize in Literature. *Doctor Zhivago* is a novel that tells the story of Yuri Zhivago who is torn between two women. Zhivago is a Russian poet and physician whose idealism and principles are tested by the horrors of World War I, the Russian Revolution, and the subsequent Russian Civil War. As Lara—his love interest—states, "The whole human way of life has been destroyed and ruined." The name "Zhivago" is derived from the Russian word 'zhizn' meaning 'life' or 'live'.

Keywords: Russian author, loss, love, marriage, Nobel Prize (Literature), Russia, Russian Revolution, war, WWI

Websites:
http://www.sparknotes.com/lit/zhivago/
http://www.kirjasto.sci.fi/pasterna.htm
http://www.pbs.org/wgbh/masterpiece/zhivago/ei_pasternak.html

Rate this book: 1 – 2 – 3   4 – 5 – 6   7 – 8 – 9

Long Books

The Good War: An Oral History of World War II
by Studs Terkel (1997) 608p, ISBN-13: 978-1565843431

Standard book equivalent: 2.3
First published: 1984

Terkel (b. 1912) is an American author and journalist who won a Pulitzer Prize in 1985 for *The Good War*. It is a narrative based on 121 oral accounts from those who lived through World War II. Terkel collected stories from both combatants and non-combatants including those from Japanese-Americans placed in internment camps, conscientious objectors, "Rosie the Riveters", senior civil servants, wives of soldiers serving overseas, and workers on the Manhattan Project. The combatants interviewed come from both the European and Pacific theaters and from several of the warring nations.

Keywords: American author, American historyoral history, Pulitzer Prize, war, WWII

Websites:
http://www.h-net.org/reviews/showrev.cgi?path=20510896221053
http://www.studsterkel.org/
http://www.usc.edu/dept/spectrum/94-95season/studs.html

Rate this book: 1 – 2 – 3   4 – 5 – 6   7 – 8 – 9

Long Books

The Grapes of Wrath
by John Steinbeck (2002) 464p, ISBN-13: 978-0142000663

Standard book equivalent: 1.8
First published: 1939

Steinbeck (1902 – 1968) was an American author who won the 1962 Nobel Prize in Literature and a 1940 Pulitzer Prize for *The Grapes of Wrath*. It is a novel about the poverty-stricken Joad family and their move from Oklahoma to California during the Dust Bowl. It follows them for about nine months as they travel to California, only to discover that it is not the land of opportunity they expected. *The Grapes of Wrath* explores themes of justice, land ownership and stewardship, and the role of government in a capitalist society. Compare with *Now in November*.

Keywords: American author, California, dust bowl, farming, Great Depression, Nobel Prize (Literature), Oklahoma, poverty, Pulitzer Prize

Websites:
http://www.sparknotes.com/lit/grapesofwrath/
http://www.gradesaver.com/classicnotes/titles/grapeswrath/
http://www.aresearchguide.com/wrath.html

Rate this book: 1 – 2 – 3   4 – 5 – 6   7 – 8 – 9

Long Books

The Iliad
by Homer, Ian Johnston (Translator) (2006) 544p, ISBN-13: 978-0977626908

Standard book equivalent: 2.7
Dates to at least the 6th century BC

Homer (c 8th century BC) was a Greek poet. Traditionally, he is believed to have been blind. *The Iliad* is a narrative poem about the Trojan War. It starts with Achilles quarrelling with the Greek commander, Agamemnon, because Agamemnon took away his prized girl. The story is surprisingly violent, following the twists and turns of the war as the gods divide up glory among the warriors. It includes neither Paris's seduction of Helen nor the Trojan horse incident, which were added by other authors.

Keywords: Greek author, ancient Greece, Trojan War, Troy, war

Websites:
http://www.sparknotes.com/lit/iliad/
http://www.mala.bc.ca/~johnstoi/homer/iliad_title.htm
http://www.cliffsnotes.com/WileyCDA/LitNote/id-26.html

Rate this book: 1 – 2 – 3   4 – 5 – 6   7 – 8 – 9

Long Books

The Innocents Abroad
by Mark Twain (2003) 652p, ISBN-13: 978-0486428321

Standard book equivalent: 2.5
First published: 1869

Mark Twain (1835 – 1910) is a pseudonym for American author Samuel Clemens. *The Innocents Abroad* is a nonfiction travelogue that sold over 70,000 copies in its first year and remained the best-selling of Twain's works throughout his lifetime. The book chronicles his 1867 tour of Europe and the Holy Land with stops in such places as Tangier, Marseilles, Paris, Venice, Rome, and Constantinople. The book reveals Twain to be a man with great powers of observation, and a keen sense of humor, as he describes the people and places he encounters on his tour.

Keywords: American author, Constantinople, Middle East, Paris, Rome, travel

Websites:
http://128.143.22.16/railton/innocent/iahompag.html
http://www.romeartlover.it/Twain.html
http://www.common-place.org/vol-04/no-03/wasserstrom/

Rate this book: 1 – 2 – 3   4 – 5 – 6   7 – 8 – 9

Long Books

Invisible Man
by Ralph Ellison (2002) 448p, ISBN-13: 978-0375507915

Standard book equivalent: 1.7
First published: 1952

Ellison (1913 – 1994) was an American author who won the 1953 National Book Award for *Invisible Man*. It is a novel about a young black man's search for truth and self-identity and the racism that permeates society. It is set during the 1930s in both the South and New York City. The title refers to the protagonist being invisible from society. Two important themes of the book are the effects of racism on the self-identity of African Americans and the dangers of stereo typing, regardless of whether it comes from Whites or African Americans.

Keywords: African American author, African American experience, National Book Award, New York City, prejudice, racism, the South

Websites:
http://www.sparknotes.com/lit/invisibleman/
http://www.gradesaver.com/classicnotes/titles/invisibleman/
http://www.kirjasto.sci.fi/rellison.htm

Rate this book: 1 – 2 – 3   4 – 5 – 6   7 – 8 – 9

Long Books

The Kite Runner
by Khaled Hosseini (2004) 400p, ISBN-13: 978-1594480003

Standard book equivalent: 1.5
First published: 2003

Hosseini (b. 1965) is an Afghan American author and physician. *The Kite Runner* is a novel that follows the story of Amir, the privileged son of a wealthy businessman in Kabul, and Hassan, the son of Amir's father's servant. As children they lead an idyllic life together in the Afghanistan of the early 1970s. They fly kites, tell stories and play as children do everywhere to occupy their time. Then, there is a betrayal and ultimately salvation as their relationship takes unexpected turns.

Keywords: Afghan author, American Author, Afghanistan, betrayal, coming-of-age, friendship

Websites:
http://www.khaledhosseini.com/
http://www.bookpage.com/0306bp/fiction/kite_runner.html
http://query.nytimes.com/gst/fullpage.html?res=9504E0DF123FF930A3575BC0A9659C8B63

Rate this book: 1 – 2 – 3   4 – 5 – 6   7 – 8 – 9

Long Books

Les Miserables **
by Victor Hugo; Lee Fahnestock, Norman MacAfee (translators) (1987) 1488p, ISBN-13: 978-0451525260

Standard book equivalent: 5.7
First published: 1862

Hugo (1773 – 1823) was a French author, and statesman. *Les Miserables* is a novel set in early-19th century Paris. It is about how people's actions affect the lives of others, and how God works in these actions for the ultimate good. The protagonist is Jean Valjean an ex-convict (convicted of stealing food to eat) who is struggling to redeem himself through good works. His initial jail sentence had been lengthened from five to nineteen years because of numerous escape attempts. He was an angry man when finally released. This story follows his life after prison.

Keywords: French author, France, Paris, poverty, prison

Websites:
http://www.online-literature.com/victor_hugo/les_miserables/
http://www.sparknotes.com/lit/lesmis/
http://www.btinternet.com/~glynhughes/squashed/lesmiserables.htm

Rate this book: 1 – 2 – 3   4 – 5 – 6   7 – 8 – 9

Long Books

The Magic Mountain
by Thomas Mann (1996) 720p, ISBN-13: 978-0679772873

Standard book equivalent: 2.8
First published: 1924

Mann (1875 – 1955) was a German author and winner of the 1929 Nobel Prize in Literature. *The Magic Mountain* is a novel about Hans Castorp, a modern Everyman. He spends seven years in a Swiss sanatorium for tuberculosis patients where he meets people, including one named Naphta, who are representative icons of pre-war Europe. Hans leaves the sanatorium to become a soldier in World War I. Naphta is interesting, given the history of 1930s and 1940s Germany—he is a Jewish-born Jesuit who defends the use of terror and the taking of life for the sake of ideals.

Keywords: German author, Europe, medicine, Nobel Prize (Literature), Switzerland, war, WWI

Websites:
http://www.littlebluelight.com/lblphp/indivwork.php?wkey=202
http://www.bookrags.com/shortguide-magic-mountain/
http://www.kirjasto.sci.fi/tmann.htm

Rate this book: 1 – 2 – 3   4 – 5 – 6   7 – 8 – 9

Long Books

Main Street
by Sinclair Lewis (1998) 400p, ISBN-13: 978-0486406558

Standard book equivalent: 1.5
First published: 1920

Lewis (1885 – 1951) was an American author and winner of the 1930 Nobel Prize in Literature. *Main Street* is a novel set in Gopher Prairie, Minnesota. The protagonist is Carol Milford, a physician's wife who is disenchanted with her small-town life. She tries to change the ugliness, dullness and ignorance she sees in Gopher Prairie, but becomes frustrated at the effort. *Main Street* is noted as an early example of feminist literature by an American male author.

Keywords: American author, feminism, medicine, Midwest, Nobel Prize (Literature)

Websites:
http://www.bookrags.com/studyguide-mainstreet/
http://www.kirjasto.sci.fi/slewis.htm
http://etext.virginia.edu/toc/modeng/public/LewMain.html

Rate this book: 1 – 2 – 3   4 – 5 – 6   7 – 8 – 9

Long Books

The Naked and the Dead
by Norman Mailer (2000) 736p, ISBN-13: 978-0312265052

Standard book equivalent: 2.8
First published: 1948

Mailer (b. 1923) is an American author. *The Naked and the Dead* is a semi-autobiographical novel about a soldier in the South Pacific during World War II. The story follows a band of reconnaissance soldiers on an island in the Pacific. It opens with the initial assault on the Japanese-held island. We follow the soldiers' progress through the jungle and learn about their lives through a series of personal flashbacks. The book has a broad range of characters from a variety of ranks in the army. The interplay between the ranks is a major part of the plot.

Keywords: American author, Asia, war, WWII

Websites:
http://www.bookrags.com/studyguide-nakeddead/
http://books.guardian.co.uk/departments/classics/story/0,,105147,00.html
http://www.kirjasto.sci.fi/nmailer.htm

Rate this book: 1 – 2 – 3   4 – 5 – 6   7 – 8 – 9

Long Books

Native Son
by Richard Wright (2005) 544p, ISBN-13: 978-0060837563

Standard book equivalent: 2.0
First published: 1940

Wright (1908 – 1960) was an American author. He was the grandson of slaves and a member of the Communist Party, for which he suffered under McCarthyism. *Native Son* is a novel set in 1930s Chicago. The protagonist is 20-year-old Bigger Thomas, a black man who accidentally kills a white woman. Bigger is driven by despair, frustration, and poverty. He is doomed—trapped in a downward spiral that will lead to prison or death. *Native Son* is a powerful argument that criminals are not born, they are created through environmental influences.

Keywords: African American Author, American author, African American experience, Chicago, crime, Great Depression, poverty, prejudice, prison, racism

Websites:
http://www.sparknotes.com/lit/nativeson/
http://www.gradesaver.com/classicnotes/titles/native/
http://www.kirjasto.sci.fi/rwright.htm

Rate this book: 1 – 2 – 3   4 – 5 – 6   7 – 8 – 9

Long Books

The Octopus
by Frank Norris (2004) 508p, ISBN-13: 978-1419175862

Standard book equivalent: 1.7
First published: 1901

Norris (1870 – 1902) was an American author. *The Octopus* is a novel about the struggle of California wheat farmers in the San Joaquin valley against the powerful Pacific and Southwestern Railroad monopoly. It is based on the Mussel Slough incident. *The Octopus* is part of an unfinished trilogy. It focuses on wheat production. The next book, *The Pit* (1903), is about speculation and trading at the wheat exchange in Chicago. The third book was to deal with the export of wheat. Norris used the technique of literary naturalism to explore the issues of environmental determinism and social justice.

Keywords: American author, agriculture, business, California, environment, farming, railroad, San Joaquin Valley, wheat

Websites:
http://www.litencyc.com/php/sworks.php?rec=true&UID=31
http://www.bookrags.com/studyguide-octopus/
http://www.gutenberg.org/etext/268

Rate this book: 1 – 2 – 3   4 – 5 – 6   7 – 8 – 9

Long Books

Schindler's List
by Thomas Keneally (1993) 400p, ISBN-13: 978-0671880316

Standard book equivalent: 1.5
First published: 1982

Keneally (b. 1935) is an Australian author who won the 1982 Man Booker Prize for *Schindler's Arc* (published in the U.S. as *Schindler's List*). It is a novel based on the true story of how German war profiteer and prison camp director Oskar Schindler came to save more than 1,000 Jews from the gas chambers during World War II. Keneally uses the actual testimony of Schindler's Jews to portray the courage and cunning of a man in the midst of unspeakable evil. Also, see *The Good Man of Nanking: the Diaries of John Rabe*.

Keywords: Australian author, Germany, holocaust, Jewish experience, Man Booker Award, war, WWII

Websites:
http://www.nnbtv.dircon.co.uk/Books/2001/Schindler.html
http://www.bookrags.com/studyguide-schindlerslist/
http://books.guardian.co.uk/departments/history/story/0,6000,389879,00.html

Rate this book: 1 – 2 – 3   4 – 5 – 6   7 – 8 – 9

Long Books

Silent Spring
by Rachel Carson (2002) 400p, ISBN-13: 978-0618249060

Standard book equivalent: 1.5
First published: 1962

Carson (1907 – 1964) was an American author and marine biologist. *Silent Spring* is an environmental classic about the effects of indiscriminate pesticide use. It is often cited as the book that launched the environmental movement and is credited for getting DDT banned in the U.S. in 1972. The chemical industry strenuously attacked the book's conclusions when it was first published, but much of its tenets were soon broadly accepted. It also is a good introduction to ecology and has chapters about soils and the water cycle.

Keywords: **American** author, woman author, DDT, ecology, **environment**, nature, science

Websites:
http://www.rachelcarson.org/
http://www.uneco.org/ssalgoreintro.html
http://www.bookrags.com/studyguide-silentspring/

Rate this book: 1 – 2 – 3   4 – 5 – 6   7 – 8 – 9

Long Books

Sophie's World: A Novel about the History of Philosophy by Jostein Gaarder (1996) 544p, ISBN-13: 978-0425152256

Standard book equivalent: 2.1
First published: 1995

Gaarder (b. 1952) is a Norwegian author. *Sophie's World* is a whimsical mystery novel that is written as a dialogue between a fifteen year-old Norwegian girl and the mysterious fifty year-old Alberto Knox. Gaarder interweaves the dialogue with a history of philosophy in an entertaining tour of many of the world's greatest philosophers. Alberto serves as Sophie's mentor lecturing her on each philosopher's contribution—from the pre-Socratic Greeks through Jean-Paul Sartre and Simone de Beauvoir. All the while Sophie is attempting to learn who Alberto is and why she is receiving mysterious packages.

Keywords: Norwegian author, fable, mystery, philosophy

Websites:
http://reader.homestead.com/sophie.html
http://teenink.com/Past/2001/November/Books/SophiesWorld.html
http://www.levity.com/rubric/sophie.html

Rate this book: 1 – 2 – 3   4 – 5 – 6   7 – 8 – 9

Long Books

Two Years Before the Mast: And Twenty-Four Years After by Richard Henry Dana (2004) 432p, ISBN-13: 978-0766182219

Standard book equivalent: 1.7
First published: 1840, revised in 1869

Dana (1815 – 1882) was an American author and politician. He was a Harvard student recovering from measles when he decided to recuperate at sea as a common sailor. In 1834 he joined a two-year voyage rounding Cape Horn to deliver cargo to California. *Two Years Before the Mast* is a detailed chronicle describing his experiences in various ports and daily life at sea. Twenty-four years later he revisited California to update himself on what happened to old acquaintances during the Gold Rush. He added a narrative of those experiences as an appendix.

Keywords: American author, biography (men), California, sea

Websites:
http://www.sandiegohistory.org/bio/dana/dana.htm
http://onlinebooks.library.upenn.edu/webbin/book/lookupname?key=Dana%2C%20Richard%20Henry%2C%201815-1882
http://www.btinternet.com/~glynhughes/squashed/twoyearsbeforethemast.htm

Rate this book: 1 – 2 – 3   4 – 5 – 6   7 – 8 – 9

Long Books

The World Is Flat: a Brief History of the Twenty-first Century
by Thomas L. Friedman (2006) 608p, ISBN-13: 978-0374292799

Standard book equivalent: 2.3
First published: 2005

Friedman (b. 1953) is an American journalist and author. *The World Is Flat* is a nonfiction look at technological developments during the twentieth century. What Friedman means by "flat" is "connected". Connected refers to the lowering of trade and political barriers and the technical advances of the digital revolution. Those developments have made it possible to do business instantaneously across the planet. Globalization is driven not by major corporations or giant trade organizations like the World Bank, but by individuals all over the world with Internet access. America's reaction to this reality will determine her competitiveness in the world marketplace.

Keywords: American author, politics, technology, trade

Websites:
http://www.thomaslfriedman.com/
http://www.sciencefriday.com/pages/2005/Jun/hour2_062405.html
http://www.nytimes.com/2005/05/01/books/review/01ZAKARIA.html?ex=1272600000&en=1b84e47e745ea7ca&ei=5088&partner=rssnyt&emc=rss

Rate this book: 1 – 2 – 3   4 – 5 – 6   7 – 8 – 9

Appendix

Forty Additional Great Books

Fiction

1. *The Autobiography of Miss Jane Pittman*, Ernest Gaines
2. *The Brothers Karamazov,* by Fyodor Dostoevsky
3. *Childhood's End,* by Arthur C. Clarke
4. *The Eternal Moment, and Other Stories,* by E. M. Forster
5. *Far from the Madding Crowd,* by Thomas Hardy
6. *Grendel,* by John Gardner
7. *The House of the Seven Gables,* by Nathaniel Hawthorne
8. *Journey to the Centre of the Earth,* by Jules Verne
9. *Laments: A Bilingual Edition,* by Jan Kochanowski, Stanislaw Baranczak (Translator), Seamus Heaney (Translator)
10. *Moby-Dick,* by Herman Melville
11. *Me Dying Trial,* by Patricia Powell
12. *Melal,* by Robert Barclay
13. *The Once and Future King,* by T.H. White
14. *Roots: The Saga of an American Family,* by Alex Haley
15. *The Sailor Who Fell from Grace with the Sea,* by Yukio Mishima
16. *A Tomb for Boris Davidovich,* by Danilo Kis
17. *The Ways of White Folks,* by Langston Hughes
18. *The World According to Garp,* by John Irving
19. *World's Fair,* by E. L. Doctorow
20. *Wuthering Heights,* by Emily Bronte

Appendix

Nonfiction

1. *The Bondage of the Will*, by Martin Luther
2. *Challenging Nature: The Clash of Science and Spirituality at the New Frontiers of Life*, by Lee M. Silver
3. *Colour Bar: The Triumph of Seretse Khama and His Nation*, by Susan Wilson
4. *Eichmann in Jerusalem: A Report on the Banality of Evil*, by Hannah Arendt
5. *An Enquiry Into the Nature and Causes of the Wealth of Nations*, by Adam Smith
6. *Free to Choose: A Personal Statement*, by Milton & Rose Friedman
7. *Geronimo: His Own Story*, by Geronimo, & S. M. Barrett
8. *Hen's Teeth and Horse's Toes*, by Stephen Jay Gould
9. *Lucky: A Memoir*, by Alice Sebold
10. *Maybe I'll Pitch Forever*, by Leroy "Satchel" Paige, David Lipman
11. *Nine Hills to Nambonkaha: Two Years in the Heart of an African Village*, by Sarah Erdman
12. *The Origin of Species by Means of Natural Selection*, by Charles Darwin
13. *Power, Sex, Suicide: Mitochondria and the Meaning of Life*, by Nick Lane
14. *PT 105*, by Dick Keresey
15. *Quaker Spirituality: Selected Writings*, by HarperCollins Spiritual Classics
16. *The Souls of Black Folk*, by W.E.B. Dubois
17. *Struck by Lightning: The Curious World of Probabilities*, by Jeffrey S. Rosenthal
18. *Sufferings in Africa: The Astonishing Account of a New England Sea Captain Enslaved by North African Arabs* by James Riley
19. *Varieties of Religious Experience: A Study of Human Nature*, by William James
20. *What Evolution Is*, by Ernst Mayr

Indices

Author Index

(Nobel Prize in Literature winners are in bold-face. Pulitzer winners are indicated with an '*')

Abbott, Edwin A. *47*
Achebe, Chinua *122*
Ackerman, Diane *312*
Adichie, Chimamanda Ngozi *99*
Aeschylus *141*
Agee, James * *40*
Ahmed, Leila 198
Aidoo, Ama Ata *29*
Albee, Edward *165*
Allfrey, Phyllis S. *88*
Alvarez, Julia *63*
American Poetry & Literacy Project *176*
Anderson, Sherwood *135*
Angelou, Maya *228*
Appelbaum, Stanley *150*
Armstrong, Karen *332*
Ashe, Arthur *205*
St Augustine *326*

Bailey, John *241*
Baldwin, James *54*
Banville, John *106*
Beah, Ishmael *240*
Beckett, Samuel *164*
Bellow, Saul *108*
Benson, Herbert *314*
Best, Joel *291*
Biko, Steve *230*
Bissinger, H.G. *218*
Black Elk *195*
Black Hawk *197*
Blais, Madeleine *232*
Bolt, Robert *154*
Borges, Jorge Luis *45*
Boss, Alan, 307
Bowles, Paul *111*

Bradbury, Ray *66, 117*
Brazell, Karen *199*
Brossard, Chandler *1*
Brown, Dee *341*
Browning, Christopher, R. *256*
Buber, Martin *325*
Buck, Pearl * *56*
Burns, Robert *185*
Byock, Jesse L. *173*

Caesar, Julius 200
Calderon de La Barca, Pedro *150*
Calvino, Italo *16*
Camus, Albert *95*
Carpenter, John & Bogdana *179*
Carpentier, Alejo *71*
Carson, Ben *298*
Carson, Rachel *357*
Carter, Rubin *262*
Cather, Willa *39, 98*
Chadwick, Henry *326*
Charles, Daniel *308*
Chaucer Geoffrey *175*
Chekhov, Anton *140*
Chevalier, Tracy *53*
Chittick, William *329*
Chopin, Kate *14*
Coates, Carrol F. *128*
Coe, Michael D. *272*
Coe, Sophie D. *272*
Coelho, Paulo *4*
Coetzee, J.M. *129*
Coghill, Nevill *175*
Cohen, Stanley *220*
Cold Mountain (Han-Shan) *180*

Author

Collingham, Lizzie *204*
Confucius *323*
Conrad, Joseph *60*
Crane, Stephen *101*
Criddle, Joan D. *271*
Cullen, John *120*

The Dalai Lama *248*
Dana, Richard Henry *359*
David-Neel, Alexandra *249*
Davis, Sampson 257
Dawkins, Richard *316*
de la Pena, Jose Enrique *280*
de Mier, Fray Servando Teresa *247*
de Onis, Harriet *71*
de Sales, Francis 331
Delaney, Elizabeth & Sarah *223*
Dellinger, Susan *259*
Diamant, Anita *102*
Dickens, Charles *31*
Divakaruni, Chitra Banerjee *79*
Dobie, Kathy *255*
Dolot, Miron *213*
Dorris, Michael *136*
Douglass, Frederick *252*
Doyle, Sir Arthur Conan *61*
Duckett, Alfred *229*
Dryden, Ken *219*

Eliot, George *114*
Eliot, T.S. *156*
Ellis, Joseph J. * *217*
Ellison, Ralph *348*
Emecheta, Buchi *69*
Eshun Ekow *196*
Equiano, Olaudah *239*
Esquivel, Laura *74*
Euripedes *142*
Evans, Ann Llewellyn *335*

Fadiman, Anne *264*

Fagles, Robert *346*
Fahnestock, Lee *350*
Fast, Howard *8*
Farah, Nuruddin *52*
Fakhruddin 'Iraqi *329*
Faulkner, William *10*
Figiel, Sia *133*
Fischer, Louis *212*
Fisher, Helen *321*
Fitzgerald, F. Scott *59*
Forster, E.M. *64*
Fossey, Dian *299*
Foster, Frances Smith *233*
Foster, Thomas *227*
Fox, Douglas, C. *190*
St Francis de Sales *331*
Frank, Anne *192*
Frankl, Viktor *245*
Franklin, Benjamin *193*
Friedlander, Michael W. *285*
Friedman, Thomas L. *360*
Frobenius, Leo *190*
Fromm, Erich *324*

Gaarder, Jostein *358*
Gamow, George *313*
Gandhi, Mahatma *212*
Gardner, Martin *310*
Gawande, Atul *291*
George, Andrew *169*
Goethe, Johann Wolfgang von *147*
Goodall, Jane *302*
Golding, William *75*
Goleman, Daniel *295*
Gould, Laura L. *290*
Gonick, Larry *289*
Gourevitch, Philip *277*
Grafton, John *207*
Greene, Graham *96*
Grene, David *141, 142, 143*
Grossman, Edith *254*

Author

Haddon, Mark *36*
Haley, Alex *338*
Hamill, Pete *278*
Hamilton, Rita *172*
Handal, Nathalie *186*
Handford, S.A, *200*
Hansberry, Lorraine *161*
Hansen, Ron *12*
Harris, Joanne *30*
Harvey, Andrew *328, 336*
Hawking, Stephen *288*
Hayes, Bill *296*
Heaney, Seamus *167*
Hearth, Amy Hill *223*
Heim, Michael Henry *125*
Heller, Joseph *342*
Helvarg, David *286*
Hemingway, Ernest * *44, 85*
Herbert, Zbigniew *179*
Hersey, John *226*
Hesse, Hermann *113*
Hilton, James *76*
Hinton, S.E. *89*
Homer *83, 346*
Hope, Anthony *97*
Hossein, Nasr Seyyed *329*
Hosseini, Khaled *349*
Hrabel, Bohumil *125*
Holleman, Marybeth *300*
Hubbell, Sue *319*
Hugo, Viktor *350*
Hunt, Rameck *257*
Hurston, Zora Neale *121*
Huxley, Aldous *21*

Ibsen, Henrik *146*
Irving, Washington *103*

Jackson, Donald *197*
Jacobs, Harriet *233*
James, William, *334*
Jenkins, George *257*
Jerome, Fred *211*

Johnson, James Weldon *13*
Johnson, Josephine W. * *82*
Johnston, Ian *346*
Jones, Edward P. *77*
Judson, Olivia *294*

Kafka, Franz *126*
Kahn, Ashley *242*
Kahn, Roger *340*
Kazantzakis, Nikos *138*
Keckley, Elizabeth *194*
Keller, Helen *266*
Kelly, Fanny *251*
Keneally, Thomas *356*
Kesey, Ken *86*
Ketchum, Richard M. *206*
Keyes, Daniel *48*
Khadra, Yasmina *120*
Kidd, Sue Monk *107*
King, Thomas *78*
Kingston, Maxine Hong *281*
Klipper, Miriam Z. *314*
Kolata, Gina *215*
Knowles, John *109*
Koestler, Arthur *37*
Kosinski, Jerzy *91*
Kotlowitz, Alex *270*
Kourouma, Ahmadou *128*

Laciste, Grace *73*
Lahiri, Jhumpa * *67*
Lane, Helen *247*
Lardner, Ring *137*
Lawton, Manny *263*
le Carre, John *118*
Lee, Chang-Rae *80*
Lee, Harper * *123*
Levy, Stuart B. *284*
Lewis, C. S. *105*
Lewis, H. W. *320*
Lewis, Sinclair *352*
Liebling, A.J. *268*
Liebow, Elliot *269*

Author

Litton, Helen *234*
Longfellow, Henry Wadsworth *168, 170*

Maalouf, Amin *203*
MacAfee, Norman *350*
MacIntyre, Ben *244*
Mahfouz, Naguib *9*
Mailer, Norman *353*
Malamud, Bernard * *46*
Mam, Teeda Butt *271*
Mamet, David * *148*
Mann, Thomas *351*
Marquez, Gabriel Garcia *32, 254*
Martel, Yann *73*
Martinez, Ruben *201*
Masin, Barbara *221*
Masur, Louis P. *189*
Mathabane, Mark *236*
Matt, Daniel C. *327*
Maxwell, William *116*
McCullough, David *235*
McKay, Nellie Y. *233*
McPherson, James Alan * *43*
McPherson, James M. *216*
Mead, Margaret *191*
Merton, Thomas *333*
Michener, James A. *23*
Michigan Historical Reprint Series *251*
Miller, Arthur *144, 145*
Miller, Walter M. *26*
Min, Anchee *17*
Mlodinow, Leonard *288*
Mori, Kyoko *112*
Morris, Desmond *311*
Morrison, Toni *119*
Murphey, Cecil *298*

Naipaul, V.S. *20*
Nathan, John *94*
Ndebele, Njabulo *50*

Negri, Paul *184*
Neihardt, John G. *195*
Nijo, Lady *199*
Noll, Mark A. *337*
Nooteboom, Cees *49*
Norman, Marsha * *157*
Norris, Frank *355*

O'Brien, Flann *11*
O'Brien, Tim *55*
O' Connor, Flannery *57*
Oë, Kenzaburo *94*
Oliver, Mary * *178*
O'Neil, Eugene *152*
Orwell, George *2, 7*
Oshinsky, David M. **258, 282*
Ovid *183*

Page, Lisa Frazier *257*
Palmer, George Herbert *83*
Pasternak, Boris *343*
Patchett, Ann *18*
Paton, Alan *34*
Paulos, John Allen *303*
Paulsen, Gary *279*
Payne, Katy *317*
Payton, Walter *253*
Peden, Margaret Sayers *92*
Peers, E. Allison *331*
Perry, Carmen *280*
Perry, Janet *172*
Philbrick, Nathaniel *231*
Plath, Sylvia *19*
Poe, Edgar Allan *1*
Pollan, Michael *287*
Porter, Roy *243*
Power, Susan *104*
Preston, Diana *339*
Price, Vincent *1*
Pynchon, Thomas *35*

Rabe, John *222*
Rampersad, Arnold *205*

366

Author

Remarque, Erich Maria 6
Rhenquist, William H. 267
Rhys, Jean 134
Rich, Louise 276
Rigden, John S. 301
Roach, Mary 318
Robeson, Paul 224
Robinson, Jackie 229
Robinson, Marilynne 62
Roosevelt, Theodore 261
Roth, Philip 58
Rulfo, Juan 92
Runciman, Steven 214
Rushdie, Salman 110

Sacks, Oliver 309
Salinger, J.D. 27
Salisbury, Gay 202
Salisbury, Laney 202
Saroyan, William 65
Sartre, Jean Paul 158
Satrapi, Marjane 93
Sayers, Dorothy L. 174
Schiff, Hilda 182
Schreiber, Marion 273
Schuyler, James 5
Schwarcz, Joe 297
See, Lisa 115
Seife, Charles 322
Selvon, Samuel 24
Shakespeare, William 139
Shaw, George Bernard 162
Shinseki, David M. 258, 282
Shiva, Vandana 265
Shelley, Mary 51
Sherman, Joan R. 177
Sijie, Dai 15
Simon, Neil * 153
Sinclair, Upton * 70
Sloane, Eric 208
Snyder, Gary Snyder * 188
Sophocles 143
Soseki, Natsume 72

Soyinka, Wole 151
Stannard, Russell 313
Stark, Peter 305
Steinbeck, John * 84, 345
Stoker, Bram 42
Stowe, Harriet Beecher 127
Strindberg, August 155
Stubbs, Aelred 230
Swanwick, Anna, 147
Switzer, Katherine 246

Tan, Amy 68
Tang, Truong Nhu 275
Taylor, Rodger 211
Taylor, William Banks 209
Tennyson, Alfred 171
St. Teresa of Avila 330
Terkel, Studs * 344
Thiong'o, Ngugi wa 132
Thomas, Lewis 306
Thomas, Piri 210
Tierno Jr, Philip M. 315
Tolan, Sandy 237
Toland, John 263
Tolstoy, Leo 130
Tuchman, Barbara W. 283
Tutuola, Amos 90
Twain, Mark 3, 347
Tyler, Anne 41

Updike, John 100

Vergil 166
Voltaire 25
Vonnegut Jr., Kurt 28

Waley, Arthur 323
Walker, Alice * 33
Washington, Booker T. 274
Watkins, S. Craig 225
Watson, James D. 293
Weller, Shane 181
Wells, H. G. 131

Author

Wells, Spencer *304*
Welty, Eudora * *87*
West, Nathanael *38*
Wheelan, Charles *250*
Wheelis, Mark *289*
Whitfield, Susan *238*
Whitman, Walt *187*
Wiesel, Elie *81*
Wilde, Oscar *149*
Wilder, Thornton * *22, 159*

Williams, Tennessee * *163*
Wilson, August * *160*
Wilson, Peter *329*
Wolfe, Tom *260*
Woolf, Virginia *124*
Wright, Richard *354*

X, Malcolm *338*

Yaeger, Don *253*

Authors by Country Index

African Authors

Algerian
Khadra, Yasmina *120*
Egyptian
Ahmed, Leila 198
Mahfouz, Naguib *9*
Ghanaian
Aidoo, Ama Ata *29*
Eshun Ekow *196*
Ivorian
Kourouma, Ahmadou *128*
Kenyan
Thiong'o, Ngugi wa *132*
Nigerian
Achebe, Chinua *122*

Adichie, Chimamanda Ngozi *99*
Emecheta, Buchi *69*
Equiano, Olaudah *239*
Soyinka, Wole *151*
Tutuola, Amos *90*
Sierra Leonean
Beah, Ishmael *240*
Somali
Farah, Nuruddin *52*
South African
Biko, Steve *230*
Coetzee, J.M. *129*
Mathabane, Mark *236*
Ndebele, Njabulo *50*
Paton, Alan *34*

Asian Authors

Afghan
Hosseini, Khaled *349*
Cambodian
Mam, Teeda Butt *271*
Chinese
Confucius 323
Cold Mountain (Han-Shan) *180*
Min, Anchee *17*
Sijie, Dai *15*
Indian
Divakaruni, Chitra Banerjee *79*
Gandhi, Mahatma *212*

Naipaul, V.S. *20*
Rushdie, Salman *110*
Shiva, Vandana *265*
Japanese
Mori, Kyoko *112*
Nijo, Lady 199
Oë, Kenzaburo *94*
Soseki, Natsume 72
Korean
Lee, Chang-Rae 80
Tibetan
The Dalai Lama 248
Vietnamese
Tang, Truong Nhu 275

Author by Country

Australian & Pacific Island Authors

Australian
Bailey, John *241*
Keneally, Thomas *356*

Samoan
Figiel, Sia *133*

European Authors

Austrian
Buber, Martin *325*
Frankl, Viktor *245*

British
Abbott, Edwin A. *47*
Armstrong, Karen *332*
Bolt, Robert *154*
Burns, Robert *185*
Chaucer Geoffrey *175*
Coghill, Nevill *175*
Collingham, Lizzie *204*
Conrad, Joseph *60*
Dawkins, Richard *316*
Dickens, Charles *31*
Doyle, Sir Arthur Conan *61*
Eliot, George *114*
Forster, E.M. *64*
George, Andrew *169*
Golding, William *75*
Goodall, Jane *302*
Haddon, Mark *36*
Harris, Joanne *30*
Hawking, Stephen *288*
Hilton, James *76*
Hope, Anthony *97*
Huxley, Aldous *21*
Judson, Olivia *294*
le Carre, John *118*
MacIntyre, Ben *244*
Naipaul, V.S. *20*
Orwell, George *2, 7*
Preston, Diana *339*
Porter, Roy *243*

Runciman, Steven *214*
Rushdie, Salman *110*
Sacks, Oliver *309*
Sayers, Dorothy L. *174*
Shakespeare, William *139*
Shelley, Mary *51*
Swanwick, Anna, 147
Tennyson, Alfred *171*
Wells, H. G. *131*
Whitfield, Susan *238*
Woolf, Virginia *124*

Czech
Hrabel, Bohumil *125*
Kafka, Farnz 126

Dutch
Frank, Anne *192*
Nooteboom, Cees *49*

French
Anonymous (*The Song of Roland*) 174
Camus, Albert *95*
David-Neel, Alexandra *249*
Hugo, Viktor *350*
de Sales, Francis *331*
Sartre, Jean Paul *158*
Voltaire *25*

German
Frobenius, Leo *190*
Fromm, Erich *324*
Goethe, Johann Wolfgang von *147*
Hesse, Hermann *113*
Mann, Thomas *351*

Rabe, John *222*
Remarque, Erich Maria *6*
Schreiber, Marion *273*

Greek
Aeschylus *141*
Euripedes *142*
Homer *83, 346*
Kazantzakis, Nikos *138*
Sophocles *143*

Hungarian
Koestler, Arthur *37*

Icelandic
Anonymous (*The Saga of the Volsungs*) *173*

Irish
Banville, John *106*
Beckett, Samuel *164*
Grene, David *141, 142, 143*
Heaney, Seamus *167*
Lewis, C. S. *105*
O'Brien, Flann *11*
Shaw, George Bernard *162*
Stoker, Bram *42*
Wilde, Oscar *149*

Italian
Caesar, Julius *200*
Calvino, Italo *16*
Ovid *183*
Vergil *166*

Norwegian
Gaarder, Jostein *358*
Ibsen, Henrik *146*

Polish
Herbert, Zbigniew *179*
Kosinski, Jerzy *91*

Romanian
Wiesel, Elie *81*

Russian
Chekhov, Anton *140*
Pasternak, Boris *343*
Tolstoy, Leo *130*

Spanish
Anonymous *(El Cid) 172*
Calderón de La Barca, Pedro *150*
de Mier, Fray Servando Teresa *247*
St. Teresa of Avila *330*

Swedish
Strindberg, August *155*

Ukrainian
Dolot, Miron *213*
Gamow, George *313*

Middle Eastern Authors

Arab
Handal, Nathalie *186*

Iranian
Satrapi, Marjane *93*

Lebanese
Maalouf, Amin *203*

Persian
Fakhruddin 'Iraqi *329*

Author by Country

North American Authors

American

Ackerman, Diane *312*
Agee, James *40*
Ahmed, Leila *198*
Albee, Edward *165*
Alvarez, Julia *63*
American Poetry & Literacy Project *176*
Anderson, Sherwood *135*
Angelou, Maya *228*
Ashe, Arthur *205*

Baldwin, James *54*
Bellow, Saul *108*
Benson, Herbert *314*
Best, Joel *292*
Bissinger, H.G. *218*
Black Elk *195*
Black Hawk *197*
Blais, Madeleine *232*
Boss, Alan *307*
Bowles, Paul *111*
Bradbury, Ray *66, 117*
Brazell, Karen *199*
Brown, Dee 341
Browning, Christopher, R. *256*
Buck, Pearl *56*
Byock, Jesse L. *173*

Carpenter, John & Bogdana 179
Carson, Ben 298
Carson, Rachel *357*
Carter, Rubin *262*
Cather, Willa *39, 98*
Charles, Daniel *308*
Chevalier, Tracy *53*
Chopin, Kate *14*

Coe, Michael & Sophie *272*
Cohen, Stanley *220*
Crane, Stephen *101*
Criddle, Joan D. *271*
Cullen, John 120

Dana, Richard Henry *359*
Davis, Sampson *257*
Delaney, Elizabeth & Sarah *223*
Dellinger, Susan *259*
Diamant, Anita *102*
Divakaruni, Chitra Banerjee *79*
Dobie, Kathy *255*
Dolot, Miron *213*
Douglass, Frederick *252*
Duckett, Alfred 229

Ellis, Joseph J. *217*
Ellison, Ralph *348*
Eliot, T.S. *156*

Fadiman, Anne *264*
Fahnestock, Lee *350*
Fast, Howard *8*
Faulkner, William *10*
Fisher, Helen *321*
Fitzgerald, F. Scott *59*
Fossey, Dian *299*
Foster, Thomas *227*
Franklin, Benjamin *193*
Friedlander, Michael W. *285*
Friedman, Thomas L. *360*

Gardner, Martin *31*
Gawande, Atul *291*

Author by Country

Goleman, Daniel *295*
Gonick, Larry *289*
Gould, Laura L. *290*
Gourevitch, Philip *277*
Grene, David *141, 142, 143*
Greene, Graham *96*

Haley, Alex *338*
Hamill, Pete *278*
Handford, S.A, *200*
Hansberry, Lorraine *161*
Hansen, Ron *12*
Hayes, Bill *296*
Hearth, Amy Hill *223*
Heller, Joseph *342*
Helvarg, David *286*
Hemingway, Ernest *44, 85*
Hersey, John *226*
Hinton, S.E. *89*
Holleman, Marybeth *300*
Hosseini, Khaled *349*
Hubbell, Sue *319*
Hunt, Rameck *257*
Hurston, Zora Neale *121*

Irving, Washington *103*

Jacobs, Harriet *233*
James, William, *334*
Jenkins, George *257*
Jerome, Fred *211*
Johnson, James Weldon *13*
Johnson, Josephine W. *82*
Jones, Edward P. *77*

Kahn, Ashley *242*
Kahn, Roger *340*
Keckley, Elizabeth *194*
Keller, Helen *266*
Kelly, Fanny *251*
Kesey, Ken *86*
Ketchum, Richard M. *206*
Keyes, Daniel *48*

Kidd, Sue Monk *107*
Kingston, Maxine Hong *281*
Knowles, John *109*
Kolata, Gina *215*
Kotlowitz, Alex *270*

Lahiri, Jhumpa *67*
Lardner, Ring *137*
Lawton, Manny *263*
Lee, Chang-Rae *80*
Lee, Harper *123*
Levy, Stuart B. *284*
Lewis, H. W. *320*
Lewis, Sinclair *352*
Liebling, A.J. *268*
Liebow, Elliot *269*
Longfellow, Henry Wadsworth *168, 170*

Maalouf, Amin *202*
MacAfee, Norman *350*
Mailer, Norman *353*
Malamud, Bernard *46*
Mamet, David *148*
Martinez, Ruben *201*
Masin, Barbara *221*
Masur, Louis P. *189*
Matt, Daniel C. *327*
Maxwell, William *116*
McCullough, David *235*
McPherson, James Alan *43*
McPherson, James M. *216*
Mead, Margaret *191*
Merton, Thomas *333*
Michener, James A. *23*
Michigan Historical Reprint Series *251*
Miller, Arthur *144, 145*
Miller, Walter M. *26*
Min, Anchee *17*
Mori, Kyoko *112*
Morris, Desmond *311*
Morrison, Toni *119*

Author by Country

Murphey, Cecil *299*

Neihardt, John G. *195*
Noll, Mark A. *337*
Norman, Marsha *157*
Norris, Frank *355*

O'Brien, Tim *55*
O' Connor, Flannery *57*
O'Neil, Eugene *152*
Oliver, Mary *178*
Oshinsky, David M. *258, 282*

Page, Lisa Frazier *257*
Patchett, Ann *18*
Paulos, John Allen *303*
Paulsen, Gary *279*
Payne, Katy *317*
Payton, Walter *253*
Peden, Margaret Sayers *92*
Philbrick, Nathaniel *231*
Plath, Sylvia *19*
Poe, Edgar Allan *1*
Pollan, Michael *287*
Pynchon, Thomas *35*

Rampersad, Arnold *205*
Rhenquist, William H. *267*
Rich, Louise *276*
Rigden, John S. *301*
Roach, Mary *318*
Robeson, Paul *224*
Robinson, Jackie *229*
Robinson, Marilynne *62*
Roosevelt, Theodore *261*
Roth, Philip *58*

Salinger, J.D. *27*
Salisbury, Gay *202*
Salisbury, Laney *202*
Saroyan, William *65*
Schuyler, James *5*
See, Lisa *115*

Seife, Charles *322*
Sherman, Joan R. *177*
Simon, Neil *153*
Sinclair, Upton *70*
Sloane, Eric *208*
Snyder, Gary *188*
Stark, Peter 305
Steinbeck, John *84, 345*
Stowe, Harriet Beecher *127*
Switzer, Katherine, 246

Taylor, Rodger *211*
Taylor, William Banks *209*
Tan, Amy *68*
Terkel, Studs *344*
Thomas, Lewis *306*
Thomas, Piri *210*
Tierno Jr, Philip M. *315*
Tolan, Sandy *237*
Toland, John *263*
Tuchman, Barbara W. *283*
Twain, Mark *3, 347*
Tyler, Anne *41*

Updike, John *100*

Vonnegut Jr., Kurt *28*

Walker, Alice *33*
Washington, Booker T. *274*
Watkins, S. Craig *225*
Watson, James D. *293*
Wells, Spencer *304*
Welty, Eudora *87*
West, Nathanael *38*
Wheelis, Mark *289*
Wheelan, Charles *250*
Whitman, Walt *187*
Wiesel, Elie *81*
Wilder, Thornton *22, 159*
Williams, Tennessee *163*
Wilson, August *160*
Wolfe, Tom *260*

Wright, Richard 354

X, Malcolm *338*

Canadian
    Dryden, Ken *219*
    Evans, Ann Llewellyn *335*
    Johnston, Ian *346*
    Martel, Yann *73*
    Schwarcz, Joe *297*

Mexican
    de la Pena, Jose Enrique *280*
    de Mier, Fray Servando Teresa *247*
    Esquivel, Laura *74*
    Rulfo, Juan *92*

Native American
    Black Elk *195*
    Black Hawk *197*
    Dorris, Michael *136*
    King, Thomas *78*
    Power, Susan *104*

South American & Caribbean Authors

Argentinean
    Borges, Jorge Luis *45*

Brazilian
    Coelho, Paulo *4*

Caribbean
    Allfrey, Phyllis S. *88*
    Naipaul, V.S. *20*
    Rampersad, Arnold *205*
    Rhys, Jean *134*
    Selvon, Samuel *24*

Colombian
    Marquez, Gabriel Garcia *32, 254*

Cuban
    Carpentier, Alejo *71*

African-American Authors Index

Angelou, Maya *228*
Ashe, Arthur *205*
Baldwin, James *54*
Carson, Ben *298*
Carter, Rubin *262*
Davis, Sampson *257*
Delaney, Elizabeth & Sarah *223*
Douglass, Frederick *252*
Duckett, Alfred *229*
Ellison, Ralph *348*
Haley, Alex *338*
Hansberry, Lorraine *161*
Hunt, Rameck *257*
Hurston, Zora Neale *121*
Jacobs, Harriet *233*

Jenkins, George *257*
Johnson, James Weldon *13*
Jones, Edward P. *77*
Keckley, Elizabeth 194
McPherson, James Alan *43*
Morrison, Toni *119*
Payton, Walter *253*
Robeson, Paul *224*
Robinson, Jackie *229*
Sherman, Joan R. *177*
Washington, Booker T. *274*
Walker, Alice *33*
Wilson, August *160*
Wright, Richard *354*
X, Malcolm *338*

Women Authors Index

Ackerman, Diane *312*
Adichie, Chimamanda Ngozi *99*
Ahmed, Leila 198
Aidoo, Ama Ata *29*
Allfrey, Phyllis S. *88*
Alvarez, Julia *63*
Angelou, Maya *228*
Armstrong, Karen *332*

Blais, Madeleine *232*
Brazell, Karen *199*
Buck, Pearl *56*

Carson, Rachel *357*
Cather, Willa *39, 98*
Chevalier, Tracy *53*
Chopin, Kate *14*
Coates, Carrol F. *128*
Coe, Sophie D. *272*
Collingham, Lizzie *204*

Criddle, Joan D. *271*

David-Neel, Alexandra *249*
Delaney, Elizabeth & Sarah *223*
Dellinger, Susan *259*
Diamant, Anita *102*
Divakaruni, Chitra Banerjee *79*
Dobie, Kathy *255*

Eliot, George *114*
Emecheta, Buchi *69*
Esquivel, Laura *74*
Evans, Ann Llewellyn *335*

Fadiman, Anne *264*
Fahnestock, Lee *350*
Fischer, Louis *212*
Fisher, Helen *321*
Fossey, Dian *299*
Frank, Anne *192*

African American / Women Authors

Goodall, Jane *302*
Gould, Laura L. *290*
Grossman, Edith *254*

Hansberry, Lorraine *161*
Harris, Joanne *30*
Hearth, Amy Hill *223*
Hill, Fanny *252*
Hinton, S.E. *89*
Holleman, Marybeth *300*
Hubbell, Sue *319*
Hurston, Zora Neale *121*

Jacobs, Harriet *233*
Johnson, Josephine W. *82*
Judson, Olivia *294*

Keckley, Elizabeth *194*
Keller, Helen *266*
Kelly, Fanny *251*
Kidd, Sue Monk *107*
Kingston, Maxine Hong *281*
Klipper, Miriam Z. *314*
Kolata, Gina *215*

Laciste, Grace *73*
Lahiri, Jhumpa *67*
Lane, Helen *247*
Lee, Harper *123*
Litton, Helen *234*

Mam, Teeda Butt *271*
Masin, Barbara *221*
Mead, Margaret *191*
Min, Anchee *17*
Mori, Kyoko *112*
Morrison, Toni *119*

Nijo, Lady *199*
Norman, Marsha *157*

O' Connor, Flannery *57*

Oliver, Mary *178*

Page, Lisa Frazier *257*
Patchett, Ann *18*
Payne, Katy 317
Peden, Margaret Sayers *92*
Plath, Sylvia *19*
Power, Susan 104
Preston, Diana *339*

Rhys, Jean *134*
Rich, Louise *276*
Roach, Mary *318*
Robinson, Marilynne *62*

Salisbury, Gay 202
Salisbury, Laney 202
Satrapi, Marjane *93*
Sayers, Dorothy L. *174*
Schiff, Hilda *182*
Schreiber, Marion *273*
See, Lisa *115*
Shelley, Mary *51*
Sherman, Joan R. *177*
Shiva, Vandana *265*
Stowe, Harriet Beecher *127*
Swanwick, Anna, 147
Switzer, Katherine, 246

Tan, Amy *68*
St. Teresa of Avila *331*
Tuchman, Barbara W. *283*
Tyler, Anne *41*

Walker, Alice 33
Welty, Eudora *87*
Whitfield, Susan *238*
Woolf, Virginia *124*

Date of First Publication Index

2000-
1831: Year of Eclipse 189
Balzac and the Little Chinese Seamstress 15
Becoming Madame Mao 17
Before the Fallout: From Marie Curie to Hiroshima 339
Bel Canto 18
Black Gold of the Sun: Searching for Home in Africa and Beyond 196
Blue Frontier: Saving America's Living Seas 286
The Botany of Desire: A Plant's-Eye View of the World 287
A Briefer History of Time 288
Complications: A Surgeon's Notes on an Imperfect Science 291
Crossing Over: A Mexican Family on the Migrant Trail 201
The Cruelest Miles: The Heroic Story of Dogs and Men in a Race against an Epidemic 202
The Curious Incident of the Dog in the Night-Time 36
Curry: A Tale of Cooks and Conquerors 204
Damned Lies and Statistics: Untangling Numbers from the Media, Politicians, and Activists 292
Dr. Tatiana's Sex Advice to All Creation: the Definitive Guide to the Evolutionary Biology of Sex 294
Einstein on Race and Racism 211
Five Quarts: A Personal and Natural History of Blood 296
Founding Brothers: The Revolutionary Generation 217
Gauntlet: Five Friends, 20,000 Enemy Troops, & the Secret That Could Have Changed the Course of the Cold War 221
The Genie in the Bottle: 64 All New Commentaries on the Fascinating Chemistry of Everyday Life 297
Heart of the Sound 300
Hip Hop Matters: Politics, Pop Culture, and the Struggle for the Soul of a Movement 225
How to Read Literature like a Professor: a Lively and Entertaining Guide to Reading between the Line 227
Hydrogen: The Essential Element 301
In the Heart of the Sea: The Tragedy of the Whaleship Essex 231
Islam: A Short History 332
The Journey of Man: A Genetic Odyssey 304
The Kite Runner 349

Publication Date

Last Breath: Cautionary Tales from the Limits of Human Endurance 305
The Lemon Tree: An Arab, a Jew, and the Heart of the Middle East 237
Life of Pi 73
A Long Way Gone: Memoirs of a Boy Soldier 240
Lords of the Harvest: Biotech, Big Money, and the Future of Food 308
The Lost German Slave Girl: The Extraordinary True Story of Sally Miller and Her Fight for Freedom in Old New Orleans 241
A Love Supreme: The Making of John Coltrane's Masterpiece 242
Madness: A Brief History 243
The Man Who Would Be King: The First American in Afghanistan 244
Marathon Woman: Running the Race to Revolutionize Women's Sports 246
Naked Economics: Undressing the Dismal Science 250
Never Die Easy: The Autobiography of Walter Payton 253
The Only Girl in the Car 255
The Pact 257
Persepolis: The Story of a Childhood 93
Polio: An American Story 258
Purple Hibiscus 99
Red Legs and Black Sox: Edd Roush and the Untold Story of the 1919 World Series 259
Roofwalker 104
The Sea 106
The Secret Life of Bees 107
The Secret Life of Germs: What They Are, Why We Need Them, and How We Can Protect Ourselves Against Them 315
Shinto Norito - A Book of Prayers 335
Snow Flower and the Secret Fan 115
Stiff: The Curious Lives of Human Cadavers 318
The Swallows of Kabul 120
Teachings of the Hindu Mystics 336
The Twentieth Train: The True Story of the Ambush of the Death Train to Auschwitz 273
Why We Love: The Nature and Chemistry of Romantic Love 321
The World Is Flat: a Brief History of the Twenty-first Century 360
Zero: The Biography of a Dangerous Idea 322

Publication Date

1990s

African-American Poetry: An Anthology, 1773-1927 177
The Antibiotic Paradox: How the Misuse of Antibiotics Destroys Their Curative Powers 284
At the Fringes of Science 285
Atticus 12
A Border Passage: From Cairo to America—A Woman's Journey 198
Cats Are Not Peas: A Calico History of Genetics 290
Changes: A Love Story 29
Chocolat 30
Days of Grace 205
Decisive Day: The Battle for Bunker Hill 206
Down on Parchman Farm: The Great Prison in the Mississippi Delta 209
Emotional Intelligence 295
The Essential Kabbalah: The Heart of Jewish Mysticism 327
The Essential Mystics: Selections from the World's Great Wisdom Traditions 328
The Following Story 49
Flu: The Story of the Great Influenza Pandemic of 1918 and the Search for the Virus That Caused It 215
For Cause and Comrades: Why Men Fought in the Civil War 216
Friday Night Lights: A Town, a Team, and a Dream 218
Gifted Hands: The Ben Carson Story 298
Girl with a Pearl Earring 53
Glengarry Glen Ross 148
The Good Man of Nanking: The Diaries of John Rabe 222
Having Our Say: The Delany Sisters' First 100 Years 223
Holocaust Poetry 182
How the Garcia Girls Lost Their Accents 63
In These Girls, Hope is a Muscle 232
Interpreter of Maladies 67
The Irish Famine: An Illustrated History 234
Life along the Silk Road 238
Looking for Earths: The Race to Find New Solar Systems 307
Lost in the City 77
Lost in Yonkers 153
Medicine River 78
The Mistress of Spices 79
Native Speaker 80
A Natural History of the Senses 312

Publication Date

News of a Kidnapping 254
*Ordinary Men: Reserve Police Battalion 101 and the Final
    Solution in Poland* 256
The Red Tent 102
Shizuko's Daughter 112
Silent Thunder: In the Presence of Elephants 317
Sophie's World 358
The Spirit Catches You and You Fall Down 264
Stolen Harvest: The Hijacking of the Global Food Supply 265
Tell Them Who I Am: The Lives of Homeless Women 269
*There Are No Children Here: The Story of Two Boys Growing Up
    in Urban America* 270
The True History of Chocolate 272
Turning Points: Decisive Moments in the History of Christianity
    337
Waiting for Aphrodite: Journeys into the Time before Bones 319
Waiting for the Barbarians 129
Waiting for the Vote of the Wild Animals 128
*We Wish to Inform You That Tomorrow We Will be Killed with
    Our Families: Stories from Rwanda* 277
Where We Once Belonged 133
Why Flip a Coin? The Art and Science of Good Decisions 320
Why Sinatra Matters 278
Winterdance: The Fine Madness of Running the Iditarod 279
*Worse than Slavery: Parchman Farm and the Ordeal of Jim Crow
    Justice,* 282
A Yellow Raft in Blue Water 136

1980s

The Alchemist: A Fable about Following Your Dream 4
American Primitive 178
The Cartoon Guide to Genetics 289
Chronicle of a Death Foretold 32
The Color Purple 33
Crusades through Arab Eyes 203
Dinner at the Homesick Restaurant 41
Execution by Hunger: The Hidden Holocaust 213
Fools and Other Stories 50
The Game 219
The Good War: An Oral History of World War II 344
Gorillas in the Mist 299
Housekeeping 62
Innumeracy: Mathematical Illiteracy and Its Consequences 303

Publication Date

The Joy Luck 68
Kaffir Boy: The True Story of a Black Youth's Coming-of-age in Apartheid South Africa 236
Like Water for Chocolate 74
The Man Who Mistook His Wife for a Hat: And Other Clinical Tales 309
'night, Mother 157
The Piano Lesson 160
Schindler's List 356
Shame 110
So Long, See You Tomorrow 116
Some Survived: An Eyewitness Account of the Bataan Death March and the Men Who Lived Through It 263
The Supreme Court 267
To Destroy You Is No Loss: The Odyssey of a Cambodian Family 271
A Vietcong Memoir: An Inside Account of the Vietnam War and Its Aftermath 275

1970s

Arabian Nights and Days 9
A Bend in the River 20
The Boys of Summer 340
Bury My Heart at Wounded Knee: An Indian History of the American West 341
Elbow Room 43
From a Crooked Rib 52
The Game They Played 220
Going After Cacciato 55
I Never Had It Made: An Autobiography of Jackie Robinson 229
I Write What I Like: Selected Writings 230
In the Shadow of Man 302
Joys of Motherhood 69
The Lives of a Cell 306
Mr. Cogito 179
The Optimist's Daughter 87
The Relaxation Response 314
The Right Stuff 260
The Selfish Gene 316
The Sixteenth Round: From Number 1 Contender To #45472 262
Sula 119
Too Loud a Solitude 125
Turtle Island 188

Publication Date

The Woman Warrior: Memoirs of a Girlhood among Ghosts 281

1960s
April Morning 8
The Autobiography of Malcolm X 338
The Bell Jar 19
Cat's Cradle 28
Catch 22 342
The Crying of Lot 49 35
The Double Helix: A Personal Account of the Discovery of the Structure of DNA 293
Down These Mean Streets 210
The Essential Gandhi: An Anthology of His Writings on His Life, Work, and Ideas 212
The Fall of Constantinople 1453 214
The Fixer 46
Flowers for Algernon 48
Goodbye, Columbus 58
I Know Why the Caged Bird Sings 228
Johnstown Flood 235
The Lion and the Jewel 151
A Man for All Seasons 154
My Land and My People: The Original Autobiography of His Holiness the Dalai Lama of Tibet 248
The Naked Ape 311
New Seeds of Contemplation 333
The New World of Mr. Tompkins 313
One Flew Over the Cuckoo's Nest 86
The Outsiders 89
The Painted Bird 91
A Personal Matter 94
Rabbit, Run 100
Silent Spring 357
Something Wicked This Way Comes 117
The Spy Who Came In from the Cold 118
To Kill a Mockingbird 123
Weep Not, Child 132
Wide Sargasso Sea 134
Who's Afraid of Virginia Woolf? 165

1950s
Alfred and Guinevere 5
The Art of Loving 324

Publication Date

The Baron in the Trees 16
The Bridges at Toko-Ri 23
Brighter Sun 24
A Canticle for Leibowitz 26
The Catcher in the Rye 27
The Crucible 144
A Death in the Family 40
Doctor Zhivago 343
Go Tell It on the Mountain 54
A Good Man is Hard to Find 57
Here I Stand 224
The Illustrated Man 66
Invisible Man 348
Lord of the Flies 75
Mathematics, Magic and Mystery (Cards, Coins, and Other Magic) 310
Night 81
Old Man and the Sea 85
The Orchid House 88
The Palm-Wine Drinkard and My Life in the Bush of Ghosts 90
Pedro Paramo 92
A Raisin in the Sun 161
Seize the Day 108
A Separate Peace 109
The Sweet Science 268
Things Fall Apart 122
Waiting for Godot 164
Zimmermann Telegram 283

1940s

1984 2
And Keep Your Powder Dry: An Anthropologist Looks at America 191
Animal Farm 7
Anne Frank: The Diary of a Young Girl 192
Between Man and Man 325
Cry, the Beloved Country 34
Darkness at Noon 37
The Death of a Salesman 145
Ficciones 45
Hiroshima 226
The Human Comedy 65
The Kingdom of This World 71

Publication Date

A Long Day's Journey into Night 152
Man's Search for Meaning 245
The Naked and the Dead 353
Native Son 354
The New World of Mr. Tompkins 313
No Exit and Three Other Plays 158
The Plague 95
The Power and the Glory 96
The Screwtape Letters 105
The Sheltering Sky 111
A Streetcar Named Desire 163
We Took to the Woods 276
Zorba the Greek 138

1930s

African Genesis: Folk Tales and Myths of Africa 190
As I Lay Dying 10
At Swim-Two-Birds 11
Black Elk Speaks 195
Brave New World 21
The Day of the Locust 38
The Good Earth 56
The Grapes of Wrath 345
Lost Horizon 76
Murder in the Cathedral 156
Now in November 82
Of Mice and Men 84
Our Town 159
Their Eyes Were Watching God 121

1920s

All Quiet on the Western Front 6
Bridge of San Luis Rey 22
Death Comes for the Archbishop 39
A Farewell to Arms 44
The Great Gatsby 59
The Magic Mountain 351
Main Street 352
My Journey to Lhasa 249
The Professor's House 98
Saint Joan 162
Siddhartha 113
To the Lighthouse 124

Publication Date

    The Trial 126

1910s
    The Autobiography of an Ex-Colored Man 13
    Howards End 64
    Kokoro 72
    Winesburg, Ohio 135
    You Know Me Al 137

1900s
    The Cherry Orchard 140
    Hound of the Baskervilles 61
    The Jungle 70
    The Octopus 355
    Pragmatism: A New Name for Some Old Ways of Thinking 334
    The Story of My Life 266
    Up from Slavery: An Autobiography 274

19th Century
    18 Best Stories by Edgar Allan Poe 1
    101 Great American Poems 176
    The Adventures of Huckleberry Finn 3
    African-American Poetry: An Anthology, 1773-1927 177
    The Awakening 14
    Behind the Scenes in the Lincoln White House: Memoirs of an African-American Seamstress 194
    Black Hawk: An Autobiography 197
    A Christmas Carol 31
    Courtship of Miles Standish 168
    The Declaration of Independence and Other Great Documents of American History 1775-1865 207
    Diary of an Early American Boy: Noah Blake 1805 208
    A Doll's House 146
    Dracula 42
    Evangeline 170
    Faust Part One 147
    Flatland: A Romance of Many Dimensions 47
    Frankenstein 51
    Heart of Darkness 60
    Idylls of the King 171
    The Importance of Being Earnest 149
    Incidents in the Life of a Slave Girl 233

Publication Date

Les Miserables 350
Miss Julie 155
The Innocents Abroad 347
Memoirs of Fray Servando Teresa de Mier 247
Narrative of my captivity among the Sioux Indians. By Fanny Kelly. With a brief account of General Sully's Indian expedition in 1864, bearing upon events occurring in my captivity 251
Narrative of the Life of Frederick Douglass 252
The Prisoner of Zenda 97
The Red Badge of Courage 101
Rip Van Winkle and Other Stories: And Other Stories 103
Rough Riders 261
Selected Poems 187
Silas Marner 114
Two Years Before the Mast: And Twenty-Four Years After 359
Uncle Tom's Cabin 127
Walk in the Light & Twenty-Three Tales 130
The War of the Worlds 131
With Santa Anna in Texas: A Personal Narrative of the Revolution 280

18th Century

African-American Poetry: An Anthology, 1773-1927 177
The Autobiography of Benjamin Franklin 193
Candide 25
The Declaration of Independence and Other Great Documents of American History 1775-1865 207
The Life of Olaudah Equiano 239
Poems and Songs 185

17th Century

3 by Shakespeare: A Midsummer Night's Dream, Romeo and Juliet and Richard III 139
Introduction to the Devout Life 331
Life Is a Dream/La Vida es Sueno 150

16th Century

Interior Castle 330

14th Century

Confessions of Lady Nijo 199

Publication Date

Troilus and Criseyde 175

13th Century
Fakhruddin Iraqi: Divine Flashes 329
The Saga of the Volsungs 173

12th Century
The Poem of the Cid: Dual Language Edition 172

11th Century
The Song of Roland 174

10th Century
Beowulf 167

8th Century
The Collected Songs of Cold Mountain 180

4th Century
Confessions 326

Earlier
Aeneid 166
The Analects of Confucius 323
The Complete Greek Tragedies: Aeschylus II 141
The Complete Greek Tragedies: Euripides V 142
The Complete Greek Tragedies: Sophocles I 143
The Conquest of Gaul 200
The Epic of Gilgamesh 169
The Iliad 346
The Metamorphoses: Selected Stories in Verse 183
The Odyssey 83

Keyword Index

A

absurdism, 25, 95, 125, 126, 164, 165, 342
abuse, 3, 33, 107, 228, 233, 240
Adams, John, 217
adventure, 3, 4, 49, 73, 75, 76, 97, 244
Afghanistan, 120, 244, 349
Africa, 190
    Central, 20, 60, 277
    East, 52, 132
    North, 95, 111
    South, 34, 50, 129, 230, 236
    West, 29, 69, 90, 99, 122, 128, 151, 196, 239, 240
African American experience, 43, 77, 123, 160, 161, 177
    men, 13, 54, 205, 224, 229, 252, 253, 257, 262, 274, 338, 348, 354
    women, 33, 119, 121, 194, 223, 228, 233
agriculture, 56, 82, 265, 308, 355
Ahmed, Leila, 198
AIDS, 205
Alamo, 280
Alaska, 202, 279, 300
alcoholism, 12, 100, 152, 165
American history
    18th Century, 197, 206, 217, 267
    19th Century, 194, 195, 197, 216, 231, 235, 241, 251, 252, 261, 267, 280, 341
    20th Century, 195, 201, 202, 209, 211, 220, 225, 226, 242, 259, 260, 263, 267, 268, 282, 283, 340, 344
American Revolution, 8, 206, 217
ancient, 83, 102, 141, 142, 143, 166, 169, 183, 200
ancient Greece, 346
Angelou, Maya, 228
anthropology, 190, 191, 269, 272, 304, 305, 311, 312, 321
antibiotics, 284
apartheid, 34, 50, 230, 236
apples, 287
Arab experience, 9, 186, 203, 237
Ashe, Arthur, 205
Asia, 80, 263, 264, 271, 275, 353
assimilation, 58, 63, 67, 68, 196, 198, 201, 281
astronomy, 307
atomic bomb, 28, 226, 339

Keyword

Augustine of Hippo, 326
Auschwitz, 81, 245, 273
autism, 36
aviation, 23, 260

B

Babylonia, 169
Baltimore, 41
baseball, 137, 229, 259, 340
basketball, 100, 220, 232
Bataan Death March, 263
Becket, Thomas, 156
Belgium, 273
betrayal, 109, 114, 115, 119, 139, 171, 173, 192, 349
Biko, Steve, 230
biography
    men, 154, 156, 193, 195, 196, 197, 200, 205, 210, 212, 222, 229, 236, 239, 244, 247, 248, 252, 253, 261, 262, 263, 274, 275, 278, 280, 291, 298, 326, 338, 359
    women, 162, 192, 194, 198, 199, 223, 228, 233, 246, 251, 255, 271, 281
biology, 284, 287, 289, 290, 293, 294, 296, 299, 300, 302, 304, 306, 308, 309, 312, 315, 316, 317, 318, 319, 321
biotechnology, 265, 308
Black Hawk, 197
Black Sox, 259
blind, 266
blood, 296
Boston, 67, 246
botany, 287
boxing, 262, 268
Brooklyn Dodgers, 229, 340
bubonic plague, 95
Buddhism, 113, 248, 249
Bunker Hill, 206
bureaucracy, 105, 125, 126, 342
Burns, Robert, 185
business, 31, 148, 355

C

cadavers, 318
Caesar, 200
California, 35, 38, 65, 68, 79, 84, 264, 345, 355, 359
Cambodia, 264, 271
Canada, 78, 170
cancer, 253
cannabis, 287

Keyword

card tricks, 310
Caribbean, 88
carnival, 117
Carson, Ben, 298
Carter, Rubin "Hurricane", 262
cats, 290
central Asia, 238
change, 125
chemistry, 297, 301
Chicago, 70, 104, 148, 161, 253, 270, 354
Chicago Bears, 253
child soldier, 240
children, 5, 75, 270
chimpanzees, 302
China, 15, 17, 56, 68, 115, 180, 222, 249, 281, 323
chocolate, 30, 272
Christianity, 130, 326, 330, 331, 333, 337
Christmas, 31
Cincinnati Reds, 259
civil rights, 209, 211, 223, 229, 230, 236, 338
Civil War, 101, 216
Cogito, Mr., 179
cold war, 118, 221
Colombia, 254
colonialism, 20, 60, 88, 122, 129, 131, 132, 151, 198, 244, 247
Coltrane, John, 242
comedy, 139, 149
coming-of-age
    female, 15, 17, 33, 62, 63, 112, 133, 228, 255
    male, 6, 8, 13, 27, 48, 65, 89, 101, 109, 132, 236, 349
communism, 221
Confucius, 323
Congo, 60
conservation, 300, 317
Constantinople, 214, 347
contemplation, 333, 335
Crete, 138
crime, 36, 61, 354
crops, 265, 308
cross-cultural, 20, 63, 67, 68, 76, 78, 80, 104, 111, 122, 136, 138, 196, 197, 198, 201, 210, 251, 264, 281
Crusades, 203, 214
Cuba, 261
culture, 191
CUNY, 220
Curie, Marie, 339
curry, 204
Czechoslovakia, 125, 221

Keyword

D

Dalai Lama, 248
David-Neel, Alexandra, 249
DDT, 357
death, 10, 39, 40, 112, 157, 318
decadence, 38, 56, 59
decision-making, 320
Delaney, Sarah & Elizabeth, 223
Denmark, 167
depression, 157
desert, 111
devil, 105, 147
dictatorship, 2, 7, 17, 37, 75, 128, 129, 213
disaster, 22
disease, 95, 215, 258, 264
DNA, 289, 290, 293, 316
dogs, 202, 279
Dominica, 88
Dominican Republic, 63
Douglas, Frederick, 252
drugs, 210, 240, 254
dust bowl, 345
dystopia, 2, 21, 26

E

ecology, 286, 357
economics, 250
Egypt, 4, 198
Einstein, 211, 339
El Cid, 172
elephants, 317
England, 31, 61, 64, 114, 134, 156, 171, 196
environment, 286, 300, 355, 357
epistolary novel, 33, 42, 105
Equiano, Olaudah, 239
Eshun, Ekow, 196
Europe, 91, 351
exoplanets, 307

F

fable, 4, 7, 9, 16, 25, 47, 73, 85, 103, 147, 171, 190, 358
family, 5, 40, 41, 62, 68, 69, 72, 74, 82, 87, 92, 94, 98, 99, 100, 107, 108, 112, 114, 124, 145, 146, 152, 153, 157, 160, 161, 163, 270
famine, 213, 234
farming, 82, 234, 265, 345, 355

feminism, 14, 29, 33, 52, 68, 69, 74, 115, 120, 121, 146, 155, 162, 198, 246, 281, 352
flood, 235
flu, 215
food, 70, 74, 79, 204, 234, 272, 308
football, 218, 253
France, 30, 55, 174, 350
Frank, Anne, 192
Franklin, Benjamin, 193, 217
friendship, 72, 84, 109, 115, 116, 119, 121, 138, 257, 349

G

Gandhi, 212
gangs, 89
Gaul, 200
genetics, 289, 290, 293, 304, 316
genocide, 200, 213, 271, 277
Georgia, 33
Germany, 81, 118, 222, 256, 273, 283, 356
germs, 284, 315
Ghana, 29, 196
gorillas, 299
graphic book, 93, 289
Great Depression, 38, 82, 84, 123, 160, 345, 354
Greece, 138
greed, 31, 92

H

Haiti, 71
Harlan, Josiah, 244
hero, 166, 167, 169, 171, 172, 173, 174, 175
high school, 218, 232
Himalayas, 76
Hinduism, 336
hip hop, 225
Hiroshima, 28, 339
history, 200, 203, 204, 213, 214, 215, 234, 237, 238, 239, 243, 244, 247, 254, 256, 258, 271, 272, 280, 284, 332, 337, 339
hockey, 219
Hollywood, 38
holocaust, 81, 182, 192, 245, 256, 273, 356
homeless, 269
horror, 1, 42, 51, 103, 117
hydrogen, 301

Keyword

I

Iceland, 173
ice-nine, 28
Idaho, 62
Iditarod, 279
immigrants, 24, 63, 67, 68, 70, 80, 201, 210, 281
immortality, 49
India, 67, 73, 79, 113, 204, 212, 265
innumeracy, 303
inspirational, 4, 33, 85, 107, 205, 228, 253, 257, 298, 324
invertebrates, 319
Iran, 93
Ireland, 11, 106, 234
Islam, 198, 203, 214, 329, 332, 338
Italy, 16, 44

J

Jacobs, Harriet, 233
Jamaica, 134
Japan, 72, 94, 112, 199, 226, 263
jazz, 242
Jefferson, Thomas, 217
Jewish experience, 46, 58, 102, 108, 182, 192, 237, 256, 273, 356
Joan of Arc, 162
Judaism, 325, 327

K

Kabbalah, 327
Keckley, Elizabeth, 194
Keller, Helen, 266
Kelly, Fanny, 251
Kenya, 132
kidnapping, 254
King Arthur, 171
Korea, 23, 80
Korean War, 23

L

Lincoln, 194
literature, 227
logotherapy, 245
London, 24, 196
Long Island, 59
loss, 12, 106, 170, 343

Keyword

love, 12, 14, 15, 29, 32, 44, 48, 52, 58, 87, 92, 97, 106, 107, 111, 112, 114, 136, 168, 170, 181, 321, 324, 343

M

magic tricks, 310
magical realism, 16, 71, 74, 90, 92, 105
Man Booker Award, 73, 106, 356
Mao, 15, 17
marathon, 246
marriage, 9, 14, 17, 24, 29, 100, 111, 146, 151, 159, 165, 343
Martians, 131
massacre, 222, 277, 341
math, 47, 303, 310, 320, 322
Mathabane, Mark, 236
Mau Mau, 132
McCarthyism, 144, 224
medicine, 202, 215, 243, 257, 258, 264, 284, 291, 296, 298, 305, 306, 309, 315, 351, 352
medieval, 203, 238
memory, 106, 116
mental illness, 19, 27, 36, 86, 157, 243, 309
metaphysics, 184
Mexico, 12, 74, 92, 96, 201, 247, 280, 283
microbiology, 315
Middle East, 237, 347
midlife crisis, 100, 106, 108, 145
Midwest, 82, 98, 116, 117, 119, 135, 251, 352
Miller, Sally, 241
Missouri, 3
Montreal Canadiens, 219
morality, 130, 158
More, Thomas, 154
motherhood, 69, 107, 136, 157
music, 225, 242, 278
Muslim experience, 93, 120, 198, 203
mystery, 5, 12, 61, 118, 358
mysticism, 327, 328, 330, 336
mythology, 83, 183

N

Nanking, 222
Nat Turner's Rebellion, 189
Nation of Islam, 338
National Book Award, 55, 116, 231, 348
Native American experience, 78, 104, 136, 195, 197, 251, 341
nature, 111, 178, 188, 276, 279, 286, 299, 300, 302, 357

Netherlands, The, 53
neurology, 309
New England, 159, 165, 168, 206, 232, 276
New Orleans, 14, 163, 241
New York City, 27, 54, 63, 80, 108, 145, 153, 210, 220, 340, 348
Nibelungs, 173
Nigeria, 69, 90, 99, 122, 151, 239
Nijo, 199
Nobel Prize
    Literature, 9, 10, 20, *32, 44, 56, 75, 84, 85, 94, 95, 108, 113, 119, 129, 151, 152, 156,* 162, *164,* 167, *254, 343, 345, 351, 352*
    Peace, *212, 248*
    Physiology or Medicine, *293*
Nome, 202, 279
nuclear war, 26

O

Ohio, 135
Oklahoma, 89, 345
Oppenheimer, 339
optimism, 25
oral history, 344

P

Pacific Ocean, 73, 231, 286
Pakistan, 110
parable, 130
Parchman Farm, 209, 282
Paris, 275, 347, 350
PEN/Faulkner Award, 18
PEN/Hemingway Award, 62, 77, 80, 104
Pennsylvania, 235
Persia, 329
Peyton, Walter, 253
Philippines, 263
philosophy, 158, 323, 324, 325, 334, 358
physics, 288, 301, 313, 339
pilots, 23, 260
Pittsburgh, 160
pogrom, 46
Poland, 150, 256
polio, 258
politics, 2, 21, 28, 71, 110, 128, 129, 154, 156, 189, 224, 275, 339, 360
potatoes, 234, 287
poverty, 52, 201, 209, 210, 269, 270, 282, 345, 350, 354
power, 86, 144, 162

pragmatism, 334
Prague, 125
predestination, 150
prejudice, 30, 48, 89, 123, 161, 210, 223, 224, 228, 229, 262, 338, 348, 354
primates, 299, 302, 311
Prince William Sound, 300
prison, 209, 210, 262, 282, 338, 350, 354
psychology, 243, 245, 295, 314, 324
Puerto Rico, 210
Pulitzer Prize, 22, 33, 40, 43, 44, 46, 56, 67, 70, 82, 85, 87, 123, 148, 153, 157, 159, 160, 163, 178, 188, 217, 258, 282, 344, 345

R

Rabe, John, 222
racism, 3, 13, 34, 54, 107, 123, 127, 129, 132, 161, 209, 210, 211, 223, 228, 230, 236, 262, 282, 338, 348, 354
railroad, 355
reading, 227
relationships, 324, 325
relaxation, 314
religion, 26, 39, 54, 73, 76, 93, 96, 99, 105, 110, 113, 120, 147, 150, 156, 162, 189, 247, 248, 323, 325, 326, 327, 328, 330, 331, 332, 333, 335, 336, 337, 338
Robeson, Paul, 224
Robinson, Jackie, 229, 340
Roland, 174
Rome, 166, 183, 200, 347
Roosevelt, Theodore, 261
roughing-it, 276
Roush, Edd, 259
running, 246
Ruritania, 97
Russia, 37, 46, 140, 213, 343
Russian Revolution, 343
Rwanda, 277, 299

S

Salem, 144
Samoa, 133
San Joaquin Valley, 355
Santa Ana, 280
satire, 7
science, 284, 285, 287, 288, 289, 290, 291, 292, 293, 296, 297, 298, 299, 300, 301, 302, 303, 304, 305, 306, 307, 308, 309, 310, 312, 313, 314, 315, 316, 317, 318, 320, 321, 322, 339, 357
science fiction, 21, 26, 28, 48, 51, 66, 131

Scotland, 124
Scrooge, 31
sea, 85, 231, 286, 359
senses, 312
sex, 294
shame, 110
Sherlock Holmes, 61
Shinto, 335
short-stories, 1, 24, 43, 45, 50, 57, 58, 63, 66, 67, 77, 103, 104, 130, 135, 137
Sierra Leone, 240
silk, 238
Sinatra, Frank, 278
Sioux, 251
slavery, 71, 111, 127, 189, 194, 233, 239, 241, 252, 274
social class, 64, 134, 149, 155
solar system, 307
Somalia, 52
South, 10, 33, 87, 107, 123, 209, 282, 348
South Africa, 34, 50, 212, 230, 236
South America, 18, 22, 32
Southwest, 39
space, 307
Spain, 4, 172, 247
Spanish-American war, 261
sports, 137, 205, 218, 219, 220, 229, 232, 236, 246, 253, 259, 262, 268, 279, 305, 340
sports scandal, 220, 259
spy, 118
Stalinism, 2, 37, 213
statistics, 292
Sufism, 329
suicide, 12, 72, 112, 157
Supreme Court, 267
Switzer, Katherine, 246
Switzerland, 351

T

Tang, Truong Nhu, 275
technology, 28, 51, 125, 339, 360
tennis, 205, 236
terrorism, 18
Thomas, Piri, 210
Tibet, 76, 248, 249
time, 49, 288, 313
Togo, 128
tolerance, 30, 46, 48, 99
totalitarianism, 2, 21, 37, 126

Keyword

trade, 238, 360
tragedy, 139, 140, 141, 142, 143, 144, 145, 148, 152
Transylvania, 42
travel, 249, 347
Trinidad, 24
Trojan War, 346
Troy, 166, 175, 346
tulips, 287
Tuskegee, 274

U

U.S. Air force, 260
Ukraine, 213
United States, 191

V

vaccines, 258
Vermeer, 53
Vietcong, 275
Vietnam, 55
Vietnam, war, 275
violence, 75, 109, 120, 138, 230, 233, 271
Volsungs, 173

W

war, 6, 8, 23, 44, 55, 65, 71, 81, 83, 91, 101, 109, 131, 162, 192, 197, 200, 203, 206, 216, 222, 226, 237, 240, 244, 256, 261, 263, 271, 273, 277, 283, 339, 341, 342, 343, 344, 346, 351, 353, 356
Washington D.C., 77, 269
Washington, Booker T., 274
Washington, George, 217
West Indies, 134
whaling, 231
wheat, 355
winter, 202, 279
witchcraft, 144
women, 102, 136, 199, 269, 281
work, 70
World Series, 259
WWI, 6, 44, 283, 343, 351
WWII, 65, 81, 91, 109, 192, 222, 226, 256, 263, 273, 342, 344, 353, 356

Keyword

Z

zero, 322
Zimmerman telegram, 283

'*'-Level Books (less challenging)

1. *18 Best Stories by Edgar Allan Poe* 1
2. *101 Great American Poems* 176
3. *The Adventures of Huckleberry Finn* 3
4. *The Alchemist: A Fable About Following Your Dream* 4
5. *Alfred and Guinevere* 5
6. *All Quiet on the Western Front* 6
7. *Animal Farm* 7
8. *Anne Frank: The Diary of a Young Girl* 192
9. *April Morning* 8
10. *The Autobiography of Benjamin Franklin* 193
11. *The Autobiography of Malcolm X* 338
12. *Behind the Scenes in the Lincoln White House: Memoirs of an African-American Seamstress* 194
13. *The Bridges at Toko-Ri* 23
14. *Brighter Sun* 24
15. *A Christmas Carol* 31
16. *Courtship of Miles Standish* 168
17. *The Crucible* 144
18. *The Death of a Salesman* 145
19. *Evangeline* 170
20. *Favorite African Folktales* 45
21. *The Genie in the Bottle: 64 All New Commentaries on the Fascinating Chemistry of Everyday Life* 298
22. *Gifted Hands: The Ben Carson Story* 298
23. *Girl with a Pearl Earring* 53
24. *Go Tell It on the Mountain* 54

Keyword

25. *The Good Earth* 56
26. *A Good Man is Hard to Find* 57
27. *Hound of the Baskervilles* 61
28. *How the Garcia Girls Lost Their Accents* 63
29. *The Human Comedy* 65
30. *In These Girls, Hope is a Muscle* 232
31. *The Illustrated Man* 66
32. *Life on the Run* 240
33. *The Lion and the Jewel* 151
34. *A Long Day's Journey into Night* 152
35. *Lost Horizon* 76
36. *Lost in the City* 77
37. *Lost in Yonkers* 153
38. *Narrative of my captivity among the Sioux Indians. By Fanny Kelly. With a brief account of General Sully's Indian expedition in 1864, bearing upon events occurring in my captivity* 252
39. *Never Die Easy: The Autobiography of Walter Payton* 253
40. *The Odyssey* 83
41. *Of Mice and Men* 84
42. *Old Man and the Sea* 85
43. *Our Town* 159
44. *The Outsiders* 89
45. *The Pact* 257
46. *Persepolis: The Story of a Childhood* 93
47. *The Piano Lesson* 160
48. *The Prisoner of Zenda* 97
49. *A Raisin in the Sun* 161
50. *The Red Badge of Courage* 101

Keyword

51. *Rip Van Winkle and Other Stories* 103
52. *Shizuko's Daughter* 112
53. *Snow Flower and the Secret Fan* 115
54. *Some Survived: An Eyewitness Account of the Bataan Death March and the Men Who Lived Through It* 264
55. *Something Wicked This Way Comes* 117
56. *Stiff: The Curious Lives of Human Cadavers* 318
57. *The Story of My Life* 267
58. *To Kill A Mockingbird* 123
59. *The War of the Worlds* 131
60. *Weep Not, Child* 132
61. *Winesburg, Ohio* 135
62. *Winterdance: The Fine Madness of Running the Iditarod* 279

Keyword

'**'-Level Books (challenging)

1. *The Analects of Confucius* 323
2. *And Keep Your Powder Dry: An Anthropologist Looks at America* 191
3. *The Antibiotic Paradox* 284
4. *As I Lay Dying* 10
5. *At Swim-Two-Birds* 11
6. *At the Fringes of Science: With a New Epilogue* 285
7. *The Bell Jar* 19
8. *Between Man and Man* 325
9. *Candide* 25
10. *A Canticle for Leibowitz* 26
11. *Catch 22* 342
12. *Darkness at Noon* 37
13. *Down on Parchman Farm: The Great Prison in the Mississippi Delta* 209
14. *Emotional Intelligence* 295
15. *The Essential Kabbalah* 327
16. *The Essential Mystics* 328
17. *Flatland: A Romance of Many Dimensions* 48
18. *The Following Story* 49
19. *How to Read Literature like a Professor* 227
20. *Hydrogen: The Essential Element* 302
21. *The Journey of Man: A Genetic Odyssey* 305
22. *Kokoro* 72
23. *Les Miserables* 350
24. *The Lives of a Cell* 306

Keyword

25. *A Love Supreme: The Making of John Coltrane's Masterpiece* 242
26. *Lucky: A Memoir* 243
27. *Madness: A Brief History* 244
28. *Metaphysical Poetry: An Anthology* 184
29. *Naked Economics: Undressing the Dismal Science* 250
30. *New Seeds of Contemplation* 334
31. *The New World of Mr. Tompkins* 313
32. *'night, Mother* 157
33. *No Exit and Three Other Plays* 158
34. *The Painted Bird* 91
35. *The Selfish Gene* 316
36. *Shame* 110
37. *Siddhartha* 113
38. *Tell Them Who I Am: The Lives of Homeless Women* 269
39. *To the Lighthouse* 124
40. *Too Loud a Solitude* 125
41. *Waiting for Godot* 164
42. *Who's Afraid of Virginia Woolf?* 165
43. *Why Flip a Coin? The Art and Science of Good Decision* 320
44. *Worse than Slavery: Parchman Farm and the Ordeal of Jim Crow Justice* 282
45. *Zero: The Biography of a Dangerous Idea* 322

Reading Log

	Title	Standard Book Equivalent	Rating
1			
2			
3			
4			
5			
6			
7			
8			
9			
10			
11			
12			
13			
14			
15			
16			
17			
18			
19			
20			

Reading Log

	Title	Standard Book Equivalent	Rating
21			
22			
23			
24			
25			
26			
27			
28			
29			
30			
31			
32			
33			
34			
35			
36			
37			
38			
39			
40			

Reading Log

	Title	Standard Book Equivalent	Rating
41			
42			
43			
44			
45			
46			
47			
48			
49			
50			
51			
52			
53			
54			
55			
56			
57			
58			
59			
60			

Reading Log

	Title	Standard Book Equivalent	Rating
61			
62			
63			
64			
65			
66			
67			
68			
69			
70			
71			
72			
73			
74			
75			
76			
77			
78			
79			
80			

LaVergne, TN USA
19 August 2009

155101LV00005B/72/A